The Poets' Jesus

THE POETS' JESUS

Representations at the End of a Millennium

PEGGY ROSENTHAL

OXFORD

UNIVERSITY PRESS

2000

OXFORD

UNIVERSITY PRESS

Oxford   New York

Athens   Auckland   Bangkok   Bogotá   Buenos Aires   Calcutta
Cape Town   Chennai   Dar es Salaam   Delhi   Florence   Hong Kong   Istanbul
Karachi   Kuala Lumpur   Madrid   Melbourne   Mexico City   Mumbai
Nairobi   Paris   São Paulo   Singapore   Taipei   Tokyo   Toronto   Warsaw

and associated companies in
Berlin   Ibadan

Copyright © 2000 by Peggy Rosenthal

Published by Oxford University Press, Inc.
198 Madison Avenue, New York, New York 10016

Oxford is a registered trademark of Oxford University Press

Library of Congress Cataloging-in-Publication Data
Rosenthal, Peggy.
The poets' Jesus : representations at the end
of a millennium / Peggy Rosenthal.
p.   cm.
Includes bibliographical references and index.
ISBN 0-19-513114-2
1. Christian poetry—History and criticism.   2. Religious poetry—
History and criticism.   3. Jesus Christ—In literature.   I. Title.
PN1386.R67   2000
809.1′9351—dc21   99-23029

1 3 5 7 9 8 6 4 2

Printed in the United States of America
on acid-free paper

To Robert Atwan,
who suggested I write this book
and
William H. Shannon,
who insisted I keep at it

Preface

The start of the third millennium seems a logical time to reassess what poets have made of the person from whose birth, as it is traditionally dated, we in fact count these millennia. Poetry has always been a privileged medium through which a culture talks of, and to, its gods. Poetry, that is, searches and stretches language to probe the questions of life's ultimate meanings that people everywhere have asked. Even where Jesus of Nazareth is not claimed as Incarnate God, even where that claim is dismissed out of hand, he still engages poets because he raises those questions of ultimate meaning that language about gods is meant to serve. Christianity's core story—of the God who became human so that humankind might come to its own divine fullness—hasn't lost its appeal for poets after these two thousand years. The story evidently so resonates with poetry's classic task that even in cultures not predominantly Christian, and even in this past century, which has defined itself (at least in the West) as "secular" or "post-Christian," Jesus remains a figure that poets seek out. In the ways that they configure him, in the poets' Jesus of different times and places, we can see how different peoples are making sense of what it means to be human in relation to the divine.

I wrote *The Poets' Jesus* simply because this subject, of inherent interest for cultural history, hadn't been treated for fifty years and hence needed to be revisited. When my co-editors and I were collecting poems on Jesus for our anthology *Divine Inspiration: The Life of Jesus in World Poetry* (Oxford, 1998), we were amazed to discover that the most recent book discussing our subject, in any of the languages we were able to search, was *The Christ of the Poets,* published in 1948 by a Vanderbilt University professor of English literature named Edwin Mims. It is a good, solid study, but a couple of its basic assumptions are out of date, interestingly enough in ways that illustrate major changes of outlook during the twentieth century's second half. Mims's title subject is "Christ"; mine is "Jesus," because many of the poets I discuss wouldn't think of calling Jesus of Nazareth the Christ of Christian faith. And, though you can't tell from the title, Mims's poets are all from Britain and the United States, a limitation that's no longer acceptable. Mims himself complains that the previous book on the subject, called *The Christ of English Poetry* and published in England in 1908, treats "only some of the medieval poets, Shakespeare, Milton, and Browning." Mims is justifiably pleased to be extending the range to the English metaphysical poets, other Victorians, and United States poets up to his own present time, including some American "Negro poets." But to us today, this range feels narrow, claustrophobic. The parochial assumption that a study of "literature" really meant "English literature" and no more—still the mode when I was in graduate school in the 1960s—no longer stands. We now assume that there is more in the world worth studying than our own products, and any book claiming a large sweep in its title has to reach beyond the English-speaking lands. So in *The Poets' Jesus* I have aimed, as my collaborators and I did in *Divine Inspiration,* for something of a global range. I've had the advantage of writing after twenty years or so of an energetic effort by educators, translators, and publishers to make available in English, with helpfully knowledgeable introductions, editions of the best contemporary poets of Africa, the Arab countries, Latin America, and Asia. Where these poets treat the figure of Jesus—which they do, as we'll see, to a surprising extent—I've been able to draw them into my discussion.

I'm sure I have fallen short, however, in the range of my poets and in other respects that whoever treats the subject anew fifty years hence will legitimately complain of in her preface. I'm sorry I won't be around then to have the fun of seeing how *The Poets' Jesus* will appear out of date. My guess, my hope, is that my omission of certain cultures will be noted and corrected. India, for instance, must surely have produced a substantial body of poetry on Jesus, since Christianity has thrived in parts of the Indian subcontinent since the fourth century; but even through native Indian contacts I have been unable to get my hands on much of the literature. Another way I hope that *The Poets' Jesus* will appear outdated is in my masculine pronoun for God, perhaps even for Christ. An exciting theology of gender-inclusive language for God is just now in the making. But since it needs to be further explored and refined before it enters the general discourse, to have incorporated it into this book—that is, into a discussion whose focus isn't that theological issue itself—would have been a distraction.

There is, however, much scholarship that I have directly and gratefully made use of: in theology, biblical exegesis, literary history, literary criticism, literary biography. Since the primary audience I have in mind for this book is the general reader rather than academics, I've kept most of these source references out of the body of the text, acknowledging my debts in the endnotes. Here I will mention only the outstanding book to which everyone studying the history of images of Jesus is indebted: Jaroslav Pelikan's *Jesus through the Centuries.* Since its publication in 1985, this immensely readable survey, grounded in a lifetime of scholarship, has both enlightened the general reader and provided a solid base for further study. In writing *The Poets' Jesus* I have seen my project as trying to supplement Pelikan's in two ways. Poetry enters only occasionally into his book (his cultural history draws mostly from the visual arts, the theology, and the political and ecclesial institutions of an era), so I've wanted to let poetry tell its special version of the story, enhanced by a few illustrations from the visual arts. And, while Pelikan spreads his attention fairly evenly across these twenty centuries, I focus mainly on the last, because it produced a remarkable variety of poetic treatments of Jesus of which scarcely any notice has been taken. Concentrating in detail on these recent poetic configurations of Jesus has allowed me to offer, through them, some cultural analysis of these turbulent past hundred years.

So my opening chapter moves quickly through the first eighteen hundred years of poetic transformations of Jesus, watching them go by as if on a stage that has been set by the theological, philosophical, social, and literary assumptions of each main era. That is, I picture Jesus as a dramatic character whom poets of succeeding epochs cast in changing roles. I certainly don't claim this theater metaphor to be original. It's quite the opposite: all the world has been a stage many times over. But the very familiarity of the metaphor is what makes it convenient. It allows me to describe changing cultural contexts as stage sets and to point to where Jesus is placed on stage, what costumes he wears, what roles he plays, and who or what else is out there with him. The metaphor, I should clarify, isn't meant to imply either irreverence toward Jesus or a belief that he is in reality no more than a stagey or staged figure, recast by each era for its own purposes. Jesus himself (and this is precisely what many poets across those early centuries are stretching their language to try to express) escapes all such castings, which are our human imagination's efforts to "place" him in the drama of our existence.

After this opening chapter I move at a more leisurely pace, so that we can get to know better both the poets and the Jesus they configure. In chapter 2, we'll spend some time with "Jesus as Romantic Hero," because this nineteenth century figure, fashioned jointly by the theology and poetry of the era, is the precursor of nearly everything that happens to the twentieth-century poets' Jesus. The first thing that happens, as we'll see in chapter 3, "Sliding into Modernism: Jesus Pale and Shrunken," is that Jesus suffers a radical diminishment; he is reduced—by the waning of religious faith—to a merely human figure, undignified, weak, even wimpy. These modernist configurations of Jesus take us into the twentieth century. From there, for reasons I detail further at that point, we can't move chronologically: the major twentieth-century poetic configurations of Jesus take shape almost simultaneously throughout the century. So I've grouped them by the roles they give to Jesus, sometimes also grounding a chapter in a place where that role was predominant. Chapter 4 stays mainly with Western culture in its "Crisis of the Secularized West: Postmodernism's Jesus as Antihero"; here we have a poets' Jesus who acts out postmodernism's cynicism or who is a product of its flippant play with the meaninglessness of meaning. Chapter 5 moves to "Crucified Africa: The Politicized Jesus of Africa and Beyond." Here we'll see poets of the African continent and diaspora fashioning two sorts of figures of Jesus, both rooted in their people's unique political experience: he becomes an archetype of their people's suffering spread over the earth, but he is also set down intimately amid their tribal cultures, joining the native dance in one spot, contending against native gods in another. Chapter 6, "Archetypal Christ: Arabic Poetry and Other Wastelands," follows political configurations of Jesus into other anguished areas of the world, starting with the Arab Middle East, whose post–World War II poets conflate Jesus with the mythical gods of death/rebirth narratives set in a wasted desert landscape. Much of the twentieth-century stage, we'll go on to see, is envisioned by poets all over the globe as a vast wasteland, blasted by world wars, genocides, totalitarian brutality, nuclear terror. The last part of chapter 6 and the whole of chapter 7, "Jesus Absent," look at various ways that poets have set Jesus onto this grim stage or have kept him deliberately off it, configuring a Jesus Forgotten or Pushed Aside—by the century's forces of evil or, more positively, by humankind's own creative powers—or a Jesus Waited For in the dark. Chapter 8, "Between Absence and Presence: Playing around with Jesus," has a lighter feel; here the poets' Jesus starts to return to the scene, but teasingly, taking part in typical late-twentieth-century spiritual dramas that are still going on. Finally, with chapter 9, "Jesus Present," Jesus openly takes center stage, and with much of the hopeful character of his first fifteen hundred years, as contemporary poets reimagine for their own day some of his original Gospel roles.

Though I offer this preview of the book in terms of the metaphor of roles and staging, that metaphor itself doesn't play a major role in my exposition after chapter 1. Its only purpose there, and in other places where it does come in, is to help sharpen our view of how Jesus is being configured by the poets under study. But overuse of it would distract attention from my main interest: the poetry itself. Getting to know this poetry has been the great joy of writing this book. In fact, my purpose in writing wasn't just to present certain poems that illustrate a thesis; it was also to communicate something of the feel of becoming intimate with fine poems. When I teach courses on poetry to adults—one of my favorite things to do—many are astonished at how poetry can speak to them, can enter their lives, once they become comfortable reading it. Often they have been scared off by the calculated obscurity of certain modes of modern verse. Or they had been put off, if they attended college during the past twenty years, by literature courses that engaged them in theory rather than in the primary text (an approach that is fortunately passing, as indeed it must, since literature itself—not our theories about it—is what touches the soul and so will last). In addition, the hype of the electronic age has been telling them that the printed word is obsolete. It isn't. Nothing can replace the profoundly tactile experience of holding a book in one's hand while lingering with the whole mind and body over lines composed by a poet whose aim is to invite (rather than to intimidate) reflection. I tried in this book to pass on poetry's invitation by writing in a tone that shares with the reader the adventure of entering the poets' world. If reading the book leads readers on to more of the poems, I'll be happy.

Acknowledgments

Thanks, first, to David Impastato, whose generous correspondence helped me think through many of the ideas in this book and whose anthology *Upholding Mystery* opened to me new worlds of contemporary poetry. When I started writing books twenty years ago, I told myself that a main purpose of this solitary and unremunerative occupation was to make friends. So it has been a delight to find that through the writing of this book has come not only my friendship with David but also our current collaboration in offering retreats and courses on poetry and spirituality around the country.

My thanks to the scholars and clergy who graciously read parts of the manuscript or responded to particular queries I sent their way: Ralph Anderson, Issa J. Boullata, Jonathan Chavez, John Gatta, Joseph Hart, Dennis O'Brien, James Torrens, S. J., and Susan Wolfson. Thanks to Marvin Mich, former dean of St. Bernard's Institute, for offering me the opportunity to teach a graduate seminar on some of the material in the book. As an independent scholar, I'm grateful for the resources made available by the National Coalition of Independent Scholars. For energetic help in locating art work, thanks to Gregory Wolfe, editor of *Image: A Journal of the Arts and Religion,* and to Eugene Chung, O.C.S.O. Thanks, too, to the artists who donated their work.

Susan Chang, my initial editor at Oxford, enthusiastically supported this project from the start; I wonder if readers realize the extent to which the very existence of the books they read depends on an editor's supportiveness. Elissa Morris, my new editor, picked up the ball with energy and good humor. Robert Milks, my production editor, carried the project through to completion with the conscientious professionalism I treasure at Oxford. To all three, my thanks for being so delightful to work with. To my agent, John Wright, continued thanks for his indispensable role in bringing this and all my previous books to light.

As ever, thanks to my husband, George Dardess, my life partner in all things. From breakfast table conversations to reading and rereading and re-rereading the manuscript at various stages, George has combined the loving encouragement of a helpmeet with the sharp critical eye of a professional colleague, even composing a sentence here and there when I got stuck. I can't imagine having written the book without his companionship. Finally, thanks to my parents, Marge and Ken Zierler, for a home that has always stimulated a love of literature and the best values it transmits.

A briefer version of chapter 6 appeared as "Christ in the Desert of Twentieth Century Poetry," in *Cross Currents,* Spring 1997. An expansion of the discussion of Vassar Miller in chapter 9 appeared as "Knowing in the Bones: The Poetry of Vassar Miller," *Christian Century,* May 21–28, 1997. All biblical quotations in the book use the New Revised Standard Version.

Contents

The Poets' Jesus

Jesus as Christ and More

The First Eighteen Centuries

Entering my city's local history museum, you come first to a blank video screen. A press of the button starts off an animated simulation of the geological changes at the very spot where you're standing, from the Earth's beginning to the present moment. In a mere 120 seconds you see molten lava cool into a crust over which slides a glacier that melts into a rushing river whose force carves out walls that deepen into the gorge and waterfall that you can see in real life outside the museum window.

Reading this opening chapter will have to be something like the experience of watching that video. To cover eighteen hundred years of poetry on Jesus, we'll have to be in fast-forward mode. And to keep the images from going by in a blur, I'll be able to sketch only broad outlines. Too much detail at such a speed would clutter and confuse the picture. Since, as I noted in the preface, the main metaphor through which we're watching Jesus move through the centuries' poetry isn't geological but theatrical, the sketches are of brief scenes from key epochs, noting names he is given and major roles he is made to play.

JESUS STEPS ONTO the stage of world history in the role of Christ. This is the first title that his followers gave him after his crucifixion, as word spread among them that God had raised him from the dead. Being Jews, they were familiar with the figure of "Messiah," a Hebrew word meaning "anointed one." Applied in their Scriptures to certain kings or high priests especially chosen by God, the title was commonly used by Jews at the time for the person God would send to lead Israel to ultimate freedom. Living in Greek-speaking communities, they used the Greek term for Messiah: *Christos*. So sure were they that Jesus of Nazareth was the Christos awaited by Israel that they made this role his very name, calling him Jesus Christ or even just Christ and soon calling themselves Christians. All the other roles that Jesus is called on to play for the Christianity of the next seventeen hundred years are elaborations of this one. Christ is his core identity.

In the earliest known poetry on Jesus, he is already Messiah and more. This poetry took the form of hymns, composed by the first Jewish Christian communities to celebrate and explain what it meant to them that Jesus had been resurrected from death. Some of these poems have been lost, but we have those that were incorporated into the writings that became the New Testament, and what they do with Jesus is astonishing. In the grand hymn that Paul places in his letter to the Philippians (Phil. 2:6–11), two symmetrical but contrasting sets of strophes swoop Jesus from the heights to the depths and then back up again. In the first set, starting off "in the form of God," he "empties" himself into the "slavery" of "human form," then "humbles himself" even further to the point of "obediently" accepting death on a cross. In this downward course, termed by scholars "kenotic" (the hymn's Greek word for "emptying"), most commentators see Jesus playing but also reversing Adam's role. That is, rather than grasping at his divine likeness as Adam had done in disobedience to God, Jesus obeys God's will and lets himself fall into death. From this nadir, in the hymn's second part God rewards Jesus' obedient suffering by "exalting" him with "the name above every other name," so that the poem ends by proclaiming "Jesus Christ is Lord." This is quite a position for Jesus of Nazareth to have reached within a couple decades after his death, and it is upheld and elaborated in the other early hymns and by Paul throughout his letters. We're numbed by now to the formulation "Jesus Christ is Lord," but its claims were unprecedented in Jewish history. In the formula, an itinerant preacher who had suffered the most disgraceful death of his day, the crucifixion meted out to common criminals, receives not only the appellation "Christos" but also a title that commands worship: "Lord." With this title comes the extraordinary suggestion that Jesus is himself divine.[1]

There is no doubt about Jesus' divinity in another famous hymn, composed around the end of the first century. This is the poem that forms the prologue of John's Gospel, where Jesus is announced as Logos: as the Word who was "in the beginning," the Word through whom all things came into being, the Word who indeed "was God." No higher claim for Jesus can be made. And at the same time, in one of the most influential lines of Christianity ever written, this very "Word became flesh and lived among us." With this line, the Incarnation as a definite concept enters Christianity. We're so used to hearing Jesus defined doctrinally as the Incarnate Son of God that it's easy not to notice that only with the Fourth Gospel, a fairly late New Testament work, is Jesus unequivocally presented as Incarnate Son—as, that is, a preexistent divine being who became a particular human being by taking on flesh in Mary's womb. Of course, Jesus as Son of God had been born of Mary in the Gospels of Matthew and Luke, but these writers didn't speculate on his life before this moment of his birth. And marvelous early hymns like the one in Colossians 1:15–20 had cast Jesus in the role of Wisdom, the fertile figure of Jewish tradition who lived from the beginning with God and through whom all creation was made. But it was the genius of John's prologue and indeed his whole Gospel to conflate these roles, so that preexistent divine life belonged without question to the particular human person named Jesus of Nazareth.

These hymns far from exhaust the roles that Jesus plays in the first-century writings that would later be gathered as the New Testament. Though these writings are primarily prose, and my subject is the poets' Jesus, it is important at least to note his main New Testament roles since they're the source of nearly all the poetic configurations of him over the succeeding centuries. The New Testament suggests so many titles and terms for Jesus that I can offer only a partial list, like reading spottily from the cast of characters that he plays. There are the major christological roles, that is, the names that try to specify Jesus' role in the divine plan. Besides the ones we've already seen in the hymns—Messiah, Lord, Word, and God—Jesus is called Teacher, Prophet, High Priest, Savior, Son of Man, and Son of God. (He isn't given all these titles by every New Testament writer, nor do different writers necessarily mean the same thing by the terms they do share, nor are scholars agreed on which of the titles Jesus used of himself.) Jesus also steps, in the course of the New Testament, into several Old Testament roles: besides Wisdom and the new Adam, he is cast as the Suffering Servant of Isaiah. Moreover, he plays many other roles in the New Testament that don't have names attached to them: he goes through the Synoptic Gospels proclaiming the kingdom of God, forgiving sins, healing ills, and implying that these activities are really dimensions of a single action, which is God's salvation of humankind. John's Jesus performs some of these activities, but he's more likely to stand still and put on a series of metaphorical costumes, announcing them with the declaration "I am": I am, he says, the Good Shepherd, the Vine, the Bread of Life, the Light of the World, the Resurrection, the Way, the Truth, and the Life. In the New Testament book of Revelation, Jesus adds, "I am the Alpha and the Omega," the first and last letters of the Greek alphabet, hence the beginning and end of all.

CHRISTIAN POETRY OF THE second and third centuries continues this proliferation of roles for Jesus, as do the prose works in which the poems are embedded. "Poetry" wasn't for these early Christians a genre apart from their basically prose apologetics, catechesis, apocryphal stories, and exhortations to pagans. Writing in order to clarify the Gospel message, defend it from heresy, and spread it beyond the Jewish communities into the rest of the Greco-Roman world, they might burst into a hymn of praise at any moment. They could barely contain their gratitude to God for redeeming all creation in this Jesus Christ who, as preexistent and everlasting Logos, draws into himself all things in the cosmos. "All things" increasingly meant, for these writers, everything good in Jewish scripture, Greek philosophy, and pagan religion; all had foreshadowed Christ and hence were now gathered into him, transformed into his glorious redemptive being. Far from thinking that they needed to choose among the titles for Jesus, then, the second- and third-century Christian writers celebrated their concatenation of images for Christ as the very truth they were proclaiming.

So in the hymns of this era, Jesus takes on multiple roles simultaneously— or as simultaneously as a sequential art form like poetry can permit. The hymn with which the important second-century theologian Clement of Alexandria ends his catechetical treatise *Paedagogus* is a chain of names for Jesus inspired by images from the Bible and Plato and pagan lore, all fused by the triumphant figure of "Christ the King": "[y]ou who bridle colts untamed . . . invincible Word, . . . you the Shepherd, Cultivator, . . . Fisher of men, . . . you the Wing that lifts to heaven all the company of saints, . . . Jesus Christ, celestial Milk out-pressed from a young bride's fragrant breasts, which are your Wisdom's graces." Clement's point is not that we're to picture Jesus changing his form with every image, but that in him all these figures are triumphantly made one. He is the harmony of the cosmos. He is even "the New Song" itself, Clement adds in a treatise that, aiming to convert Greeks, draws into Christ both Plato's cosmic harmony and the legendary power of musicians like Orpheus and Amphion to tame beasts and move stones. "My minstrel," Clement asserts, is greater still, because he "tamed the most intractable of all wild beasts—human beings," moving their stony hearts to know the truth. A poem in the (probably) third-century apocryphal Acts of John elaborates Jesus' role as Music. Telling his disciples at the Last Supper to join hands in a circle around him, Jesus sings a hymn defining himself as Lord of the Dance. In successive turns of phrase punctuated by his followers' "Amen," he spins out image after image in which he encompasses both ends of an action—"I will be born, / And I will bear. / I will eat, / And I will be eaten"—then draws his disciples into the reciprocity of the dance: "I am lamp to you / who see me. / I am a mirror to you / who know me. / . . . Now if you follow my dance, / see yourself / in Me who am speaking." The poem certainly does feel like a product of the Johannine community, turning into song the Fourth Gospel's theme of Jesus' mutual indwelling with his disciples.[2]

The important church councils of Nicaea (AD 325) and Chalcedon (AD 451) were convened in order to regulate some of the runaway language for Jesus, as it was going wild not so much in hymns as in theologies defined by the councils as heresies, being formulated by people who, in good faith, couldn't conceive how Christ could be at once both fully human and divine. The councils defined Jesus doctrinally as indeed "one person in two natures," "true God from true God" yet "born of the Virgin Mary" as true "man." Mary, further, was defined at the Council of Ephesus (AD 431) to be Theotokos, Mother of God, a title that made her the key human actor in the Christian drama of salvation through Jesus. Interestingly enough, these pronouncements that bound the faithful to the terms of a common creed did nothing to bind the imaginations of Christian poets. Quite the contrary. Secure in the core facts of the drama, the poets were free to sink their imaginations into the mystery of this Christ who "became what we are in order that we might become what he is," as the second-century theologian Irenaeus had put it, or—in the influential fourth-century formulation of Athanasius—"became human that we might become divine."

Or, in the words of the fourth-century Syriac poet Ephrem, concluding one of his nearly thirty Nativity hymns: "the Deity imprinted itself on humanity, / so that humanity might also be cut into the seal of Deity." Ephrem's coinage metaphor here is one of literally hundreds of images that burst from his fertile mind as he pondered, in the complex stanzaic forms of Syriac verse, the Nicene Creed's gracious plot of human salvation through Jesus. As a teacher in the Christian school of his native Mesopotamian city of Nisibus and later as a deacon in the church at Edessa, Ephrem wrote hymns of such poetic brilliance and theological insight that they quickly spread through the Eastern Church, translated into Greek, Coptic, Ethiopic, Armenian, and Arabic, as well as into the Latin of the Western Church before long. His influence on the Christian imagination is incalculable; his verses are staples in the Eastern liturgy still today.

Ephrem wrote on many themes, but he keeps returning to the Incarnation as the pivotal wonder: the paradox that the Lord of creation would lower himself into the very womb of his creature in order to lift all creation back up to his own blessed heights. It is the basic drama of the Philippians hymn: Jesus descends, emptying himself of divinity to take on our lowly human form, then rises to glory as Lord of the cosmos. But for Ephrem, writing after three centuries of theological development, Jesus' descending/ascending movement hinges on the incarnational moment, the mind-bending marvel that Ephrem never tires of trying to imagine anew in strophe after strophe. Reading him can be like riding an amusement park tilt-a-whirl, as we sweep down and up in a nonstop sequence of paradoxical turns. "Blessed is the Shepherd Who became the sheep for our absolution. / Blessed is the Vineshoot that became the cup of our salvation. . . . / Blessed also is the Ploughman Who Himself became / the grain of wheat that was sown. . . . / His Fruit was mingled with our human nature to draw us out toward Him Who bent down to us." This is only a small sample, from a single hymn; it's hard to think of an inversion metaphor for Jesus that Ephrem didn't come up with. Many involve Mary. Eager to defend the fairly new doctrine of the Virgin Birth from its challengers, Ephrem often sets the paradoxical salvific drama right in Mary's womb or at her breast. "As indeed He sucked Mary's milk / He has given suck—life to the universe. / As again He dwelt in His mother's womb / in His womb dwells all creation." That Jesus should be imaged as mother is perfectly natural for Ephrem; there is nothing in creation that Jesus is not. So: "He is the Living Breast of living breath; / by His life the dead were suckled, and they revived." And, linking two images not invented by Ephrem but elaborated by him inventively—Jesus clothing himself in our human flesh so that we can wear the robes of his glory, and the Resurrection as a Second Birth—Ephrem has Mary say: "He bore me also / in a second birth. I put on the glory of Him / Who put on the body, the garment of His mother."

Since, as I write, the recovery of women's dignity in Christian history is a lively enterprise among many scholars, it's worth noting that women play a large and strikingly positive role in Ephrem's telling and retelling of Jesus' salvation story. Possibly because of Ephrem's eagerness to present Mary in a favorable light, he chooses New Testament women as models for the personal relation to God that Jesus offers his followers. The Samaritan woman at the well

(John 4:1–42) "is a type of humanity / that He leads step by step." The hemorrhaging woman (Mark 5:25–33; Matthew 9:20–22; Luke 8:42–48) rejoices that while Jesus "dried up" her blood, "He made flow" the "font of her love." Even Old Testament women are defined by their love for Jesus. Ephrem praises the sexual activities of Ruth and Tamar, for example, as showing their true yearning for Christ.[3]

If we step back to look at Jesus as he is presented by Ephrem and the poets of the preceding two centuries, we see him firmly at center stage of the very meaning of the cosmos. He stands there not as a mere man named Jesus of Nazareth but as the Christ whose glorious divinity the poets can configure only by naming role after role, title after title, image after image that he takes into himself. Surrounding him on the stage, which is a timeless and boundless expanse, is every past biblical figure that could conceivably *prefigure* Christ's uniquely salvific intervention in history. This casting of Old Testament characters and events as "types" foreshadowing the Christian story (an interpretive strategy known as typology) had begun as early as Paul's epistles, for instance his calling Adam a type of Christ in the letter to the Romans; taken for granted by Ephrem's time, typology would continue to intrigue the Christian imagination for more than a millennium. I've noted that Ephrem's Greek-speaking predecessors sometimes cast figures from philosophy and pagan lore as foreshadowings of Christ as well. But a more striking difference between Ephrem and the earlier poets is in the feasts that they present as the high point of the Christian drama. For second- and third-century Christian poetry, the central feast is Easter, the celebration of Christ's triumph as King who draws all things in the cosmos harmoniously into his victory over sin and death. While Ephrem does celebrate Easter, his heart and his poetic imagination are at the Nativity, at that moment when the preexistent divine Lord Jesus, by his Incarnation, graciously reduces himself to his creation's measure so as to gift creation with his measureless divinity.

IT'S HARD TO THINK OF where the poets' Jesus could go after such a glorious beginning. He is already all things, all metaphors, all symbols. But poetry is never deterred by the grandeur of its antecedents. As the Christian cultures of East and West began to diverge around the fourth century, the East into the culture of the Byzantine era and the West into the Latin culture of the Roman Empire, poets continued to elaborate Jesus' roles and the scenes around him.

For the great sixth-century Byzantine poet Romanos, the theater metaphor has nearly literal force, since Romanos's fame rests on his versified sermons that dramatize, in delightful invented dialogue, the biblical text for each feast of the Eastern Church calendar. A deacon in the church at Emesa, near Beirut, Romanos created his verse-drama homily form in order to engage his congregation in the biblical stories that all, to Romanos's mind, reenacted the one tremendous theological drama of the Incarnation: that cosmic encounter of divinity and humanity in the person of Christ. So, no matter which Gospel story Romanos is expanding into verse dialogue, it tends to slip at some point into the paradox of Jesus' two natures as human and as God. For instance, in his verse sermon on the hemorrhaging woman who touches the hem of Jesus' cloak in hope of being healed, Romanos has Christ explain that the crowds pressing in on him "do not touch my divinity / but she, in touching my visible robe, / Clearly grasped my divine nature, / And took possession of health." The puns on "touch" and "grasp" (comparable in the original Greek) are typical of Romanos's wordplay, as is the elaboration of Jesus' speeches way beyond what he says anywhere in the Gospel texts.[4]

Meanwhile, in the West, Jesus was being set by the poets into a very different sort of scene. After Constantine's conversion made Christianity socially acceptable, Christians started studying and even teaching in the Roman schools, and the Latin classical poets became their model. One charming result was the fourth-century hymns of the Spaniard Prudentius, considered the first great Christian poet of the West, whose Gospel scenes take place in a Virgilian pastoral landscape. Christ the Shepherd seeks the parable's one lost sheep through "silvan mazes"; finding it, he carries it back to "open woodland, / Where the lush grass bends its green leaves, and laurels / Shade the glassy streamlet of living water / Ceaselessly flowing."[5]

The fact that Prudentius lived in Spain yet wrote in Latin on Christian themes shows how quickly the Roman Empire spread Christianity. Prudentius and all Western writers from the fourth century to around the fourteenth were citizens of a Europe that had Latin as its common language and Roman Christianity as its common culture. The immense output of medieval Latin Christian poetry was written primarily for specific feasts on the Church calendar or for specific parts of the Mass or of the monastic daily Liturgy of the Hours. It was created to be chanted or sung, to put the dogmas of faith in a pleasing form for a congregation largely unable to read. As liturgical poetry, it was inherently public poetry, meant to express communally held beliefs. And occasioned as so much of it was by Church feasts, it was tied less and less to the figure of Jesus. Saints' feast days crowded the Church calendar, and the family of saints was ever-growing, as foundational biblical ones like the Virgin Mary and Peter were joined by scores of figures, both legendary and historical, held up by the Church as models of the Christian life. So the medieval stage of Christian poetry fills with characters whose stories, while gaining meaning only in relation to Christ, upstage him as the drama's immediate focus.

No matter who in the family medieval poetry is focusing on, the character tends to be clothed in typological style. For the casting of Jesus, a favorite typological figure is the Cross as Tree, which has remained on the stage of the poets' Jesus to our day. In the Adam/Christ typological pairing, the wooden Cross had early become the antitype of the Tree in the Garden of Eden: "the Lord . . . by his obedience in the tree renewed and reversed what was done by disobedience in connection with a tree," wrote Irenaeus in the second century. So we'd expect to see the Cross as Tree in the stage setting of the Christian story. Yet soon it is more than just a stage prop; it becomes a character almost in its own right, a figure standing for Christ's victory. The Cross itself, made by Paul a sign of Christ's triumph over death, had taken off as the banner symbol of Christian triumph in the fourth century, after Constantine came to believe he had won a battle because he obeyed the command of a dream to fight under the sign of the Cross. This victory was the impetus for Constantine's conversion, after which he emblazoned the Cross on the helmets and shields of the Roman imperial army. Marched through Christendom now in full martial style, the Cross turned its "type," the Tree, into a figure of triumph. So the sixth-century poet Fortunatus addresses his 'Vexilla Regis prodeunt,' which became the favorite processional hymn of the Middle Ages, not to Christ but to the triumphant "Tree of beauty and of light," dyed "with royal purple," from which "God reigns." Two centuries later, an anonymous Anglo-Saxon poet clearly familiar with the Fortunatus tradition goes further and has the Tree enact the suffering of Christ's Passion, in the astonishing poem known as *The Dream of the Rood.* As the poem's main speaker, the sentient Tree so intimately shares the story of "the noble king" who "climbed me" that "I was oppressed by sorrows," it says; "sore wounded" with the soldiers' weapon-points and "drenched in moisture," "I yet bowed humbly."[6] We've seen the poets' Jesus take into himself all things in creation; here we see a created thing take Jesus into itself.

DURING THE SUBSEQUENT five hundred years or so, up through the high Middle Ages, something extraordinary happens on the stage of the poets' Jesus, as well as in the arena of Christian prose treatises and visual art. Everything we've seen so far remains on stage: the typological figures, the swelling family of saints, all created things from a grain of wheat to the angels. But now all are patterned into grand allegorical systems that link every detail of the cosmos in intricate correlations. At first glance, it's hard to see where Christ himself is amid these minute correspondences of, say, each part of the human body to a particular heavenly body and to an attribute of a personified Virtue, all numerologically proportioned. Yet the point is that there's no place, no correspondence, no proportion where he isn't. As Love Incarnate, the Cosmic Christ gives the universe its meaning, which is to be ordered toward God. The entire universe is inscribed in Christ: he is the ground of its ordering; without him, nothing can make sense. So although we don't see on stage the human person of Jesus of Nazareth, his Incarnation is the condition of possibility and the backlighting for all that we do see. In, for instance, the allegory of Virtues as dramatized in the twelfth-century verse play *Ordo Virtutum,* by Hildegard of Bingen, all we see on stage are the brilliantly arrayed personified Virtues, along with the Devil and the human Soul who is torn between them. Yet the Virtues win out precisely because, as they sing in the prologue, "we shine with the Word of God"

Vision Two *of Hildegard of Bingen's* De operatione Dei, *artist unknown. In this thirteenth century illumination of one of Hildegard's prose visions, the entire cosmos is inscribed in the breast of Christ, whose arms arc into an all-embracing sphere. Proceeding from the bearded Godhead, Christ is the Love from and toward whom the universe is perfectly ordered. Concentric spheres symbolize the cosmic elements through whose rays of light Divine Love streams; animal figures symbolize specific virtues through whose breath Divine Love pulses. All aim toward the human figure. "Humanity stands in the midst of the structure of the world," Hildegard writes, because "humanity is powerful in the power of its soul." It can do great good or evil depending on how the soul engages the particular virtues connected to each bodily organ. Scala/ Art Resource, NY.*

who "grows bright in human shape"; we are "building up the limbs of his beautiful body." In the finale, Christ himself even speaks through them, reminding the Father that his tired limbs are the people struggling right now to put on the jeweled Virtues, which will complete his glorious body on earth.[7]

The images throughout Hildegard's poetry draw on the cosmology that she systematically expounded in two visionary prose treatises. Since she was a consummate person of her age—abbess of the monastery she founded, moralist, scientist, composer, poet, and apocalyptic prophet whose visions had been approved by the pope—the configurations of Jesus in her poetry serve well as our example of his ways of appearing in medieval verse. In the liturgical poems that Hildegard composed for her nuns to sing, which she collected under the title *Symphony of the Harmony of Celestial Revelations,* the explicit subject is, as we'd expect, more often Mary or a saint than Jesus. Yet, as we'd also expect, he is ever-present, in metaphor, as the meaning of their meaning. He is the light, the blossom, the dawn, that issued from Mary. He is "heaven's harmonies" that "rang" from her womb. He "put on vestments / woven of flesh / cut from a woman / born of Adam / to bleach the agony out of his clothes." We've seen these images before; medieval poets are striving not for originality but for an ever fuller vision of their inherited truth. Hildegard's intensely compressed vision, however, generates striking new condensations of the standard symbols. "Hence the heavens dropped dew upon the grass," she writes of the Virgin, "and the whole earth was made glad, / because her womb brought forth wheat, / and because the birds of heaven / had nests in it." Hildegard is tracing here the classic parabolic sweep of the Philippians hymn, but in her hands the hymn's successive moments—Christ's descent through the Incarnation to the Crucifixion, followed by his ascent in the Resurrection—are compacted into a single allegorical metaphor cluster. The "wheat," born of the Spirit's dew watering the earth of Mary's womb, is both the eucharistic bread recalling Christ's sacrificial death and also the tree where birds nest, an image Jesus uses in the Gospels for the kingdom of heaven toward which his Resurrection will draw all creation. Ephrem, too, made vivid metaphors of the basic christic drama of the Philippians hymn, but Hildegard's vision, eight hundred years later, differs. Both poets are energized by the wonder of the Incarnation; but while Ephrem produces successive paradoxes imagining ever anew the mystery of God made human, Hildegard fills in more and more allegorical details all connected within a single unifying cosmology.[8]

While Hildegard puts her fully articulated cosmology into prose and draws from it in her poetry, Dante does it all together, two centuries later, in the poem that represents the literary high point of the Middle Ages. Dante's pilgrim journey in the *Divine Comedy* is an orderly passage through a universe where every detail of human behavior has meaning in relation to the divine love made known in Christ. But though systematized, the *Commedia*'s world isn't the least static. It buzzes with the political and social life of Dante's own day, as the people he meets speak their regrets and desires, their advice and warnings, their blessings and curses from the place in the cosmic order where their actions have put them. And always we are propelled through that order by the poet's personal moral drama—his desire to learn where he has gone astray and to mend his ways so as to pursue the good—and by the terza rima stanzas whose interlocking rhymes pulse forward with a threefold rhythm meant to evoke the Holy Trinity, that threefold love of God toward which human nature is (in Dante's view) inexorably drawn. When Dante gets to Paradise, not only is everything surging upward toward the absolute presence of "the Love that moves the sun and the other stars," but all the holy souls along the way are spinning in the joy of this love. It is in the *Paradiso,* of course, that Christ is most vividly present, and always as light, which is the medium of the heavenly realm. So he shines forth in canto 14 as a Cosmic Cross of divine rays along which the holy souls blissfully scurry, glittering like stars drawing their light from his. And he is the Radiant Substance that dazzles Dante's sight in canto 23 when Beatrice gives him a glimpse of Christ Triumphant, "the wisdom and power which opened / a road between the earth and heaven."[9]

But at the very same time that the medieval stage of the poets' Jesus fills with this Cosmic Christ in whom every creature and idea and institution in the universe finds its place, another stage that could hardly look more different is being set up. It is the devotional stage, empty of all but two or three figures yet filled with feeling. The Franciscan order, founded in the thirteenth century, was the main force behind the scenes of this new emotionally rich spirituality rooted in a recovery of the humanity of Jesus. In step-by-step prose handbooks, the most influential of which was the *Meditationes Vitae Christi,* Franciscan piety directed attention especially to Jesus on the Cross, so as to evoke identification with his suffering. "Begin at his head and look down to his toe," directs one of the many poeticized versions of the *Meditationes.* "You'll find no meaning but anguish and woe." These lines were composed in Middle English; I've only modernized the language a bit. All over Europe, the message and mood of the *Meditationes* was being put not only into Latin poems like the lyrical *Philomela* of John Pecham, but also into vernacular verse composed for the peasantry. The simple, vivid language was meant to move listeners literally to tears: tears of pity and sorrow for Jesus' suffering, of repentance for their own current sins (which continued to draw out his torments even now), of loving desire to share his pain. "Alas, Jesus, my sweet," the poets cry; "now they drive cruel nails into your dear flesh, now your face pales, now your sides stream red with blood!" The poems out of which I've formed this composite verse are even more drenched in pathos, using devices like the dramatic present tense and a speaker pictured so close to Jesus' body that he can peer deep into the gory detail of each of the Five Wounds.[10]

After a millennium of exalted titles for Jesus, the devotional appeal to his humble *humanitas* is quite startling. He is addressed tenderly by his personal name, Jesus. He wears not the Triumphant King's glorious crown but his original crown of thorns from the Gospel narrative. His title, taken from one of Isaiah's descriptions of the Suffering Servant (53:3), is Man of Sorrows. He is also very much the Son of Mary, who becomes Mother of Sorrows. In the visual art as well as the popular poetry produced by this devotional movement, Mary's grief at the foot of the Cross is so intensely imagined that the theme becomes the double passion of Mother and Son. Or even, we could say, the triple passion of the poet in there with them, so passionately does the poet long to share their pain. "Holy Mother! pierce me through: / In my heart each wound renew / Of my Savior crucified," begs the poet in the most famous product of this genre, the fourteenth-century Latin poem *Stabat Mater,* which stands Mary right next to her Son, "through her heart, his sorrow sharing, / All his bitter anguish bearing." The heart is clearly where the action is on the thirteenth- and fourteenth-century devotional stage. Mary's heart is emotionally pierced by the sword that wounds her Son, who in some poems and paintings offers a literally bleeding, cloven heart to the beholder. The poet in turn, as beholder become actor in the scene, not only wrings his own heart in shared anguish with Mother and Son but also offers it back, as in the line of the fourteenth-century English poet Richard Rolle: "Jesu, receive my heart, and bring me to thy love."

THE LINE COULD ALMOST have come from John of the Cross (1542–1591), whose poems of mystic love between the soul and Christ are treasures of Spanish lyrical verse. Yet with John of the Cross, we enter a radically different literary and religious world from that of medieval devotion. In between had come the Italian Renaissance, with its invention of subjectivity and of lyrical verse forms to express the poet's personal shifts of mood and mind, especially in states of love. In between had also come the beginning of the Protestant Reformation, which broke up the comprehensively integrated medieval world in ways we'll return to. For John and his Spanish compatriots, the most directly felt force was the Catholic Counter-Reformation, which so rigorously forbade unorthodox ideas that creative thinkers turned in on themselves merely for survival. That at least is one explanation for the rich body of mystical literature produced in sixteenth-century Spain, including the classic works of Fray Luis de León and of John's own mentor, Teresa of Avila.

In the mysticisms of all religious traditions, the predominant figure of God is Lover. For John of the Cross, the Lover is Jesus configured specifically as Bridegroom: loving spouse of humankind, of the Church, and of the poet's own soul. John gets this figure of Jesus from Christianity's longstanding allegorical reading of the biblical Song of Songs, but John's poetic recastings are so fresh that they still engage readers today. In one of his ballads using a popular lilting Spanish verse form, he imagines the Father and Son in heaven before the Incarnation, discussing the need for the Son to take on human form. It is a nonbiblical scene that other poets of various eras have enjoyed imagining: picturing, we could say, the scene that must have preceded that first moment of the Philippians hymn where Jesus voluntarily descends into flesh. In the dialogue of John's ballad, Father and Son both see the descent as the Bridegroom's embrace of his bride by taking on her "likeness," for in the law of "perfect love" (says the Father), the lover "becomes like" his beloved for their mutual "delight." The response of the human soul to this self-sacrificing gesture of divine love is what John elaborates in his most famous—indeed, beloved—poem, 'The Dark Night.' Taking on the role of bride, the poet describes himself so "inflamed" by love that he rushes into the dark night to a union with the Beloved in which both are "transformed," fused into one: "amado con amada / amada en el amado trasformada." That play between the words for "lover" and "transformed" is untranslatable, and I've yet to see an English rendition of the poem that fully conveys its seductiveness: John's frankly erotic language pulses through the intriguing verse form of the lira, which pulls the reader forward with its rhyme scheme staggered between long and short lines.[11]

The Italian Renaissance verse forms that John is drawing on continue to shape the poets' Jesus of the seventeenth-century baroque all over the continent and even across the Atlantic Ocean, where European literary culture followed mercantile and missionary concerns. The Petrarchan sonnet, invented for the theme of secular love, was especially suited—with its play of emotion and wit, its acrobatic mental twists—for elaborating the core Christian paradox of a God loving us so much that he became human to make us divine. In sacred sonnets like those of Miguel de Guevara (1585?–1646?), an Augustinian monk who worked among the indigenous peoples of New Spain, the poet adapts the love sonnet's tropes to play with what it means to exchange love with such a Lord. In the celebrated "I am not moved to love thee, my Lord God," probably by Guevara, the poet stands before the Cross much like the poet on the medieval devotional stage. Yet here on the baroque stage, the head as much as the heart is where the action is. Teasing out a different sense of being "moved" in nearly every line, caressing the sound and multiple signification of words, the baroque poet seems as much in love with his own language as with his Lord. And in love with stretching the configurations of love itself into baroque poetry's infamous conceits: those jarring metaphors that yank together images from different conceptual worlds, pulling taut their meanings as if tempting them to snap. In one poem from an astounding sequence of five hundred twenty sonnets composed by the Frenchman Jean de La Ceppède (1548–1623) to picture instant by instant the four Gospels' final chapters, the poet prays to follow Jesus by escaping his own worldly distractions like the young man who escaped arrest at Gethsemane by slipping out of his clothes (Mark 14:51–2). And the Polish poet Zbigniew Morsztyn (1620?–1690?), taking an epigraph from the Song of Songs in one of his cycle of one hundred thirteen 'Emblems,' breathlessly runs after his Beloved only to find him "nakedly" stretched on the cross as on a bed stripped of pillow and sheet, "his only bedding" his torment and pain.[12]

Baroque poetry doesn't limit Jesus to the figure of Lover. The Renaissance revival of classical literature had made pastoral a popular mode, and Jesus as Shepherd is again on stage, in the guise in which we last saw him in the Virgilian pastoral of Prudentius. The prolific Spanish writer Lope de Vega (1562–1635) pulls off the feat of fashioning Jesus as at once both Shepherd and Lover in his much-quoted sonnet 'Shepherd who with your tender calls.' Sor Juana Inés de la Cruz (1651–1695), the brilliant poet of New Spain (now Mexico), who transformed into dazzling baroque every genre she touched, has Jesus triple his roles in her liturgical verse play *The Divine Narcissus*. The title character, who is Christ in classical dress, in one scene appears as a shepherd calling for the Gospel's lost sheep as for his beloved who has strayed: "Braving these rugged woods / until my feet are torn," says the Crucified Jesus as Narcissus as Shepherd Lover, "I leave the flock behind, / to follow your foolish steps; / still you spurn this love of mine, / though for you I've left the other ninety-nine." This isn't the Christ of the earliest Christian centuries, who draws all images into himself by his newly redemptive being. What holds together these multiple figures of Jesus isn't the energy of a new theological vision but the poet's own wit. Not that Sor Juana's figures of Jesus aren't perfectly orthodox; indeed, in her villancicos, dance songs commissioned by the Church to instruct and entertain the peasantry at religious festivals, Jesus appears in forms easily recognized by the common people: Word, Baby (at the Nativity), and of course Lover. But Sor Juana plays word games with the Word, makes puns on the Baby's crying at his birth for our sins for which he'll die, and turns the Baby God into Cupid wounding us with his arrows of love, all in the joyful beat of a traditonal folk dance pattern.[13]

Behind all this baroque intellectual sparkle, with its perception of a reality so fragmented and unstable that only the poet's wit could yank together its disparate elements, lay the complex of forces—most notably those of the Protestant Reformation—that had ripped apart the harmoniously ordered medieval universe. I think it's safe to say that nothing in European life and thought was left untouched by the Reformation and its ripple effects (perhaps too gentle a metaphor, considering the turbulent storms and even the literal wars of tidal wave force that reconstructed not only the ecclesial but also the political landscape). For our subject of the poets' Jesus, the point we need to focus on is where the Reformation touched—indeed, took firm hold of—Christianity's central character, as it did from the start in Luther's determined recasting of Jesus as a living presence. Translating the Gospels into the German people's own tongue so that they could make the Word of God their very own, preaching sermons that spurned allegorical exegesis in favor of concrete application of Scripture to current daily life, Luther offered, as Jaroslav Pelikan aptly summarizes it in *Jesus through the Centuries,* "a depiction of Jesus marked by such freshness of language that Jesus became a sixteenth-century contemporary." Luther's liturgical and sacramental reforms were aimed at encouraging each believer's personal encounter with this living Jesus. To this end, he radically diminished the priest's role as intermediary and fostered full congregational participation at Mass, for instance through more singing of hymns, many of which Luther himself composed.

Luther's immeasurable impact on subsequent poets' Jesus came not through his hymn texts, however, but through the direct personal relation with God's Word—in the living Christ and in the living vernacular Scripture—that his entire movement pushed. The most dramatic result for poetry can be seen on the stage of the seventeenth-century religious verse that we know best in English through such poets as John Donne, George Herbert, Henry Vaughan, and Edward Taylor. I don't mean to imply that Luther was the sole producer and director of this unprecedented staging. Calvin and the other major Protestant reformers went even further in relocating the Christian life from what they condemned as external ritual trappings to the interior of the believer's soul, where a prescribed psychospiritual plot was expected to be followed: from sorrow for one's sins to desperate longing for Christ's mercy to gratitude for sanctification through Christ's grace. Also encouraging a prescribed course of self-examination were the Counter-Reformation guidebooks that aimed to co-opt the Protestant inculcation of personal contact with Jesus while also correcting the emotionalism of the earlier Franciscan *Meditationes* with a theologically sophisticated engagement of the intellect. These sixteenth-century guided meditations on the life of Christ, most influentially the *Spiritual Exercises* composed by Ignatius, were immensely popular with believers of all the burgeoning Christian denominations on the continent and in England. The combined effect on Christian poetry of these various guided self-examinations was a radical relocation, an interiorizing, of the Christian drama. The entire stage—props and scenery, curtains and floorboards, all the characters including Jesus himself—is now set up within the poet's own soul.[14]

Sometimes a poem's plot lies precisely in this inward transposition of the story. Citing the disciple's question to Jesus in John 1:38—"Where are you staying?"—Vaughan's poem 'The Dwelling-Place' moves through various proffered answers, all external locales (fountain, mountain, star), to conclude: "But I am sure, thou dost now come / Oft to a narrow, homely room, . . . My God, I mean my sinful heart." Edward Taylor toys with the "wonder" of Jesus' "renting" as home the poet's own heart in his 'Meditation 2.24' on the key incarnational line of John 1:14, "the Word became flesh and lived among us." The mutual indwelling of Jesus and his followers is a motif of John's Gospel, playfully developed as early as the third-century poem that we looked at, on Jesus as Lord of the Dance. But Taylor's treatment can't be imagined in any century but the seventeenth. Unique to his time is not only the baroque style of wit that for Taylor is grateful play with God's gracious Word, plus the particularizing of the Incarnate Word's "flesh" as the poet's very own, but also an internalizing of the whole typological universe. In the single phrase "Thou'lt tent in mee," Taylor makes all these characteristically seventeenth-century moves. Teasing out conceits on his own "flesh" as Christ's "house" or "tabernacle" or "tent" in which Christ shares (via a pun on the Latin *tentare*) the poet's personal *temptations,* Taylor also draws in several tabernacles and tents where God dwells in the Old Testament. These are standard typological figures: Ephrem and Hildegard, to take two poets whose incarnational images we've seen as representative of their eras, might have used these types to prefigure the Incarnation as God's ultimate tabernacling on earth. But while Ephrem would have played with the paradox of Christ's tenting in Mary's womb so as to bring us all into his heavenly tent, and Hildegard would have set the Old Testament tent in its orderly place in an objectified system of cosmological meaning, Taylor houses the tent under the poet's own skin.[15]

Seeing the whole Christian drama acted out within the poet's self seems strikingly modern, and this internalizing certainly helps explain, along with the baroque delight in language games, the twentieth century's affinity for poetry of the seventeenth. So it's important to clarify what is happening, and not happening, on the internalized seventeenth-century devotional stage. These poets never thought for an instant that Christ lived *only* in their own selves; there isn't the shred of a solipsistic danger such as Wallace Stevens flirts with in, say, his 'Final Soliloquy of the Interior Paramour.' Nor, in casting Christ within their own psychospiritual drama, were the seventeenth-century poets setting themselves apart from other people or puffing themselves up with divinity, as the Romantics would later do. To the contrary, as they saw it, personal engagement with Christ was what joined them with other Christians, in the story of human sin and divine grace that all shared.

All shared as well a figure of Jesus who is remarkably free from the denominational contentiousness of Reformation ecclesial and secular politics. Looking at the seventeenth-century poets' Jesus, one would usually be hard put to tell if he is Protestant or Catholic. The Lover to whom the Augustinian monk Guevara confesses unworthiness in his sonnets is certainly akin to the Anglican priest Herbert's "Love," who famously "bade me welcome: yet my soul drew back, / Guiltie of dust and sinne." The Bridegroom whom the Carmelite John of the Cross chases into the night is also pursued by the Puritan minister Taylor through a series of passionate meditations on the Song of Songs. Even so protesting a Protestant as John Milton (1608–1674) casts in his poetry a Jesus who for the most part would be welcome in Rome. Much has been made of Milton's "heretical" Arianism: his conviction, clearly stated in his prose, that Jesus, though the Christ, is not of equal rank with God the Father. But this aspect of Milton's Jesus hardly comes into play in *Paradise Lost.* There a quite orthodox Christ steps right out of Colossians 1:16 and the Nicene Creed to orchestrate the world's creation in accord with their line that "through him all things were made," while in another scene he arranges with the Father to become fallen humankind's Redeemer in doctrinal terms that Anselm would have approved.

Nor is there anything heretical or even particularly Protestant in the Jesus of *Paradise Regained*. The poem's drama lies in the human Jesus' resisting Satan's temptations in the desert by coming to fuller understanding of his own identity as Christ, but this identity is never in doubt. Milton's interest in the poem is one that intrigued the Christianity of the second to fourth centuries: pondering the fine points of how Jesus can be both human and divine. What's new is putting the pondering in Christ's own mind. It is Milton's version of the interior stage that seventeenth-century poets were setting for Jesus. Not sharing his poetic contemporaries' absorption in their inner relation to Christ, Milton is absorbed instead—at least in *Paradise Regained*—in Christ's inner relation to himself.

At the same time that the seventeenth century poets' Jesus is being drawn inward, he is also being transported outward across the globe. We've seen him move across the Atlantic in the verses of Guevara and Taylor and Sor Juana, but there he remains in Western poetic modes. The real cultural leap he makes in this century is over to China, with the Jesuit missions. The Jesuits' converts there tended to be from the literati class, educated people who, at a time of intellectual and spiritual restlessness, were already shifting back and forth among Taoism, Confucianism, and Buddhism, searching for the best answers to life's ultimate questions. Those who found more satisfactory answers in the Lord of Heaven Teaching, as Christianity was called, still had to relate their new religion to their culture's classic teachings, especially those of Confucius. Among the writings of these converts that survived the official persecution of Christianity that had set in by the middle of the eighteenth century, there is a range of nuanced responses to the challenge.[16] For the scholar Zhang Xingyao (1633–1715), who was baptized in a Jesuit community whose motto was "Supplement Confucianism and displace Buddhism," Christianity was a harmonious continuation of Confucianism. The Jesus of Zhang's treatises and poems (all literati wrote poetry as a matter of course) is the sage-incarnation of the Lord of Heaven, who can help lead people back to the purity of Confucius's moral teachings. But the renowned painter and poet Wu Li (1631–1718), though comfortable with Confucian moral precepts, was struck by a radical uniqueness in Christianity. Learning of the Incarnation had astounded him. After his baptism at about age forty-four, he set himself the bold task of creating the first Christian Chinese poetry, putting into traditional Chinese verse forms his thoroughly sophisticated understanding of Christian theology. As a good literatus, Wu Li followed Chinese poetic conventions as much as he could. But often he couldn't, and this was the very point of his unprecedented mood and message. His poetry's tone of ecstatic joy, represented by exclamation points in the English translation, had been unheard of in his culture's verse. And he had to invent new poetic language for Christian concepts that had no counterparts in the Chinese classics. As much as possible, he draws on classical Chinese images: heaven as a "mountaintop," for instance, toward which we can ascend on a "ladder." But Wu Li's mountaintop has a spiritual topography foreign to the Chinese heaven:

as "the palace of the Lord," it is the place from which "one day, a baby boy came down to earth" to "save our souls from their destructiveness." Wu Li's heaven is also our own "native land," but because the devil keeps us ensnared in our fallen state, "the heaven in our nature / we let wither away." So we are powerless to ascend the ladder to heaven on our own, as Confucian moral teaching exhorts. Only when the ladder becomes "the wonder of the Cross!"—a term and concept previously nonexistent in Chinese—can we "fall in behind Jesus, / look up with reverence towards the top of that mountain, / follow His every step." Since Jesus' role as redemptive mediator between heaven and earth had no precedent in Chinese thought, and the Incarnation took place in a land so far away, Wu Li is eager to stress the universality of Christian redemption. So while one poem declares that "the Lord came down from Heaven / to show His grace in the distant West," another exclaims "His grace goes wide!" And in another (Wu Li never tires of finding new phrasing for what to him is the ultimate wonder):

> Jesus
> came down and was born,
> came down to save us and redeem
> ten thousand countries, distant places.

BACK IN THE distant place where Jesus had grown to doctrinal maturity, the poets' Jesus was about to suffer a shock: the electric shock of the European Enlightenment, whose lightening bolts aimed to numb his divine nature and nullify his redemptive role. Gathering most of its energy from French philosophes like the satirically charged Voltaire and the brilliantly volatile Diderot, the Enlightenment struck out at Christianity as "superstitious fanaticism." Inspired by the urbane skepticism that they found in the ancient classics recovered by the Renaissance, enthusiastic about the rational methods of the new science, the philosophes declared an end to "the Christian millennium" that had been fettering natural human reason and devastating Europe with its internecine wars. With the goal of "bringing people back to common sense," as Rousseau put it, the Enlightenment proudly announced the start of a secular age. The fundamental faith of the age was to be in human reason; "natural philosophy," unaided by revelation, would discover all the truths and values that humankind needs. The Enlightenment platform touted eclecticism and tolerance over dogma, practical morality over theological speculation, and, above all, the autonomy of the freely inquiring human person. "Freethinking" was the rage; everything was now subject to criticism; Voltaire praised Montaigne because "he always knows how to doubt." Nothing was sacred—least of all religion. Though God was still in the picture for most philosophes, he stayed vaguely in the background, desiring human good. Religion was fine as long as it toed the Enlightenment line and didn't make, in the name of "revelation," higher claims than human reason itself could assert. Miracles, by definition contrary to nature, were out of the question since nothing could disrupt the order of nature, not even God. The so-called miracles recounted in the Gospels were simply "ridiculous," snorted Voltaire, and the story of Jesus' resurrection a "fantasy." The Christianity approved by the Enlightenment—and adopted by a remarkable number of influential clergy, so much are people creatures of their age—was an ethical system and no more. Kant summed up the eighteenth century when he declared religious belief a matter of moral judgment by one's own conscience and posited Jesus as model of moral perfection.[17]

Where did this leave the poets' Jesus? Not much in evidence, actually. In such a climate, he was hardly likely to inspire the Muse. Poetry itself is not much in evidence anyway among the French philosophes; their favored literary forms were the treatise, the dictionary, and that consummate rationalist product, the encyclopedia. In England, the eighteenth century did turn out grand poetry in the public mode: didactic, satirical, always moral. On the rare occasions when Jesus enters this poetic stage, he tends to be spared the satiric barbs that are shot at Christianity, but he is less adored than respected, as a sublime moral teacher. Teacher was indeed one of his original New Testament roles, but now it is practically the only one he is left with. He is sometimes still called Christ, but—in the wake of the new biblical criticism, which we'll hear more of in the next chapter—even sincere Christians were no longer quite sure what this title meant. It's a sign of the times that Alexander Pope could write his poem *Messiah* solely for the pleasure of rendering Isaiah's prophecy as Virgilian eclogue, without the least interest in the Christian Messiah per se. Even the devout poet Christopher Smart, so publicly fervent in his religious expression that his rationalist contemporaries locked him up as insane, writes extravagantly joyous verse celebrating the Creator God but not making much of Jesus. In a few Gospel parables that he versifies, Smart uses them and Jesus for moral lessons right in the Enlightenment mode.[18]

A more piously treated Jesus does appear in the poetry of a religious revival that arose in reaction to the bland moralism that rationalist Christianity had become. Pietism (as the evangelical movements in Germany, England, and the United States were collectively called) deliberately addressed the believers' feelings that were so scoffingly ignored by rationalist intellectualism. The hymns written for evangelical worship are of uneven poetic quality, but some of the best are still sung today. They put into verse the pietist themes of personal experience of the living Jesus and confidence in one's personal salvation. Jesus is "my dear Redeemer" whose praise is sung in Charles Wesley's popular 'O for a Thousand Tongues,' while Isaac Watts gratefully and famously "survey[s] the wondrous Cross." Surely the most extensive poetic expression of evangelical feeling is, however, not a hymn but the nine-thousand line *Night Thoughts,* which the British poet Edward Young published in 1742–46. Begun after the death of his wife, this blank verse case for immortality rests firmly on orthodox

Christian consolation. Addressing with a sense of urgency a libertine young man called Lorenzo, the poem insists that it is only because of "Religion! Providence!"—because "the ransom was paid" for you, because "to man the bleeding cross has promised all," because "He rose!"—that "thine is redemption . . . Redemption!" There aren't quite as many exclamation points as words in *Night Thoughts,* but the count is close. They are the punctuation mark of the poet's faith that "to believe, Lorenzo! is to feel." Young's belief is certainly in Jesus as "Son of Heaven," "King of glory," and so on; a more generalized "Deity" who ensures human immortality is, however, much more on the scene. Though not at all to our current taste, *Night Thoughts* clearly fed a hunger in its day. The Wesley brothers quoted from it in their Methodist services; it was gobbled up all over Europe in various tongues, including Portuguese and Hungarian; in England, a favorite gift item well into the nineteenth century was a bound volume (we can scarcely imagine today such a weighty gift) comprising *Night Thoughts, Paradise Lost,* and James Thomson's *Seasons.*

A decisive element of the success of *Night Thoughts* was no doubt that it incorporated much of the rationalist worldview—its celebration of science, for instance—but subsumed natural religion into the only complete faith, which was (in the pietists' view) the Christian revelation. But the battle between a popular piety of the heart and an elitist rationalism of the head was far from over. We can see the war go on in the life of the young woman who became George Eliot, with whom we now settle down into a more calmly paced tour through the poets' Jesus of the nineteenth and twentieth centuries. We're done with the fast-forward run from scene to scene. In fact, that theater metaphor itself, which has enabled us to glimpse quickly the poetic configurations of Jesus of his first eighteen centuries, won't need to be so much at center stage. We'll be strolling around the scene ourselves, getting better acquainted with some of the poets, taking a leisurely look at their Jesus from a variety of angles. Most of the book will focus on the remarkable range of things that happen to him in the twentieth century. But to understand them, we first need a solid grounding in that transformative movement of the nineteenth: Romanticism.

TWO

Jesus as Romantic Hero

On Sunday morning, January 2, 1842, Mary Ann Evans refused to go to church with her father. This twenty-two-year-old woman, who would become George Eliot with the publication of her first fiction fourteen years later, was living with her widowed father in the English town of Coventry. Mr. Evans was an upstanding member of the Church of England, and Mary Ann had been accompanying him to church enthusiastically—indeed with the heightened enthusiasm of an evangelicalism that she had fervently embraced since mid-adolescence. But, always absorbing herself with deep seriousness in the intellectual currents of the time, she had been probing the rationalist critique of Christianity with her Coventry friends Cara and Charles Bray, whose large intellectual circle included Europe and America's leading freethinkers. Cara was holding to the strong Unitarian faith of her family, believing in a God whose goal was human goodness and in a Christ distinct from God but given as humanity's model of the perfect moral life. Charles had jumped into evangelicalism in his youth but out of Christianity altogether in early adulthood; now he was writing books of "natural philosophy." Mary Ann, wrestling with her doubts about Christianity as a revealed religion, came to a position somewhere between those of Cara and Charles. In a long letter to her father, explaining why she could no longer in good conscience go to church, she wrote:

> I wish entirely to remove from your mind the false notion . . . that I have any affinity in opinion with Unitarians more than with other classes of believers in the Divine authority of the books comprising the Jewish and Christian Scriptures. I regard these writings as histories consisting of mingled truth and fiction, and while I admire and cherish much of what I believe to have been the moral teaching of Jesus himself, I consider the system of doctrines built upon the facts of his life and drawn as to its materials from Jewish notions to be most dishonourable to God and most pernicious in its influence on individual and social happiness. . . . I could not without vile hypocrisy and a miserable truckling to the smile of the world for the sake of my supposed interests, profess to join in worship which I wholly disapprove.[1]

Mr. Evans was scandalized, a family crisis ensued, and other more orthodox Coventry friends—genuinely concerned that such radical opinions would keep Mary Ann from getting a decent husband—tried to lure her back to the conventional fold. After four months of anguish on all sides, father and daughter agreed to a compromise: Mary Ann would take her body to weekly church, but her mind would be permitted to follow its pursuits with a free conscience. Two years later it had led her to become the official English translator of the book that was creating havoc in Germany because it treated the Gospels as myth, David Friedrich Strauss's *Das Leben Jesu*.

ALTHOUGH GEORGE ELIOT wasn't a poet, I've begun with this episode from her life because it's a wonderful window onto the swirling personal/philosophical/religious currents of the tumultuous time to be covered in this chapter. Rugs pulled out from under settled Christian beliefs were getting a vigorous shaking in the blustery fresh air, turning the orthodox comforts of pew and parlor topsy-turvy and casting down Jesus himself—naked of accumulated Church doctrine—in Nazareth.

It was actually theologians who were yanking out the rugs to give them a good shaking, in order to get, themselves, a breath of new life. At the start of the nineteenth century, Protestant Christian theology felt dusty and faded. Although the evangelicalism that fired up the young Mary Ann Evans had been truly enlivening popular faith since the middle of the eighteenth century, this was a religious movement of the heart, not the intellect, and it left theology seeming stuffy and irrelevant. But what had left theology even more in the dust was eighteenth-century rationalism. With Christianity reduced to "the moral teaching of Jesus"—as the young Mary Ann would put it to her father, parroting what had become by then the popularized rationalist line—theology had faded into a moral utilitarianism.[2]

Rationalism took the life out of Christian theology in another way as well, by subjecting the Bible to historical criticism, a practice that had in fact begun in the seventeenth century. Spinoza, for one, had developed criteria for determining the historical validity of biblical passages, his purpose being to "free" human reason from the authority of religion. Enlightenment criticism then applied increasingly probing historical methods to the Bible, studying its semantics and literary style and the Jewish world it came from. The result was that late eighteenth century scholars were commonly concluding that Scripture and theological orthodoxy alike were basically "myth," in the reductive sense of mere stories. (Hence Mary Ann Evans's judgment, a half century later, that the Scriptures were "histories consisting of mingled truth and fiction." It takes time for controversial scholarly theories to be adopted by young intellectuals in the countryside, especially of another country; most of this critical scholarship was going on in Germany.) By the close of the eighteenth century, the authority of Scripture and of orthodoxy were so thoroughly undermined that theology felt irrelevant, passed by—like the drab old furniture and carpets in a room that the new generation has abandoned in favor of a stylish, open sunporch newly constructed for the house.

What saved theology were the bold moves of a few creative minds at the start of the nineteenth century. They yanked up the dusty rugs, dragged them outside, and shook them hard in the fresh air. But they were doing more than just shaking out the dust of moral piety and of an old, tired, settled orthodoxy. In this particular air was the Romantic spirit: fresh gusts of Self Confidence, of Imagination, of History's Flux as a magnificent Force. I capitalize these terms because Romanticism truly enlarged them all, in ways that I'll be elaborating throughout the chapter. For now, all we need to note is their influence on theology. Through certain thinkers open to the Romantic spirit in the air (Schleiermacher, Coleridge, and Hegel are the most significant), theology was transformatively renewed.

In a sense, what these creative philosopher-theologians did was shout *Yes!* to the trends that had seemed threats to theology before. To pietism's internalizing of religion, for instance, they said *yes,* the believer's personal experience is indeed where the action is. Yet they plunged into this action so deeply as to reconceive it as the basis of theology itself. Theology, that is, became fundamentally *subjective* for the first time; nearly two centuries later, we're still drawing out the implications of this radical shift of theology's ground from God to the believing human person. Schleiermacher especially, who had been raised in pietism, seized on its valorization of religious "feeling," which he transformed from mere sentiment into the locus of the entire life of faith. The believing *self* intuiting the infinite, the religious *subject* aware of its dependence on God, became theology's starting point.

As for rationalism's reduction of religion, Coleridge and Hegel, in their distinctly separate voices, boldly boomed *yes* to reason. (Shouting and booming seem the only adequate verbs for the grand minds of this era; Romanticism and its contemporaneous philosophies were intellectually noisy, disruptive, showily loud.) Both men, though in widely different ways, affirmed reason by raising it to the realm of transcendence. Coleridge's way was his famous distinction between Understanding and Reason: Understanding he defined as rationalism's scientific mode of reasoning, which was fine as far as it went; while Reason, the higher form of thought, went the whole way. "Whole" is, actually, Coleridge's core concept, along with the Imagination that grasps it and that is, furthermore, Reason at work. Only the Imagination can know God; Christianity for Coleridge can't be "proven" but only lived. His theology, like Schleiermacher's, bursts with the challenge to plunge into the life of faith, which for Coleridge is always a *process.*

This "process" is where Coleridge embraced the flux of history, though it was Hegel who transformed this particular rationalist threat—that Scripture is merely a historical product and hence has no authority—into religion's saving life. Hegel not only said *yes* to historical process; he elaborated his *yes* into a systematic philosophy comprehending every conceivable moment of the dialectic of mind and matter, Subject and Object, in the historical development of the Idea that culminates as Christian Truth. God and humankind meet, for Hegel, in the appearance of the God-man, who is the perfect embodiment of the Idea,

God's coming to self-consciousness in the human person—who in history appeared as the man Jesus Christ.

Christologies were key to all these creative new theologies, which said *yes* to history in a way that would radically reconceive, for the nineteenth century, its construction of doctrines of Christ. The Jesus of history, his human existence in a particular historical time, had to be, henceforth, the basis of any Christology. For our purpose in looking at Jesus' treatment by Romantic poets, the most interesting manifestation of this Christology was the genre of writing best known now by the title his English translator gave to Albert Schweitzer's famous survey of the genre: *The Quest of the Historical Jesus*.[3]

Schweitzer's 1906 book is still the definitive study of the Lives of Jesus that kept theology in turmoil through the nineteenth century, first in Germany, then in England and France as well. And I can't imagine Schweitzer's work being supplanted. It's hard to picture anyone else combining such diverse gifts: the patience to read some seventy-five dense tomes; the sympathy to sink genuinely into the point of view of each; the literary artistry to make each come alive; and the scholarly detachment to note their connections and trends. Though Schweitzer gives each *Life* its due, the one he clearly sees as central is the 1836 *Das Leben Jesu* of David Friedrich Strauss. For Schweitzer, Strauss's significance was his breakthrough "mythological" method, which overcame what had been a standoff between two camps: the supernaturalists, who stood their ground on Scripture's literal truth; and the rationalists, who stood theirs on Scripture's fiction, especially in its so-called miracles. Strauss, "liberated" (his own word) by Hegel's dialectic, found a way to shift the ground entirely: to the worldview of the Gospel writers themselves. There he saw Jewish Messianic expectations inventively engaged with the historic personality of the man Jesus. For Strauss, Scripture was certainly true—but true to the ideas alive at the time of its writing. And Scripture was certainly also myth—but "myth" in the sense no longer of mere fabrication, but of the highest form of religious understanding. Strauss's notion of "myth," in Schweitzer's approving paraphrase, was "the clothing in historic form of religious ideas, shaped by the unconsciously inventive power of legend, and embodied in a historic personality."[4]

Schweitzer, writing seventy years after Strauss, could calmly commend this solution to the century's vexed problem of how to relate the Christ of faith and the Jesus of history. But when published in Germany in 1836, *Das Leben Jesu* was considered so scandalous that Strauss lost his job as professor. And twelve years later, when Mary Ann Evans published her translation, the book caused such a sensation in the English-speaking world that for decades, as George Eliot, she was known as "the translator of Strauss." Holding in my hand now this translation, with its eight hundred pages of small print taking each Gospel passage through the most painstaking analysis, through Greek word-study and contemporaneous source documents and all the contending scholarly critiques, I'm amazed that this work could have caused such a widespread fuss. With our current public debate on controversial issues taking the rhetorical form of bumper stickers, it's wonderful to think of such dense prose being read and argued over by a wide populace.

The scandal wasn't caused only by Strauss's mythological method. Equally upsetting was his conclusion that—while Jesus did embody in his historical person the Hegelian Idea of God-manhood—the Idea is not limited to embodiment in Jesus. "Idea," Strauss writes (imitating Hegel's way of making Idea the acting subject of grammar and history alike),

> is not wont to lavish all its fulness on one exemplar, and be niggardly towards all others—to express itself perfectly in that one individual, and imperfectly in all the rest; it rather loves to distribute its riches among a multiplicity of exemplars which reciprocally complete each other. . . . And is not the idea of the unity of the divine and human natures a real one in a far higher sense, when I regard the whole race of mankind as its realization, than when I single out one man as such a realization? . . . This is the key to the whole of Christology. . . . Humanity is the union of the two natures—God become man, the infinite manifesting itself in the finite, and the finite spirit remembering its infinitude. . . . It is Humanity that dies, rises, and ascends to heaven.[5]

What's radical here isn't really that humanity takes on divine nature; orthodox Christianity since the second century had happily advanced the notion that Christ became human so that we might become divine. Strauss's radical step is to remove Christ's unique incarnational role from the interchange, leaving humanity on its own as the union of divine and human natures. Actually, in the context of the Romantic spirit in the air, Strauss's move seems a logical, even inevitable, product of its time. The previous fifty years of Romanticism in Germany and England had seen the development of a concept of humanity very much in direct touch with the divine. In the next thirty years across the Atlantic the development would be carried further, in the New World's special way; already Emerson, in the very different vocabulary and theological context of his famous 1838 Divinity School Address, was reaching a conclusion similar to that of Strauss.

It's no accident that among Romanticism's seminal minds, one (Goethe) was in Germany, home of most of this creative theology, while two (Coleridge and Emerson) combined in their own person theologian, philosopher, and poet. During the Romantic period, say from the 1770s to the 1860s (taking its largest range, from the early Goethe at one end to the influence on Renan at the other), theology and poetry engaged in a mutually enlivening interaction that hasn't been equalled since. Nor is it likely to be soon; with modernism, as we'll see, religion and poetry set off on their separate ways. But their paths during the Romantic period were closely interlaced—which is why I've had to move through the era's theology on the way toward poetry's handling of the figure of Jesus.

But now, before shifting to the paths charted by the era's major poets, I feel the need to pause and take a deep, slow breath, like the breath we might take before entering a magnificent cathedral or mosque or Hindu shrine. The major Romantic poets self-consciously constructed their lives and works as products of divine inspiration, and by and large they have indeed convinced readers that their poetry, at least at points, almost touches something sublime. Throwing their lives open to experience and their poetry open to their lives, they were gifted with the self-confidence and the imaginative powers to pull off a radical expansion of what it meant to be a poet. They enlarged the poet's role to a grandeur never before reached, or even conceived, in Western literature. If these are large egos we're meeting, they are deliberately so, because these poets saw themselves as encompassing quite frankly everything. "I know perfectly well my own egotism, / And know my omnivorous words," Whitman jauntily writes. "And would fetch you whoever you are flush with myself." We *are* fetched, I think, and by these poets' startling originality as much as by anything. The writers I'll be taking as illustrative of various relations to the figure of Jesus are each distinctly different from one another. No one could mix up the poetry—or the lives—of Goethe and Blake and Whitman. Yet they have in common the ability to persuade us that in their poetry we're in the presence of (in Wordsworth's phrase) "a more comprehensive soul."

IT IS CONVENIENT TO enter this brave new poetic world at the place where Goethe's thought intersects one of the theological controversies we've been following: the vexed question of the Gospels' authenticity. Goethe (1749–1832) had no problem accepting the Gospels' authority, he said,

> for there is in them a reflection of a greatness which emanated from the person of Jesus, and which was of as divine a kind as was ever seen upon earth. If I am asked whether it is in my nature to pay Him devout reverence, I say—certainly! I bow before Him as the divine manifestation of the highest morality. If I am asked whether it is in my nature to reverence the sun, I again say—certainly! For he is likewise a manifestation of the highest Being.[6]

The tone is *echt* late Goethe: grandly self-confident, bowing before life's source, yet without the least subservience. For Goethe, Jesus is undoubtedly divine, with "morality" assumed (as so often in this era) to be divinity's measure. But equally divine is the sun.

Nature worship was right in the Romantic mode. Even German pre-Romanticism, in a 1770s literary movement called the *Sturm und Drang* (Storm and Stress), indulged in what Goethe's early British biographer, George Lewes, calls a "hysterical enthusiasm" for Nature. Lewes was hardly a stodgy conservative; at the time of writing this great biography of Goethe in 1855, he had just left a longstanding free-love marriage (in which he cheerfully adopted the children born to his wife and her lover) to live in a scandalous permanent relationship with George Eliot. Yet the *Sturm und Drang*'s devil-may-care defiance of convention and its rage for anything "natural" were too much even for Lewes. Today most critics agree with his assessment: that worshipping a Nature conceived as no more than (in Lewes' scornful terms) "a compound of volcanoes and moonlight" is mere sentimentality, and that indiscriminate scorn of all rules as too "humdrum" for "genius" is facile adolescent behavior.[7]

The *Sturm und Drang* strikes us today as a self-parody of Romanticism. But Goethe's own major contributions to the *Sturm und Drang* manage to transcend the movement's immaturity, though he composed them when only in his early twenties. Besides the long dramatic chronicle *Götz von Berlichingen,* Goethe wrote at this time the key poems that inspired the new genre of Romantic lyric. 'Prometheus' (1774), actually a fragment of a verse drama that Goethe never completed, is famous for its brazen defiance of orthodox religion, in the name of a humanity that boldly takes its self-creation into its own hands. Goethe's Prometheus confidently declares: "Here I sit, form human beings / After my image." This god-defying, self-creating figure became for the Romantic poets the model construct for their role: the poet-genius who displaces orthodox Christianity's impoverished God by his own creative force.[8]

A few years later, in 'Harzreise im Winter' ('Harz Journey in Winter,' 1777), Goethe elaborated this sense of poetic vocation in the setting that would become Romanticism's defining landscape: the untamed Nature of wilderness brush, rushing streams, and above all (the vertical image is key) stormy mountaintops. The poem's course follows the solitary poet forging his own path up the wild mountainside, this course clearly a metaphor for poetic vocation in the spiritual wilderness that conventional religion—with its old, harsh, biblical God—has made of the world. When the poet reaches the mountain's peak, divine love is urgently invoked, to crown him as laureate:

> The solitary one clothe
> In your golden clouds,
> Wrap round with evergreen,
> Until the rose ripens again,
> The moist hair,
> Oh love, of your poet!
>
> With the dawning torch
> You shine to him
> Through the paths by night,
> Over groundless ways
> On barren fields;
> With the thousand-colored morning
> You bring laughter into his heart;
> With the searing storm
> You carry him upward on high;
> Winter streams rush from the cliffs
> Into his psalm,
> And into an altar of dearest thanks

For him the snow-hung brow
Of the feared peak is transformed,
Which with rows of spirits
Intuiting peoples wreathed.

I quote these two stanzas in full because they give us the Romantic peak experience par excellence. At the mountaintop, poetic imagination is liberated. Through natural forces—whether the wild "searing storm" or the gentle "thousand-colored morning"—divinity breaks through to the poet, who turns this revelation into poetry that is now divine utterance. His poem is a "psalm"; the mountain peak is transformed into his "altar."

A decade later, settling into the more serene wisdom of his middle and late years, Goethe rejected the youthful *Sturm und Drang*. Yet he remained, Lewes notes, "a Poet whose religion was Beauty, whose worship was of Nature." The figure of Jesus is conspicuously absent from Goethe's poetry—but not because of lack of religious faith. Though impatient with conventional piety, Goethe didn't doubt Jesus' divinity; we've seen that, with many people of his period, Goethe reverenced Jesus "as the divine manifestation of the highest morality." But as much as Goethe cared about morality in all his later works, to dramatize real human moral struggles he needed figures who manifested something less (hence more interesting) than moral perfection.

Meanwhile, as Goethe was growing out of the tempestuous self-creation of the *Sturm und Drang,* that sensibility was maturing in England into what would become Romanticism's fully developed construction of the Individual. For the major British Romantic poets, Jesus is out of the picture because, as in 'Prometheus' and 'Harz Journey in Winter,' the role of divine representative on earth is taken over by the poet-genius in communion with natural forces. This communion was conceived as "inspiration" in a quite literal, etymological sense: "spirit" entering "into" the poet. A favorite image for poetic inspiration was the wind-harp, or Aeolian lyre, which makes music as the breeze flows through its strings. Coleridge in his poem 'The Eolian Harp' (1795), and then Shelley in his prose 'Essay on Christianity' (1815) and 'Defence of Poetry' (c.1821), elaborated the image so that the lyre was the poet's imagination, "trembl[ing] into thought" and producing "divinest melody" (i.e., poetry), as over it swept the breeze that was "the breath of universal being," "at once the Soul of each, and God of all." When we associate Romanticism with fresh Spring breezes reinvigorating the spirit, as I did earlier in describing nineteenth-century theological renewal, we're carrying on this key image of the Aeolian harp. With such an image of the creative process, poetry of course had to be written—or at least imagined as written—in the open fields. So Wordsworth starts *The Prelude,* his major autobiographical poem (addressed to his friend Coleridge), "O there is blessing in this gentle breeze," the countryside air in which he can gratefully escape from city confinements and "breathe again!" open to "Aeolian visitations."

Though Shelley was vehemently anti-Christian, Coleridge and Wordsworth were not; each moved through varying relations to Christian orthodoxy. Coleridge began adulthood enthusiastic about a Unitarianism merged with a radical politics of faith in human progress based on imitating Christ's good works. Later, developing a stronger sense of human sin and disillusioned with Unitarianism as too rational and optimistic, Coleridge gradually returned to the religious orthodoxy of the Church of England. Wordsworth in his youth was anticlerical enough to turn down a curacy, but the Church as a structure of social cohesion always appealed to him, and increasingly he clung to the Church of England as the best safeguard of sociopolitical order. Neither of their poetic imaginations, however, were fired up by the figure of Jesus. Coleridge does have one early poem, misleadingly entitled 'Religious Musings,' in which Jesus, "the oppressed Good Man" of Unitarianism, enters in. He is actually there, though, as a jumping-off place for Coleridge's fulminations on current political issues; the poem reads like a versified journalistic editorial. And Wordsworth's late 'Ecclesiastical Sonnets' are even less about Christ; they're a (poetically dull) history of Christianity in England. But there *is* one major British poet of the period for whom Jesus is absolutely central: William Blake (1757–1827).

BLAKE'S JESUS IS THE Romantic poet-genius and more. Critics are divided on whether to class Blake as a Romantic, but—at least in relation to the themes we're following—there's no question that Blake speaks for his time. During the years that the Goethe of the *Sturm und Drang,* and then Coleridge and his companions, were constructing the grand figure of the solitary poet whose divinely inspired will combats society's constraints, Blake was independently configuring Jesus along these very lines. I say "independently" because Blake, unlike Goethe or Coleridge and Wordsworth, never belonged to a literary group; his associations were rather with the radical political and religious communities of late-eighteenth-century London. Nor did he apparently know of the theological reimaginings going on in Germany. Yet he was reacting against the same blandly moralized Jesus and the same Enlightenment rationalism as were the creative theologians I've mentioned.

Blake came to his visions from a working-class background. Unlike the other great English poets of the era, he remained all his life a manual worker and a city-dweller, earning a living as an engraver in the midst of London's filth and noise. (This did not make him worship Nature, however; a major distinction of Blake from Romanticism is that, true mystic that he was, he could worship only God, alive in the whole universe.) The Industrial Revolution affected Blake personally; his working-class passion is speaking when his poems lash out against capitalism's creation of poverty. "London groans in pain," he writes in his prophetic poem *Jerusalem* (1804–1820), because the oppressors of Albion (Blake's name for England, and all the world, in its socially structured dimension):

mock at the Labourer's limbs: they mock at his starv'd Children:
They buy his Daughters that they may have power to sell his Sons:
They compel the Poor to live upon a crust of bread by soft mild arts.

(pl. 30, ll. 28–30)

Blake also blamed the Industrial Revolution, along with the Enlightenment's worship of Reason, for the great evil of alienation. The human person alienated from the world, divided even within itself, and deeply needing reintegration—this core Romantic theme at the heart of Schleiermacher's theology, Hegel's philosophical system, Goethe's and Coleridge's valorization of the "organic whole"—for Blake is the central concern elaborated in his notoriously complex mythological visions. But Blake's concern is the personal pain of the alienated sufferer. For these other great advocates of wholeness, alienation was a theory rather than a lived experience. And while most Romantics celebrating the integrated individual against conventional society were in fact pretty comfortable in conventional society themselves, Blake genuinely wasn't.

Besides the Industrial Revolution, the other major sociopolitical influence on Blake was the French Revolution, which began when he was thirty. Poets everywhere were stirred by this revolution, which was the dominant political force behind Romanticism's praise of "freedom"; Blake isn't unique in this. But no other English poet was so obsessed by the political dimension of freedom being acted out in France. Blake's major poems of the 1790s are inconceivable without the French Revolution, which gave him hope that tyrannies of every kind—political, economic, psychological, moral, ecclesiastical, sexual—could actually be overthrown. The revolution grounded in reality Blake's apocalyptic vision of Albion redeemed as the ideal city, called Jerusalem, which is Blake's symbol of the reintegrated human person, which is also society freed of divisions (of class, of power, of gender, of moral law), which is also the cosmic body of Jesus.[9]

And which is also . . . it's hard to stop. Every symbol in Blake's mythological system is so multilayered and also interlinked with every other that to fully explicate any one would lead into and through the intricate densities of his entire visionary world. There's probably no other poet of whom we lose so much by quoting only a few lines. First, we lose the visual images that, for Blake's engraved poems, are inseparable from the text and that present with irreplaceable immediacy the absolute *humanness* of his visionary universe ("Every thing is Human, mighty! sublime! / In every bosom a Universe expands as wings" [*Jerusalem,* pl. 38, ll. 48–9]). We lose, too, the rich texture of this world so alive with Blake's invented figures of Los and Luvah and Vala and Beulah and Enitharmon and hundreds more, who draw us into their cosmic drama even when we can't put our finger on exactly what they stand for. So it's with a sad sense of necessity that I, like everyone writing about Blake in the context of another subject, leave aside the full life of his visionary universe in order to focus on the point of particular interest, in this case, the entrance of Jesus into Blake's mythological world.

Given the radical inventiveness behind most of Blake's universe, it's remarkable how familiar and traditional his Jesus is. Deeply absorbed in the Bible, Blake drew his Jesus out of its pages, adding dimensions from the English Antinomian tradition, from Christian mystics like Jacob Boehme, and from Swedenborg's theory of cosmic Man as God. Sometimes, as in *Jerusalem,* Jesus seems to step right out of John's Gospel into Blake's mythological world:

> Jesus replied: "I am the Resurrection & the Life.
> I Die & pass the limits of possibility as it appears
> To individual perception, Luvah must be Created
> And Vala; for I cannot leave them in the gnawing Grave
> But will prepare a way for my banished-ones to return.
> Come now with me into the villages, walk thro all the cities;
> Tho thou art taken to prison & judgment, starved in the streets
> I will command the cloud to give thee food & the hard rock
> To flow with milk & wine, tho thou seest me not a season,
> Even a long season & a hard journey & a howling wilderness:
> Tho Valas cloud hide thee & Luvahs fires follow thee:
> Only believe & trust in me, Lo, I am always with thee!"
>
> [pl. 62, ll.17–29)

Blake's Jesus is also the divine person of John's Gospel who lives in mutual indwelling with humankind: "I am not a God afar off, I am a brother and friend; / Within your bosoms I reside, and you reside in me" (pl. 4, ll.18–19). Yet "brother" for Blake is loaded with a socioeconomic meaning not in the Gospel. Disaffected by this time with the French Revolution's bloody and anti-Christian "brotherhood," Blake sees in brotherhood the ideal of pre–Industrial Revolution craftsmen pooling their free imaginations to work at the ongoing task of building Jerusalem. Blake's Jesus, who is the unity of freed creative people, configures this collective salvific work. At the end of *Jerusalem,* after a painfully long series of nearly a hundred plates of Albion "groaning" for salvation (Blake's reenvisioning of the extraordinary image in Romans 8:18–23 of "all creation's groaning in bondage"), finally:

> Jesus appeared standing by Albion as the Good Shepherd
> By the lost Sheep that he hath found, & Albion knew that it
> Was the Lord, the Universal Humanity; & Albion saw his Form
> A Man, & they conversed as Man with Man in Ages of Eternity.
> And the Divine Appearance was the likeness & similitude of Los.
>
> (pl. 98, ll.3–7)

Los is Blake's symbol for the human creative faculty, that is, Imagination. Yet Imagination as Los is still oppressed and torn within itself in our divided world, whereas Jesus is Imagination unfettered by repressions and conflicts. A passage like this gives a sense of the multiple conflations in Blake's figure of Jesus: the Good Shepherd from John's Gospel is Imagination, which is Universal Humanity, who is also Albion redeemed, fully human.

We can see that Blake's Divine Humanity, as he frequently calls it, antici- pates that of David Strauss several years later: humankind as the continuous revelation of God, realized in but not limited to Jesus Christ. To Strauss's rhetor- ical question quoted earlier—"Is not the idea of the unity of the divine and hu- man natures a real one in a far higher sense, when I regard the whole race of mankind as its realization, than when I single out one man as such a realiza- tion?"—Blake would have nodded assent.

Clearly, also, a Jesus who is artistic creativity, who is Imagination at work re- deeming the world, is a figure of the Romantic era. "Jesus & his Apostles and Disciples were all Artists," Blake wrote on his undated engraving *Laocoön,* where he also inscribed: "The Eternal Body of Man is The Imagination, that is God himself, The Divine body, Jesus: we are his Members. It manifests itself in his Works of Art." When Jaroslav Pelikan, in *Jesus through the Centuries,* aptly names the nineteenth-century Jesus "The Poet of the Spirit," he is thinking not only of Blake but of the century's major theologians and biblical historians, for whom Jesus took on the aesthetic powers of the Romantic poet.

In Blake's configuration, this artist-Jesus wields his creative power like a lightning bolt, thundering with Goethe's Prometheus against Christianity itself for reducing religion to moral laws that repress true human life. With biting wit and slashing rhythm, Blake delineates this iconclastic Jesus in his late unfinished poem, 'The Everlasting Gospel':

> Was Jesus Humble? or did he
> Give any proofs of Humility?
>
> . . . .
> . . . he acts with triumphant, honest pride,
> And this is the Reason Jesus died.
> If he had been Antichrist, Creeping Jesus,
> He'd have done anything to please us:
> Gone sneaking into the Synagogues
> And not used the Elders & Priests like Dogs,
> But humble as a Lamb or an Ass,
> Obey himself to Caiaphas.

The deliberately outrageous rhymes (Creeping Jesus/to please us; Synagogues/ Dogs; Ass/Caiaphas) mock groveling obedience to the ruling religious or polit- ical powers as contrary to everything Jesus lived and died for. Rather, Jesus

His Seventy Disciples sent
Against Religion & Government.

.   .   .   .

The Publicans & Harlots he
Selected for his Company,
And from the Adulteress turn'd away
God's righteous Law, that lost its Prey.

"God's righteous Law" is official church law, with its concepts of moral vi.
and of sin, which to Blake's mind is the great enemy of full human developmen..
Only disobedience of repressive authority can free the human spirit. To illustrate his point, Blake reverses the standard lesson on the Gospel episode (Luke
2:41–49) of the child Jesus staying in the temple while his anxious parents wor-
ried about where he was. Preachers of Blake's day (like many still) commonly
used the episode to model Jesus as the perfectly obedient child, but Blake will
have none of this:

Was Jesus gentle, or did he
Give any marks of Gentility?
When twelve years old he ran away
And left his Parents in dismay.
When after three days' sorrow found,
Loud as Sinai's trumpet sound:
"No Earthly Parents I confess—
[I do] My Heavenly Father's business!
Ye understand not what I say,
And, angry, force me to obey."

ONE NEARLY CONTEMPORANEOUS preacher whom we can picture delightedly reading Blake's poem from the pulpit, if he had known of it, was Ralph
Waldo Emerson (1803–1882). Philosopher of transcendentalism, Unitarian
minister who left the Church because he couldn't believe that Christ meant to
establish the sacrament of the Lord's Supper, lecturer who exhorted American
crowds to nonconformity, essayist and poet, Emerson made something uniquely American of the Romantic spirit. An egalitarian like Blake, Emerson
filled his sense of the free individual's potential with the expansiveness of open
plains. "In the presence of nature," he wrote in his 1836 essay 'Nature,' "standing on the bare ground,—my head bathed by the blithe air, and uplifted into infinite space,—all mean egotism vanishes . . . the currents of the Universal Being
circulate through me; I am part or parcel of God." In New England Unitarianism, which had already gotten a bit stuffy, Emerson was more than a
breath of fresh air: he was a gust, practically a tornado, swirling through structures of thought and practice to scatter to the winds everything smacking of

...niformity. His advice in his Address to the Harvard Divinity ... graduating class of 1838 was to worship God not in the "decaying church" but "in the soul." (The Divinity School didn't invite him back for thirty years.)

As I already mentioned in connection with David Friedrich Strauss's conclusion to his 1836 *Das Leben Jesu*, Emerson was almost simultaneously sounding the same note as Strauss. Only substituting "Divinity" or "Deity" for the Hegelian "Idea" of God-manhood (Emerson couldn't for an instant have stood the measured structure of Hegelian moments), we can imagine Emerson saying the very line of Strauss's: Divinity "is not wont to lavish all its fulness on one exemplar, and be niggardly towards all others—to express itself perfectly in that one individual, and imperfectly in all the rest; it rather loves to distribute its riches among a multiplicity of exemplars which reciprocally complete each other." For Emerson, as for Strauss, this was meant to be a direct challenge to historical Christianity's concept of Jesus Christ. The Church "has dwelt with noxious exaggeration about the *person* of Jesus," Emerson said in his Divinity School Address. Jesus was not God any more (or less) than every person is God; Jesus was a "prophet" whose gift to humankind was to have recognized this very fact: "that God incarnates himself in man, and evermore goes forth anew." So while Coleridge grew away from Unitarianism because it had too positive a view of human nature, Emerson grew away from it because its view of human nature wasn't positive enough. In seeing humanity as divine, Emerson was taking Unitarianism's sense of human goodness and carrying it—or (more than carrying, so swirling are his metaphors) sweeping it up, swelling it—to the extreme.

Though Emerson wrote poems, I've always felt that his best poetry by far was in his essays, which move their thought through metaphor—practicing what Emerson preaches about all the world being connected through words. I'm tempted to stay with his poetic prose, so bracing like the crisp fall air. But, as we'd expect from the bits of the essays that I've quoted, Jesus hardly figures in them. And their greater significance for our subject is their influence on Walt Whitman, in whose poetry Jesus merges into the figure of the poet in a way unlike any we've yet seen. Whitman is actually more Emersonian a poet than Emerson himself, and deliberately so: Whitman modeled his poetic persona on the figure Emerson delineates in his essays, especially the essay 'The Poet.' Emerson's Poet has features of the Romantic poet we've met in Europe. He is the "genius" who interprets Nature's secrets for the rest of humankind; he "stands among partial men for the complete man"; with cosmic largeness of mind and spirit, he "traverses the whole scale of experience, and is representative of man, in virtue of being the largest power to receive and to impart"; free of mere convention, he is a "liberating god"; he "re-attaches. . . . to nature and the Whole" everything in life that has been detached from God and thus made ugly. But there's an American touch, I think, in Emerson's extravagance of image, which is almost comic in its wild expansiveness. And there's an explicit chal-

Christ on the Sea of Galilee *(1854), by Eugene Delacroix (France, 1798–1863). Delacroix called himself an agnostic but was drawn to religious subjects as a vehicle for his Romantic aesthetic, which embraced the idea that the divine resides in the artist's own soul. He painted several versions of this Gospel scene (Mark 4:38, Matt. 8:23–27, Luke 8:22–25), evidently gripped by its symbolic power. Amid terrifying storms throwing the disciples, like Delacroix, off balance—including the political and social turbulence of nineteenth-century France—the sleeping Christ is the artist's creative inner spark. "God is within us," Delacroix wrote in a journal entry that would have struck a chord with Goethe and Emerson; "it is that inner pleasure which makes us admire the beautiful, which rejoices us when we have done right and . . . which constitutes the inspiration of men of genius." The Walters Art Gallery, Baltimore.*

lenge for this poet to appear on American soil: "I look in vain for the poet whom I describe" to sing of our specifically American "incomparable materials."

Walt Whitman (1819–1892) took up the challenge. For ten years or so, while working as a journalist and a carpenter in Brooklyn, he carried Emerson's essays around to read on his lunch break. Carefully crafting his poetic self along Emerson's lines, Whitman finally presented this persona to the public in his slim self-published volume of 1855, *Leaves of Grass.* Though hardly read at the time, it has come to be revered as the greatest single volume of poetry in United States literary history.

In the 1855 *Leaves of Grass,* Whitman wrote the book on inclusiveness, a century and a quarter before this became a popular American value. The volume's major poem, untitled then but now known as 'Song of Myself,' is a song of *every* self: "In all people I see myself, none more and not one a barleycorn less"(l. 401). The poem is a celebration of what today we'd call the divine worth of every person, and it's persuasive because the deity is in the details. Whitman's justifiably famous catalogs of individuals caught in an instant of everyday life still startle us with their particularity, as if the poet is throwing a bucket of cold water on our drowsy inattentiveness and saying "Look!"

Jesus is included in the poem, but not more or less than anyone else, and not by name. He, too, enters in a catalog, this one of the poet's all-embracing faith, which takes in the entire history of world religions as Whitman understood it. (Whitman's favorite punctuation mark at the time was the ellipsis; all ellipses in my quotations are his.)

I do not despise you priests;
My faith is the greatest of faiths and the least of faiths,
Enclosing all worship ancient and modern, and all between ancient and
  modern,
Believing I shall come again upon the earth after five thousand years,
Waiting responses from oracles . . . honoring the gods . . . saluting the sun,
Making a fetish of the first rock or stump . . . powowing with sticks in the
  circle of obis,
Helping the lama or brahmin as he trims the lamp of the idols,
Dancing yet through the streets in a phallic procession . . . rapt and austere in
  the woods, a gymnosophist,
Drinking mead from the skull-cap . . . to shasta and vedas admirant . . .
  minding the koran,
Walking the teokallis, spotted with gore from the stone and knife—beating
  the serpent skin-drum;
Accepting the gospels, accepting him that was crucified, knowing assuredly
  that he is divine,
To the mass kneeling—to the puritan's prayer rising—sitting patiently in a
  pew (ll.1092–1103)

The poet knows assuredly that Jesus is divine—but not uniquely divine. Whitman is "accepting" all religions as equal revelations. This wasn't unheard of at the time. All-embracing gestures were in the nineteenth-century mode of German Romantic theology, which Emerson had read and so Whitman would have had a whiff of. But even Schleiermacher, with an expansive temperament as close to Emerson's and Whitman's as the more orderly German intellectual nature would allow, hadn't gone as far as Whitman's spiritual egalitarianism. In his early and immensely influential *Speeches on Religion* (1799), Schleiermacher had celebrated the multiplicity of religions, because no one religious form alone could comprehend the Infinite's whole grandeur. A deeply committed

Christian at his core, however, Schleiermacher still saw Christianity as religion's "highest" form. This passage from 'Song of Myself' would, I think, have given him pause. And despite Schleiermacher's own radical definition of religion as "an intuition of the Infinite" available to any person, he would have been blown over by Whitman's blustery claims, throughout the poem, that every person is actually divine.

Yet Whitman's vision goes even further: each person is *more* divine than any God. A catalog that begins "Magnifying and applying come I" goes into detail with deliberately outrageous apparent self-aggrandizement:

Taking myself the exact dimensions of Jehovah and laying them away,
Lithographing Kronos and Zeus his son, and Hercules his grandson,
Buying drafts of Osiris and Isis and Belus and Brahma and Adonai,
In my portfolio placing Manito loose, and Allah on a leaf, and the crucifix
  engraved (ll.1020–1026)

And then the magnified self becomes, as always, *each* self, with the *each* then immediately particularized:

Accepting the rough deific sketches to fill out better in myself . . . bestowing
  them freely on each man and woman I see,
Discovering as much or more in a framer framing a house,
Putting higher claims for him there with his rolled-up sleeves, driving the
  mallet and chisel (ll.1031–3)

While Whitman never makes fun of his "high claims" for other people's divinity, the claims for his own he loves to deflate with comic hyperbole. "By my life-lumps! becoming already a creator!" he laughs (l.1048). The poem is full of cosmic visions; genuine mystical experiences are clearly behind it, and wild metaphors of the poet's cosmic expansion are everywhere. Yet he inflates and deflates himself in the same breath. "Who goes there! hankering, gross, mystical nude?" he challenges himself (l. 388). Or he shouts a warning at his own expansive approach: "Unscrew the locks from the doors! / Unscrew the doors themselves from their jambs!" (ll. 503–4) He imagines himself as Cosmic Man: "My feet strike an apex of the apices of the stairs, / On every step bunches of ages, and larger bunches between the steps, / All below duly traveled—and still I mount and mount" (ll.1149–51). Yet no matter how expansive he becomes in his imagination, he never loses his down-home earthiness: "Divine am I inside and out, and I make holy whatever I touch or am touched from; / The scent of these arm-pits is aroma finer than prayer" (ll. 526–7).

As divine, the poet sometimes sounds like the Gospel Jesus, without making a point of the allusion. I hear, for instance, Jesus' words from Matthew 25:40 ("Truly I tell you, just as you did it to one of the least of these my brothers, you did it to me") in Whitman's "Whoever degrades another degrades me"(l. 504). A more explicit imitation of Christ is the long sequence in which the poet takes on specific sufferings of other people, is himself "crucified" (l. 960), then rises from the grave and resurrects the dying with his own breath. But these powers aren't only his. Repeatedly the poem returns to its opening theme of including the reader in every claim for the poet's self: "And what I assume you shall assume, / And every atom belonging to me as good belongs to you" (ll. 2–3). This all-embracing equality is the very point of Whitman's identification with Jesus in the short poem 'To Him that was Crucified,' which he put in his 1860 edition of *Leaves of Grass.* Addressing Jesus as "comrade" and "dear brother," the poet exults in how they two, along with a few other free-spirited "equals" will "labor together" walking "the whole earth over . . . / Till we saturate time and eras, that the men and women of races, ages to come, may prove brethren and lovers, as we are." For Whitman, as even more centrally for Blake, Jesus is the great egalitarian.

So much in Whitman's vision recalls Blake's Divine Humanity that it's intriguing to compare the two poet-mystics. Each time I have occasion to return to either of their worlds, which seems to be about every ten years, I find myself spellbound—as if I've never entered a world so sharp with insight into our own. Yet the feel of these two worlds could hardly be more different. Entering Blake's cosmos, you feel you need to cover your head from the hailstorm of passionate anger, and you're lost without a guide through his densely woven mythic universe. The world of 'Song of Myself' is more relaxed, a loose weave of individual threads picked up as if wherever the poet happens to cast his eye. You feel you can lie back on a river bank and let Whitman's 'Song' play around you. The weather, though it can get dark, is mainly delightful: one of those days that change every few minutes, amusing you with quick-shifting cloud formations and sunlight laughing through breeze-blown willow limbs. Yet Blake and Whitman, in their very different tones and textures, are both envisioning in their uniquely concrete ways what David Friedrich Strauss put abstractly in *Das Leben Jesu:* that "the idea of the unity of the divine and human natures" has a far greater reality "when I regard the whole race of mankind as its realization, than when I single out one man," Jesus Christ. Blake does still single out Jesus, but as the cosmic divine-human body in which all redeemed humanity participates. Whitman pictures the reverse: Jesus participating in humanity's divinity. Whitman is actually more interested in picturing humanity than Jesus; his "rough deific sketch" of Jesus is pretty sketchy indeed. But Blake sketches Jesus—figuratively and literally, too, in the drawings—with the firm outline of the Gospels' salvific figure. It is Jesus who stills Blake's storms.

Neither Blake nor Whitman had patience with conventional piety, and each voices his impatience in his characteristic way. Blake's way is scathing satire, set in a mythic world where mere piety is one of evil's deep roots. Whitman's way is the single fresh image. It's fun to see how Whitman expresses the same sentiment that we saw in Mary Ann Evans's letter to her father: "I could not without vile hypocrisy and a miserable truckling to the smile of the world for the sake of my supposed interests, profess to join in worship which I wholly disapprove." Whitman also scoffs at any "truckling":

> Whimpering and truckling fold with powders for invalids . . . conformity
>   goes to the fourth-removed,
> I cock my hat as I please indoors or out. (ll. 396–7)

"Out" is definitely, though, where he preferred to cock it. Like the other major Romantic poets (except, in this case, Blake), Whitman felt closer to God in the countryside air than in the stuffy indoors of church religion. Of the many couplets in 'Song of Myself' that make the contrast, one in particular has stayed with me over the more than thirty years since I first read it:

> Logic and sermons never convince,
> The damp of the night drives deeper into my soul. (ll. 652–3)

The alliterative d's and the monosyllabic pounding must have driven the verse into my soul like the damp of the night.

THERE ARE, HOWEVER, poets of the first half of the nineteenth century for whom church religion and the countryside air were not in conflict, whose souls were moved both by sermons and by the damp of the night. They aren't the major poets who invented Romanticism. But they're talented poets, acclaimed in their day, who remained deeply committed to Christianity as it was conventionally practiced and also wrote poetry suffused with the Romantic spirit. Our composite portrait of the Romantic Jesus wouldn't be complete without looking at how he is treated by some of these poets of conventional Christian faith.

The most interesting for our purpose is Annette Droste-Hülshoff (1797–1848), because she wrote a cycle of poems based on the Sunday Gospel texts of the whole church year. Droste-Hülshoff was a practicing Catholic, from an aristocratic Westphalian family accustomed to attending Mass in their castle's private chapel. As a gifted writer in a nineteenth-century European society not disposed to welcome women's creative talents, Droste-Hülshoff suffered in trying to prove her worth, not only to the literary world but also to her own family and—most psychologically draining—to herself. To keep her emotional bearings, she alternated between hermitic periods and spells of sociability in German intellectual circles that included A. W. Schlegel, Schopenhauer's sister, and a group of Goethe's friends. By the time she was in her forties, Droste-Hülshoff's published writing was being widely praised. Like most German authors of this late Romantic era, she wrote comfortably in many genres: fiction, drama, epic poetry, ballads, lyric verse. Though she spurned the label "Romantic," a term associated in Germany with excessive fantasizing and an archaic medieval ambiance, her lyric poetry unquestionably partakes of the European Romanticism that I've been discussing. Nature looms large in her lyric verse. Her closely observed Westphalian landscape, particularly, is the characteristic setting and symbol of her inner life. Often her lyrics place the poet herself lying in the deep grass of her favorite heathland, communing with Nature and with voices she hears from beyond the grave. Droste-Hülshoff's sense of mission as a poet is also in the grand Romantic mode—the sense of having been chosen by God to utter divine truths—though she tempers this with a typical nineteenth-century Catholic sense of sin, so that in her view the poet must suffer like Christ, must sink into humanity's sinfulness and into her own personal guilt, in order to bring healing words to humankind.

Of Droste-Hülshoff's lyrics about one-third are explicitly religious, and of these the cycle of poems on the church year, *Das Geistliche Jahr* (*The Holy Year*), form the largest part. She began composing them, as an offering to her grandmother, at a time in her twenties when she was anguished by her mishandling of two potential suitors and had self-deprecatingly concluded that her independence of mind made her unfit for marriage. Though each poem takes off from the Gospel text for that day's Mass, its subject is immediately sucked into the poet's own sense of unworthiness and guilt. She herself takes the role of whatever Gospel figure is encountering Jesus: she is Peter fishing all night in vain, fishing unsuccessfully in her own heart for the pearl of faith; she is one of the unwilling guests at the wedding feast. Even in the poems that Droste-Hülshoff composed in her forties, when she completed the cycle, her spiritual struggles continue, though now she is aware of expressing an angst not merely personal but of the zeitgeist. The rationalist and critically historical challenges to Christianity—those intellectual currents that drew Mary Ann Evans to decide that she could in good conscience dispense with conventional faith and worship—overwhelmed Annette Droste-Hülshoff like rapids dashing her whole being against rocks. Wracked by guilt that her intellect might be destroying her faith, even tormented by fears of insanity, Droste-Hülshoff identifies in these poems with the fig tree cursed by Christ or with the man possessed by a legion of devils. So raw are these poems of *Das Geistliche Jahr,* so honestly do they bare the poet's struggles against what she perceives as her sinful heart, that when she completed the book in 1839, publishers considered it too dangerously lacking in spiritual consolation to print. (After her death, it did appear, to wide praise.)[10]

Reading *Das Geistliche Jahr* today, in an age that takes religious doubt for granted, we're likely to find exhausting such genuine torment over one's soul. It's a strenuous experience to accompany Droste-Hülshoff through these spiritual dramas that tug wildly against the strict verse forms she insists on, as if determined to discipline herself *some* way. But what's especially fascinating, in relation to the study of how Jesus appears as a character in the poetry of various eras, is how this mid-nineteenth-century poet who longs for faith can't keep him fixed on her own imagination's stage. Each poem of *Das Geistliche Jahr* begins by evoking a Gospel scene where Jesus would naturally be present. But when the poet then puts herself in the scene, imagining herself as the Gospel personage encountering Jesus, he instantly vanishes. Panicked, she cries out some version of "My Lord, where are you? I can't see you!"—desperately aware that it's her own lack of faith that has clouded her vision of Christ. (For Droste-Hülshoff Jesus and Christ are interchangeable names; her doubts aren't at all of his messianic divinity, but rather of her own ability to respond properly to it.) Terms like *Nebel, Wolke, Dunst* (fog, cloud, haze) fill the poems and define their atmosphere. A poem's drama is then often the poet's groping, through her imagination's rich landscape, for some element of Nature that she can grasp as sign of her invisible Savior. That element—a breeze, a thistle, a certain tree—finally mediates Christ's grace for her, though he himself remains as if tantalizingly offstage, elusive.

A few years after completing *Das Geistliche Jahr,* during her final illness, Droste-Hülshoff did write a poem putting Jesus on center stage: 'Gethsemane.' She keeps her persona out of this poem, though her own physical suffering and fears at approaching death clearly inform her character of Jesus, and the role she constructs for him is very much the one she herself had played over and over in *Das Geistliche Jahr:* the solitary figure despairing at God's absence, which is imagined in terms of natural elements that finally become the means of consolation. Significantly, the poem's subject, the Agony in the Garden, is Jesus' most vulnerably human moment in the Gospels. 'Gethsemane' is worth quoting in full, because its Jesus is so characteristically a Romantic figure, so thoroughly a product of developments in poetry and theology alike in the early to middle nineteenth century. Coming after Romanticism had made the poet's own imagination and feelings its material, and after biblical historical criticism had made Jesus' humanness a subject, Droste-Hülshoff's Jesus in 'Gethsemane' is a human being agonizingly confronting his own death by imagining it in detail. And in his imagination, Nature—in true Romantic mode—is both the correlative of his feelings and the prime actor in his inner psychological drama.

Droste-Hülshoff's accomplishment in creating this Romantic Jesus is all the more extraordinary since she stays essentially faithful to the Gospel texts while breathing into them the Romantic spirit. To watch how she does this, we should probably have the Gospel accounts fresh in mind. Here, conflating the accounts in Matthew, Mark and Luke, are the points of the scene that are her focus. (Ellipses mark the subplot of the disciples' sleeping, which doesn't interest her.)

> Jesus went with his disciples to a place called Gethsemane . . . and began to be distressed and agitated. And he said to them, "I am deeply grieved, even to death. . . ." And going a little farther, he threw himself on the ground and prayed, "My Father, if it is possible, let this cup pass from me; yet, not my will but yours

be done." [Luke alone adds:] Then an angel from heaven appeared to him and gave him strength. In his anguish he prayed more earnestly, and his sweat became like great drops of blood falling down on the ground.

Droste-Hülshoff begins her poem at the point where Jesus has thrown himself down to pray.

As Christ lay in Gethsemane,
Face down, with closed eyes,—
The breezes seeming nothing but sighs,
And a spring,
Reflecting the moon's pale face,
Murmuring its sorrow apace,—
That was the hour for the angel to bring,
In tears, from God, the bitter cup.

Then before Christ the cross rose up.
He saw his own body hanging there
Torn and wrenched, joints jutting where
The ropes stretched each limb back.
He saw the nails, the crown.
At each thorn a drop of blood hung down.
The thunder growled under its breath.
He heard a drip. Down the cross
Softly slid a whimper, then blurred out.
Christ sighed. In every pore
Sweat found a door.

The air went dark. In the grey ocean
A dead sun swam.
Through the murk he made out
The thorn-crowned head thrashing about.
Three forms lay at the cross's foot.
He saw them lying, grey as soot.
He heard the catching of their breath,
Saw how their trembling set their clothes in motion.
Was ever love as hot as his?
He knew them, knew them well.
His heart glowed.
Still harder his sweat flowed.

The sun's corpse vanished—just smoke, black day.
Cross and sighs both sank away.
A silence grimmer than a storm's roar
Swam through starless paths of air.

No breath of life anywhere.
And, all around, a crater, burnt, empty,
And a hollow voice crying for pity,
"My God, my God, why have you forsaken me?"
Death's grip seized him.
He wept. His spirit broke.
Sweat turned blood. He shook.
His mouth formed words of pain and spoke.
"Father, if it's possible, let this hour
Pass me by."

A bolt of lightning cut the night!
In that light
Swam the cross, its martyr-symbols bright.
Hands by millions he saw reaching,
Hands large and small from near and far beseeching,
And hovering spark-like over the crown of thorn
The souls of millions yet unborn.
The murk slunk back into the ground,
While the dead in their graves their voices found.
In love's fulness Christ raised himself on high.
"Father," he cried, "not my
Will but yours be done."

The moon swam out in quiet blue.
Before him, on the dewy green,
A stem of lily stretched up its length.
Then out of the calyx-cup
An angel stepped
And gave him strength.[11]

I said earlier that Jesus takes center stage in the poem. He clearly, though, shares it with Nature, whose elements are the dramatic forces not only projecting his various psychological states but even acting on them. Droste-Hülshoff starts off by giving Jesus' feelings to parts of Nature: the breezes are his sighs, the murmuring spring his sorrow, and the moon shows us the pale face of him whose own face is hidden in the ground. Through the next three stanzas—half of the entire poem—Droste-Hülshoff has Jesus imaginatively experience his Crucifixion to come; this imagination of it, in agonizing detail, is in fact what she envisions *as* his agony in the garden. Here, too, Nature is the correlative for Jesus' suffering. The thunder growls; the sun dies; all goes dark in the air devoid of life. It is this prevision of his Crucifixion—even to hearing his cry on the Cross, "My God, why have you forsaken me?"—that causes the poet's Jesus to sweat the blood of Luke's Gospel and to utter the petition from all the Synoptics: "Father, if it is possible, let this cup pass me by." But Droste-Hülshoff then cuts into Jesus' speech as the Gospels give it. While they all move right into "not my will but yours be done," she stops and takes a stanza to envision what must have gone on in Jesus' mind for him to move from anguished petition to acceptance. In a wholly original invention, she pictures flashing over Gethsemane a bolt of lightning in which Jesus sees the salvation for millions that his Cross will win; the sight sparks his love, which gives him the courage to say: "Thy will be done." Then in the final stanza, Droste-Hülshoff elaborates Luke's detail of the angel appearing from heaven to strengthen Jesus. It is an elaboration that could only have come from a poetic sensibility shaped by an era that began with Goethe's 'Harz Journey in Winter,' an era that made Nature not only alive with human feeling but also the very medium of divine utterance to humankind. Reflecting and affirming Jesus' acceptance of the Father's will, the poem's weather clears: the sky calms to a quiet blue in which the moon shines its light. Then, in a remarkable image of Nature moved by human need, a lily offers Jesus its calyx as the cup no longer of bitterness but of hope, and from this lily's calyx—rather than from Luke's "heaven"—God's angel steps to give Jesus strength. For an orthodox Catholic poet to make a flower the heavenly abode, from which God sends his saving help, is a tribute to the force of the Romantic imagination at its maturity.

This force can be seen even more powerfully in the poetry of Droste-Hülshoff's fellow Catholic Joseph von Eichendorff (1788–1857). Famous for lyric evocations of Nature that express such rapturous longing that composers of lieder have set many to music, Eichendorff constructs his Prussian countryside as a pastoral landscape that continuously calls him "home" (his favorite word) from life's toils. God is ever-present in this landscape, spreading his grace through it; and in one poem—'The Flight of the Holy Family'—Eichendorff imagines why. Intriguingly for us, it's the one poem he wrote that brings in Jesus rather than a more generalized God. The poem pictures the Holy Family's flight through a lush landscape that's not desert Egypt but rather Eichendorff's own beloved homeland; its meadow breezes cool the family and its brooklets hold their breath so as not to betray the family's flight. In gratitude to the countryside for its protection, the child Jesus then raises his hand and "blesses the silent land," which henceforth will "dream of heaven each night."

It's a simple vision of Nature blessed by God. Neither Eichendorff nor his landscape nor his Jesus has anything of Droste-Hülshoff's angst. In his comfort with orthodox Christian Romanticism, Eichendorff is like his contemporary the British poet Felicia Hemans (1793–1835). Faithful member of the Church of England, Hemans expressed in her verse a Christian piety that helps account for her immense popularity in the Britain of her day. Religious doubts, like those that George Eliot would articulate, were starting to rattle the British, generating an anxiety that sought relief in expressions of the old certainties. Hemans is more complex than this—she has a special woman's perspective, for instance, on social issues like war—but for us what's interesting is the way her piety forms a Jesus in the Romantic mold.[12] Hemans doesn't often draw on Jesus as a figure in her poetry. Though religious sentiments suffuse her twenty-four volumes of verse, only a few poems are specifically biblical, and of these most focus on female scriptural figures. In the sonnet 'Mountain Sanctuaries,' however, Hemans does use Jesus, drawing him into Romantic poetic conventions so charmingly that I quote it here as a final example of a poem that features Jesus as Romantic hero. The poem is a gem for our study, since it not only reaches back to the Romantic lyric's beginnings in Goethe and to British Romanticism's classic Wordsworthian tropes, but it also will lead us to biblical criticism's Romantic best-seller, the *Life of Jesus* by Ernest Renan. The poem's epigraph is Matthew 14:23: "He went up to a mountain apart to pray."

> A child 'midst ancient mountains I have stood,
> Where the wild falcons make their lordly nest
> On high. The spirit of the solitude
> Fell solemnly upon my infant breast,
> Though then I prayed not; but deep thoughts have pressed
> Into my being since it breathed that air,
> Nor could I *now* one moment live the guest
> Of such dread scenes, without the springs of prayer
> O'erflowing all my soul. No minsters rise
> Like them in pure communion with the skies,
> Vast, silent, open unto night and day;
> So might the o'erburdened Son of man have felt,
> When, turning where inviolate stillness dwelt,
> He sought high mountains, there apart to pray.

I noted earlier that for Goethe and for the British poets who invented Romanticism, Jesus is out of the picture because the role of divine representative on earth is taken over by the poet in communion with natural forces. What Hemans does, in her more conventional Christian belief, is give this communion back to Jesus. But first, in good Romantic mode, she has it for herself. She begins the poem by placing herself in the Wordsworthian double moment of adulthood recollecting a childhood experience of solitude in Nature's wilds. The scene, as in Goethe's 'Harz Journey in Winter,' is a mountaintop, where the poet—in her adult reenvisioning—stands alone, moved to prayer by Nature's grandeur. Like Goethe's mountain peak, Hemans's is transformed into a place of worship even better than a church: "No minsters" can compare with these mountains rising "in pure communion with the skies." But then the two poets' peak experiences diverge. For Goethe, inventing the grand figure of the poet-genius who displaces Christ in representing the divine word in our world, Nature on the mountaintop ordains the poet as God's mediator. But Hemans, writing when this grand poetic vocation has become a convention, and eager to express her conventional Christian faith, turns the peak experience over to the Christian hero, Jesus himself. In the sonnet's final three lines, she steps aside and pictures Jesus in her place, imagining for him her own Romantic experience of prayer in the "inviolate stillness" of the "high mountains." Precisely because Hemans merges the two conventions so concisely, conflating the Romantic peak experience in Nature with the only Gospel moment where Jesus is alone, 'Mountain Sanctuaries' offers a museum piece of Jesus as Romantic hero. And it shows the Romantic Jesus coming full circle. Previously bumped aside by the new figure of Romantic poet as divine mediator, Jesus is brought back to his own Gospel place, but now sustained in the Gospel scene by Romantic Nature's up-lifting spirit.

HERE WOULD BE A fitting place to leave the Romantic Jesus. But we can't quite leave him here, because Romanticism didn't. In Ernest Renan's *La Vie de Jésus* (1863), the Romantic poets' Jesus stepped into a prose narrative that put the European public instantly under its spell: five months after publication, the book had sold sixty thousand copies in France and translations were appearing in Germany, Italy, and Holland. Renan saw himself as a historian, bringing to the French Catholic world the findings of the German Lives of Jesus while en-hancing them with his own travel experience in the lands where Jesus had lived. The enhancement was what charmed the reading public. The Galilean coun-tryside that comes from Renan's pen is "a carpet of flowers . . . swept by a per-petual breeze"; its animals are "small and extremely gentle . . . crested larks which venture almost under the feet of the traveller, little river tortoises with mild and lively eyes." For Renan, this "Nature, at once smiling and grand, was the whole education of Jesus," who "lived and grew amidst these enchanting scenes."[13] Even Albert Schweitzer—who gets so irritated by Renan's "senti-mentality" that he loses his usual scholarly demeanor and belittles the book for its particularly French "poor taste"—admits that Renan's "artistic imagination" created "a Jesus who was alive."

But alive, we'd say, to the spirit of Renan's own age. The century's biblical criticism had posited a genuinely human Jesus; the century's theology had grounded its Christology in this historical Jesus while also grounding divinity in every believing human self; the century's poetry had swelled the human self with a divine spirit infusing all of Nature. *La Vie de Jésus* perfectly blends these trends of over half a century. Formed in the image of the era's creative yet still abstract theology and historical criticism, Renan's Jesus walks the Romantic po-ets' landscape as a concrete person with moods and memories, hopes and plans. He haunts Goethe's and Hemans's mountain sanctuaries. ("Jesus seems to have had a peculiar love for the mountains," writes Renan; "it was there that he was the most inspired; it was there that he held secret communion with the ancient prophets.") Renan's Jesus breathes Emerson's "blithe air" and might say with Emerson that "in the presence of nature . . . the currents of the Universal Being circulate through me." And like Emerson's Jesus, Renan's is divine only in the sense shared by all people. That is, he was fully human and no more. He was born, says Renan, of Mary and Joseph; the story of his resurrection is pleasant legend. "He is Son of God, but all men are."

To Renan's mind, literal mortality doesn't diminish Jesus' lasting inspirational power. On the contrary, taking the terms that had come to be used to extol the Romantic Hero, Renan celebrates "this sublime person" whose "great originality" was that he represented the very best that human beings might become. But that precisely was—to many other minds—the problem. Controversy raged over *La Vie de Jésus*. While the scholarly world was scandalized by Renan's casual use of historical research and his fanciful way of *imagining* the life of this sublime person, the popular press condemned such a vividly imagined Jesus as a threat to Christian faith. Renan, like Strauss before him, lost his academic job. One critic wanted to go further and have him imprisoned under a French law that made it a crime to ridicule a religion recognized by the state.

A controversy like this always indicates that a raw nerve in the social body has been touched. The fuss isn't over a single book or author but over frightening possibilities that they bring to the fore. While a Jesus sharing Romantic mountain-peak experiences was inspirational for many readers in the nineteenth century's second half, to many others that Romantic mountaintop was the dangerous start of a slippery slope. Jesus at that point may have been sublime, but as Romantic Hero he was only human. He had nowhere to go but down.

THREE

Sliding into Modernism

Jesus Pale and Shrunken

Christ is not risen, no,
He lies and moulders low;
   Christ is not risen.

.   .   .   .

What if the women, ere the dawn was grey,
Saw one or more great angels, as they say,
Angels, or Him himself: Yet neither there, nor then,
Nor afterward, nor elsewhere, nor at all,
Hath He appeared to Peter or the Ten,
Nor, save in thunderous terror, to blind Saul:
Save in an after-Gospel and late Creed
   He is not risen indeed,
     Christ is not risen.

.   .   .   .

Eat, drink, and die, for we are souls bereaved,
Of all the creatures under this broad sky
We are most hopeless that had hoped most high,
And most beliefless, that had most believed.
   Ashes to ashes, dust to dust;
   As of the unjust, also of the just—
     Yea, of that Just One too.
   It is the one sad Gospel that is true,
     Christ is not risen!

Here is Jesus about as far down as he could go: dead and buried, dust to dust, mouldering in a grave from which he doesn't rise. These mournful verses are from 'Easter Day: Naples, 1849,' by Arthur Hugh Clough (1819–1861). A British educator and friend of Matthew Arnold, Clough wrote hundreds of poems that weren't published until after his death, when they were welcomed by the Victorian public as words right out of the collective mouth. Clough was much quoted; his poems were reprinted fourteen times before the nineteenth century's close.

In the previous chapter we saw Renan, at just this time, also positing an unresurrected Jesus. Yet for Renan, as for Emerson and Whitman and others celebrating the idea of Divine Humanity, the thought of an unresurrected Jesus was exhilarating. Jesus remained, to their minds, an inspiration precisely because he *didn't* literally rise from the grave; his divine humanity energized them because it was the same divine life shared by all human beings. But the British Victorian mind couldn't seem to find this thought uplifting. Instead it felt beleaguered by unsettling questions. What if, for instance, humankind is merely mortal, not sharing in divine life after all? Where does that leave a fundamentally human Jesus? Where does it leave us? "Bereaved" and "beliefless" is Clough's sadly disillusioned answer in this poem. We "had hoped most high," but we've been deceived in our hopes for eternal salvation, and now life has no meaning except to "eat, drink, and die." With Jesus down in the grave, the poet is down, too: depressed, hopes dashed.

Depression isn't constant for the Victorians, however. More characteristic are mood swings between despair and hope, doubt and a dutifully firm optimism. Determined not to let themselves give in to gloom, Victorian writers are always kicking themselves in the pants, as if saying: enough of this, now pull yourself out of it! So Clough, typically, appended to 'Easter Day: Naples 1849' a short poem called 'Easter Day,' which turns the first poem's sad tropes into their affirmative opposites:

> In a later hour I sat and heard
> Another voice that spake, another graver word.
> Weep not, it bade, whatever hath been said,
> Though He be dead, He is not dead.
>> In the true Creed
>> He is yet risen indeed,
>>> Christ is yet risen.

Clough is pulling himself out of his despair by force of will, but clearly his heart isn't in it. The cries of the first (much longer and more vivid) poem are the ones that ring painfully true to his feelings:

> Is He not risen, and shall we not rise?
>> Oh, we unwise!
> What did we dream, what wake we to discover?
> Ye hills, fall on us, and ye mountains, cover!
>> In darkness and great gloom
> Come ere we thought it is *our* day of doom
> From the cursed world which is one tomb,
>> Christ is not risen!

The *locus classicus* of Victorian mood swings between disillusionment and hope is Tennyson's *In Memoriam*. It's amazing that such a period piece can hold up after a century and a half, but I think it does. Tennyson struggles so honestly and openly against his grief at the early death of his close friend, Arthur Hallam, that reading the poem's one hundred thirty-one cantos—which necessarily takes many sittings, like many consolation visits to a friend of one's own—is like accompanying the poet through the long grieving process, with all its ups and downs. Yet as moved as I am by *In Memoriam,* I must admit that the way it moves me does make me a bit seasick. It's all those ups and downs, downs and ups, as the poem sways on the waves of Tennyson's alternating grief and hope. *In Memoriam* affects the reader so powerfully, I think, because the poet's swaying emotions aren't merely personal but are the metaphysical swings of his era as it reached for and then lost and then again reached for the old verities. The poet's grief isn't only for the loss of his friend; it's also for the loss of previous consolations for the loss of a friend. What has died, he fears, is the religious faith that once gave death meaning. Yet he can't let the dead faith rest in peace; he keeps trying to call it back from the grave.

Nor can he rest in his relation to Nature, that rich ground of meaning for the Romantics. *In Memoriam* is all over the place with Nature. In spots the poem is pure Romantic idyll: like Renan's gentle Nature, which was "the whole education of Jesus," Tennyson's "hill and wood and field did print the same sweet forms" on the youthful minds of Hallam and himself, while the twilight winds "came in whispers of the beauteous world"(canto 79). Yet elsewhere in the poem the wind dies down to utter silence, and those solid hills terrifyingly lose their form and "melt like mist" (canto 123). What had happened, over the fifteen years that Tennyson was composing the various cantos of *In Memoriam* (1835–1850), was that he read Sir Charles Lyell's new *Principles of Geology* (1830–1834), a work that struck the Victorian mind as literally earth-shaking.[1] Even before Darwin's *On the Origin of Species* (1859), Lyell's *Principles* and contemporaneous geological and biological works were positing an evolutionary process whereby Nature developed according to its own unfeeling laws. Victorians who were already clinging to their religious faith by a thread saw science now cutting belief's last lifeline. The voice of Nature, which to the Romantics had spoken of an omnipresent beneficent divine force—which had ordained Goethe's poet, which had made Emerson feel "part or parcel of God," which had strengthened Droste-Hülshoff's Christ at Gethsemane—was now silent. Or, worse, Nature was actively hostile to divine and human harmony: it was a blind battleground, infamously "red in tooth and claw." (This tagline commonly taken as shorthand for Darwin is indeed from *In Memoriam,* composed before Darwin's *Origin.*)

At this point in a discussion of Victorian sadness watching previously solid grounds of meaning crumble, it's customary to quote from 'Dover Beach.' And I don't see any reason to thwart the expectation. Matthew Arnold's poem, written probably during the 1850s, really does capture marvelously the heartbreaking loneliness of standing in a world no longer sustained by firm faith. Arnold sets the scene metaphorically by the shore:

> The Sea of Faith
> Was once, too, at the full, and round earth's shore
> Lay like the folds of a bright girdle furl'd.
> But now I only hear
> Its melancholy, long, withdrawing roar,
> Retreating, to the breath
> Of the night-wind, down the vast edges drear
> And naked shingles of the world.

The "shingles" are the coarse gravel beaches, grim remains of a Nature once luxuriant in its care for human concerns. The Romantic breeze that once played through the poet's mind like an Aeolian harp, inspiring the creative imagination with divine breath, is now nothing but the night-wind blowing over faith's retreating tide. All that the poet can now hear is the "melancholy, long, withdrawing roar" as faith recedes. With Tennyson and with Clough, Arnold is sounding the first mournful notes of what would become modernism. I'll define below what I mean by this much overused term, "modernism"—after we look at the major poet who was making way for it in France.

DURING THE SAME decades that 'Dover Beach,' *In Memoriam,* and Clough's "sad Gospel" were being composed, the receding infinite was also being evoked across the English Channel, in poems by Charles Baudelaire (1821–1867). He wasn't mourning, however. With a complex personality that combined the rebel and the mystic, Baudelaire was at once raging against a God who had abandoned humankind to the Devil, wallowing in the horrible ways of a miserably corrupted world, and seeking escape from this filth in an aesthetic that reconstructed infinite beauty on another plane.

Most of Baudelaire's poetry, however, is absorbed in the wallowing. The one collection of poems that he published, *Les Fleurs du mal* (1857), starts off throwing into our faces our collective human garbage:

> Stupidity, delusion, stinginess and vice
> Occupy our thoughts and overtax our force:
> We use ourselves to feed our loveable remorse
> Like beggars use their skin as pasturage for lice.[2]

This is the opening verse of the volume's prefatory poem, 'To the Reader,' which proceeds by dragging us further through the gutter of the poet's personal hell. Caressing the details of his own vices in perversely seductive language crafted to simulate the Devil's lure, the poet then implicates us in his degradation by addressing the reader directly as "my duplicate, my brother." It's fun to imagine a reader of the 1850s coming to this unflattering characterization from the nearly contemporaneous but opposite one in Whitman's 1855 'Song of Myself.' Such a reader might understandably feel a bit schizophrenic, being addressed by Whitman as his equal in divine compassion and cosmic breadth, and by Baudelaire as his equal in corruption. Or maybe this hypothetical reader would simply know, from the one poet's expansive optimism about human nature and the other's absorption in human sin, whether the poem was coming from America or France.

Personal sin does seem to be a peculiarly French literary obsession. I think of the Marquis de Sade, from whose literature of sexual cruelty the word "sadism" was coined, or, in our century, of François Mauriac's novels, minutely tracing sin's insidious pathways through the human psyche. Baudelaire, as a man of his own time, put a Romantic spin on this typically French preoccupation—turning his sin-obsessed life into his work and vice versa. But like everything else in Baudelaire, his relation to Romanticism was complex. He rejected its misty nostalgia for the medieval, its sentimentalized Nature (which enthralled his compatriot Renan), its swollen poetic ego. He did identify with the Romantic poet as rebel and as persecuted victim of a narrow-minded society; yet for Baudelaire, the grand figure of Romantic rebel was neither the poet himself nor (as it was for Blake) Jesus Christ, but Satan. Like Shelley, Baudelaire praised Milton's Lucifer as the majestic untamed hero who acts decisively even it means his damnation. And like Nietzsche a bit later in the century, Baudelaire nurtured the idea of superhuman power, whether Satanic or angelic, that could raise humanity from its petty misery.

This basically was Baudelaire's gripe against Jesus, as it was Nietzsche's: that Jesus was, finally, a wimp. Far from questioning his divinity, Baudelaire reproaches him for not fully using his divine power to combat evil in the world. Baudelaire's only poem focusing directly on Jesus, 'Saint Peter's Denial,' has precisely this theme. The poem begins with a deliberately disgusting scene of heavenly debauchery: a drunken, sadistic God, gorged on human suffering, is lulled to sleep by a symphony of our protests and sobs. Then suddenly the poet turns to address Jesus:

> —Ah! Jesus! mind the Garden and the Olive Tree!
> In pure simplicity, upon your knees you prayed
> To Him who in His heaven laughed while you were splayed
> By hangmen pounding spikes into your live anatomy.

You were foolishly innocent, the poet is saying, to demean yourself before this tyrant God. And on the Cross, he goes on, didn't "remorse / Thrust deeper than the soldier's spear into your side" as you recalled past triumphs when truly "you were lord"?—particularly that moment when, "with bravery and pride," you overturned the tables in the temple and "whipped those merchants through the doors"? Given Baudelaire's judgment that Jesus was here at his greatest, acting decisively against social evil, the poem's defiant end logically follows.

> —For me, most certainly, I shall be satisfied
> To leave a world where action fails to match the word;
> Would I might use the sword and perish by the sword!
> Saint Peter denied Jesus. . . . And he did right!

The social reformer Pierre Joseph Proudhon, whom Baudelaire knew well, had rejected Christ for exactly this reason.[3] But what is special about Baudelaire's disappointment in Christ is its context in the poet's oeuvre: it is next to Satan's active power in the world that Jesus pales. The whole of *Les Fleurs du mal* is a cosmic battle between good and evil played out on the Paris streets and in the poet's own soul; and Satan is so overpowering that, in a poem put by Baudelaire almost right after 'St. Peter's Denial,' he displaces Christ in the Catholic litany. The poem, 'The Litanies of Satan,' is the poet's perverse prayer to the Devil, with a refrain of "O Satan, pray take pity on my endless pain."

Yet Baudelaire does not worship Satan. He simply takes him seriously. Knowing from experience the terrible attraction of the demonic, he refuses to avert his gaze from what Satan is capable of in our hearts. In this unblinking focus, he is doing no more than adhering to the Catholic dogma of original sin; such, at least, was the argument of Mauriac in 1920 (protesting the banning of Baudelaire's poetry from French schools). Baudelaire only "listened to his poor soul," Mauriac said, "and he confessed it" with "a heart truly pursued by Grace." Mauriac could write sympathetically of Baudelaire because they shared a severe French Catholic vision of the human soul so enmeshed in sin that nothing short of grace can free it.[4]

Baudelaire's longing for this grace is a recurrent motif in his poetry. 'Beyond Repair' ('L'Irreparable'), for instance, after painting yet another Baudelairian picture of hell, ends with a striking change of scene, the memory of Satan vanquished by a mere fairy in a cheap theater production:

> I have sometimes seen, on the stage of a banal playhouse
>   A being, all light, gold and gauze,
> Vanquishing huge Satan;
>   But my heart, never visited by ecstasy,
> Is a theater where forever is awaited,
>   Ever, ever in vain, the Being with wings of gauze.[5]

The sense of looking in vain, of longing for a lost link, a lost ecstasy, pervades Baudelaire's famous poem 'The Swan.' Figures of exile circle around the central image of a swan escaped from its cage and distractedly dragging its plumage through the city dust, "heartsick for his lovely native lake," twisting his neck "toward heaven's cruel, ironic blue . . . / As though he would address reproaches to his God." (The image gripped the next generation of Symbolist poets, and swan poems multiplied around the world like rabbits; we'll see one in the work of the Nicaraguan Rubén Darío.)

Abandoned, like the swan, by God, the poet would have to reconnect with the transcendent himself. To this end, Baudelaire developed the aesthetic theory that so influenced poetry for the next hundred years that his works were translated into more languages than any other book except the Bible (an astounding fact that speaks volumes about twentieth-century spirituality). In this theory, a poem or a painting or a piece of music—the correspondence of the arts was key for Baudelaire—creates a "suggestive magic" that gives the soul a glimpse of "splendors beyond the tomb." The artist is an "exile amid the imperfect," reaching to "take possession, immediately, on this very earth, of a revealed paradise." The means of possession that Baudelaire saw, drawing (as had Blake) on Swedenborg, was "what a mystic religion calls *correspondence*": "the inner and secret relation of things." Relations on the horizontal plain, those perceivable by the senses, Baudelaire called "synaesthetic correspondences" (I say more about them hereafter in connection with their formative influence on the Symbolists). Vertical relations, those between the visible and invisible, were the "transcendental correspondences" already much noted by the Romantics; like Emerson, Baudelaire saw every natural thing symbolizing its corresponding spiritual reality.[6]

All art, Baudelaire said, aspires toward beauty, which he defined famously as "the infinite within the finite." Beauty had nothing of the sentimental for Baudelaire. Quite the contrary: he seized on Poe's sense of beauty as always strange, sometimes even sinister. Even, for Baudelaire (this won't surprise us), possibly satanic. His anguish over whether beauty is "from Satan or from God" is dramatized in the poem 'Hymn to Beauty,' which starts right off: "Are you from heaven's depths or hell's infinity, / O Beauty?" Yanking the poet back and forth between these two poles, the poem becomes a metaphor for all of Baudelaire's verse, for his entire imaginative being. How frayed his sensibility must have been, torn between opposing infinitudes, we can picture if we recall his British Victorian contemporaries, who were tossed between religious doubt and a determination not to lose the old comforts of belief. Their ups and downs were distressing enough; yet Baudelaire's imagination resides at both extremes of the British swing between doubt and hope. Baudelaire is deeper down than doubt, in hell—yet reaching higher than hope, to heaven.

If the British Victorian poems bemoaning lost certainties were, as I suggested, the sad prefatory notes of modernism, then Baudelaire's work can be seen—or heard—as modernism's overture.

BEFORE GOING FURTHER with the term "modernism," I need to explain the sense in which I'll use it here. It won't be the sense perhaps expected by readers familiar with the term in the context of church history. Instead, I'll be using it mainly in the sense it has in literary history, because this is the primary sense in which it shapes poetic refigurings of Jesus. However, neither the literary nor the religious movement was watertight; -isms never are. And two contemporaneous movements called by the same name were bound to ooze into each other. Furthermore, in the century since both movements began, the word "modernist" has been so flooded with meanings that its defining bounds have utterly burst; for analytical purposes, the term is awash with confusion unless some retaining walls are placed around it.

I assign here, therefore, some limiting definition to the two modernisms that bear on our subject of the poets' Jesus. For religious modernism, this will be the Protestant, not the Catholic, movement. The Catholic use of the term doesn't concern this study since it was solely an inhouse matter: a reactionary papacy used the word as a whip to lash at Catholic intellectuals' engagement with secular thought. For the Protestant movement, I adopt the definition of church historian Martin E. Marty: that the modernists were progressives who, at the turn of the twentieth century, "wanted to advance the processes of change from within the Protestant core-culture." These progressives, enthusiastically embracing the zeitgeist's evolutionary vision of social change as a process inevitably leading society toward an ever-higher integration, were eager for religion to welcome "science" into its worldview. The nineteenth-century developments that to some people threatened religious faith—historical criticism of the Bible, the quest for the historical Jesus, Darwinian evolutionary theory—were to the modernist mind all to the religious good. Not that modernists simply reduced faith to science. But, as Marty notes, "they did not want to collapse belief in the face of progress. They did not want to be merely secular, but religious, in decisively though never narrowly Christian ways."[7]

Literary modernism, however, was a movement toward the merely secular. The rest of this chapter details what this movement involved and how poetry's figure of Jesus got shrunken in the process. But for clarity's sake, I set out here a working definition: literary modernism was the aesthetic of fragmentation crafted within a weltanshauung that saw traditional cohesive structures— whether of society or church or state or literature itself—all discredited and collapsed. Literary modernism came out of Romanticism; cultural history never makes a simply fresh start. Romanticism had attacked traditional structures as empty authoritarian forms repressing the individual. But people were then left amid the devastation of crumbled structures of meaning. Modernism expressed their sense that they could no longer respond with Romanticism's heroic grandeur. Though literary modernism has spasmodic moments of wild glee at the collapse of old restrictive forms, its dominant tone is hurt and baffled. Its aesthetic is a search for ways to express its sense of fragmentation and loss, by breaking down literature's very materials themselves: syntax, character, symbol, stanza form, and so on.

The dominant spirits of religious and of literary modernism, then, could hardly be more different; this is why it's important not to confuse the terms. Religious modernism happily embraces a world moving toward integration, while literary modernism sadly watches its world fall apart. The vision of one is holistic, the other fragmented. There are meeting points: most notably, for our purposes, in their reimagining of Jesus of Nazareth; I comment on these as we come to them. But the modernism I refer to from now on, unless specified otherwise, is the literary movement.

As a literary aesthetic, modernism began with the French Symbolist movement of the 1880s, centering around the work of Mallarmé, Verlaine, and Rimbaud. Dismissing traditional religious, political, and literary structures as crumbled and discredited, the Symbolists proclaimed poetry freed from external reality. Romanticism had already interiorized poetry by making its subject the poet's personal view of the world, refashioned by Imagination. The Symbolists went the next step. Letting the discredited outer world drop away, they camped out in the mind. There they settled into the only subject they could trust, the poet's inner being as known through sense perceptions. This was far from a claustrophobic inner world, however. Baudelaire had taught them, through his theory of synaesthetic correspondences, how all the senses in concert could create their own infinitude. His poem 'Correspondences,' evoking "perfumes fragrant as an infant's flesh, / Sweet as an oboe's cry, and greener than the spring," also declared outright: "As distant, verberating echoes can resound . . . / So can each scent and hue and sound to each respond."

This poem became a Symbolist manifesto. "Scent and hue and sound" in their symbolic relations—suggested evocatively, as in music—were declared to be poetry's material. Music was for the Symbolists the privileged art because its elements (sounds) got their meaning not from an outside referent but from their own interconnections. Words, too, liberated as they now were from their referential function, could seek meaning in the same intersignifying way. Language, that is, was declared to have its own reality—a status that has been radically transformative for writing ever since. Freeing words from their need to grasp a fixed outer reality, the Symbolists also freed their meters from fixed restrictive forms, inventing their famous versification technique, *vers libre* (free verse). Thus liberated from old strictures, poetry was charged to *evoke*. Images were to be symbols evoking the poet's state of soul; rhythms were to reproduce the poet's inner life processes.

The Symbolist movement utterly transformed world poetry—though not all at once. The first dramatic impact was in Latin America, where (for reasons peculiar to Spanish literary history) poetry had been languishing for two centuries. Led by the Nicaraguan-born Rubén Darío (1867–1916), Latin American poets immediately seized on the Symbolist program to revitalize their own poetic language and vision. Rubén Darío is one of those writers that we can't imagine a literary culture having lived without; Octavio Paz calls him quite frankly the "founder" of contemporary Spanish poetry.[8] Darío's influence was so formative—not only on Latin American modernism, with which his name became synonymous, but also on Spanish-language poetry everywhere for the next century—that he can serve well here as a representative of modernism's early aesthetic and its radical refiguring of Jesus.

As early as 1888, Darío was exhorting his fellow writers toward *el modernismo*. For him the term meant literally "to be modern, current," which meant to leap into the shatteringly fresh synaesthetic moment of France. "Words should paint the color of a sound, the aroma of a star," Darío wrote in a prose manifesto; "they should capture the very soul of things."[9] To the Spanish American modernists (as they soon called themselves), the very soul of things was a cosmic harmony sensed in the individual soul and expressed by traditional Spanish versifications now recovered in experimental rhythms. The early modernist celebration of a spirit "violently alive," demolishing old structures with an energized delight in the immediately sensed color and aroma and beat, finds its expression par excellence in Darío's iconoclastic version of the Lord's Prayer, 'Paternoster to Pan':

> Our Pan, which art on earth . . .
> Bring us back your joyous kingdom
> in which you come singing . . .
>
> You are always violently alive;
> with your wild impulsiveness,
> shake your celestial horns in the sky,
> sink your goat's feet in the earth.
>
> Give us rhythm and measure
> through the love of your song;
> and through the love of your flute, give us
> this day our daily love.[10]

Such self-conscious paganism, calling on Pan in place of the Christian God, came at a price for the poet. To anyone raised in Spanish Catholicism's sin-laden world, modernism's joy in the senses felt like an outright defiance of Christianity. The Church declared the world fallen, awaiting Christ's final redemption; the poetic spirit found its own world already redeemed, naturally alive with scintillating love.

But the Spanish culture can't cast off Christ so easily. Darío held on in a couple of ways. One was to let the figure of Christ stay on the scene, but as one among many redemptive forces in the universe. Though Whitman had already relativized Christ in this way, his was a solitary vision, whereas Darío's shared in the progressive European and North American Christian theology of his time. This relativization of Jesus is a rare point on which the modernisms of literature and of church history do meet. Progressives gathering in Chicago for the unprecedented World's Parliament of Religions in 1893 claimed controversially that, in humanity's "evolutionary movement" toward unity, Jesus could hardly still be the only Way to religious truth.[11] This equalizing interfaith vision, reinforced soon by anthropological research and by Carl Jung's theory of archetypes, does undoubtedly remain a background force pushing poetry everywhere toward a figure of Christ Relativized. Later in the book we'll see this treatment of Christ, set down as an equal among other religions' gods or even merged with them, appear in the poetry of a range of twentieth-century cultures.

For Darío, it was a treatment at the service of his own anxiety. Like his French contemporaries, Darío often felt lost in the evocative world of his senses, seeking an elusive ideal beauty that could never quite be grasped. Romanticism had already claimed for art a revelation independent of religion, and the Symbolist modernists were extending the poet's role as "seer" who penetrates infinity and becomes a voice for the Eternal. Darío luxuriated in the role. Yet in his poetry, as his hypersensual language reaches for the Infinite, revelation keeps retreating beyond the horizon—over which hangs only a cosmic question mark. Reading Darío, I seem to hear Debussy's *Pelléas et Mélisande,* stretching out its shimmering anticipatory strains toward a resolution that remains forever as if just one more phrase away, consummation continually postponed in an eternity of preorgasmic intensity. Darío's signature poem, 'I seek a form . . . ,' is the essence of Debussy (and Monet and Mallarmé) in fourteen lines. Opening with a statement of his core poetic impulse—"I seek a form that my style cannot discover"—Darío fashions a sequence of lush metaphors attempting to grasp the elusive "word that runs away." But what he finally comes up against is a form of Baudelaire's Swan, which for Darío is a grand sensual image of the universe as interrogation: "the neck of the great white swan, that questions me." Where does this leave the poet? Anguished questions of where he is, of who he is, inform whole poems. Trying to get his bearings in relation to traditional cultural signposts, he sometimes draws on Christ—but, deliberately, as only one among many potentially signifying markers. In the poem 'Knight,' he tests identities: "I am a semicentaur . . . I imitate the Minotaur . . . I sing to Proserpina," and finally, "I am Satan, and I am Christ / dying between two thieves— / Oh where do I exist?"

His 'Christmas Sonnet' stays with a Christian scene, but only to suggest, finally, the poet's sad alienation from it. After first evoking the manger scene in the hushed tones of conventional piety, the poet breaks off:

> This vision rises within me, and multiplies
> in gorgeous details, in a thousand rich marvels,
> because of the sure hope of most divine good
>
> of the Virgin, the Child, and outlawed Saint Joseph;
> and I, on my poor donkey, ride toward Egypt,
> with no star any longer, and far from Bethlehem.[12]

This is Darío's other way of holding on to the figure of Christ: clinging for an instant, only to say goodbye. Finding the moment when the holy family is exiled and apparently lost, he puts himself into the scene—then leaves himself there, as if that were the end of the story. The Christian story with its "sure hope of most divine good" will go on, but without the poet. I don't know of a more poignant expression of the modernist sense of loss. Traditional faith is lovingly evoked, but as an exquisite impossibility for the modern person. Readers with English as their native poetic idiom will hear (though Darío probably didn't) the rippling echoes of Dover Beach's "melancholy, long, withdrawing roar" as faith's tide recedes.

'Paternoster to Pan' and 'Christmas Sonnet' are two sides of a modernist coin stamped with the figure of Christ. On the bright side, joyous sensuality parodies the central prayer of Jesus, and religious faith is cast exuberantly to the winds; on the dark side, Jesus remains in gorgeous detail, while the poet rides quietly off into shadow, sadly but inexorably distancing himself from the hope of past faith. "Darío's aesthetic is a kind of Orphism that does not exclude Christ (though it admits him as nostalgia rather than presence)," Paz writes.[13] Christ as nostalgia: it's a figure that modernism newly brings on the scene.

LITERARY MODERNISM'S NEXT major moment came in Britain after the turn of the century, when Ezra Pound and T. S. Eliot refocused the Symbolist vision onto the fragment. Pound, who loved propagandizing, invented the title *Des Imagists* for a 1914 anthology of poems based on refined modernist principles of "the exact word." Symbolist poetry-as-music was too hazy for the Imagists, who preferred the analogy of poetry as sculpture: each image, in this new imperative, had to be "hard and clear." While Amy Lowell, an indefatigable propagandist herself, carried on the Imagist cause in the United States, Pound campaigned on the continent for a cultural regeneration that he was convinced (aided as he was by having one of the century's larger egos) only poetry could bring about. Among Pound's protégés was T. S. Eliot, who had actually discovered Symbolism on his own but owed to Pound the early promotion of his poetry. Pound even had a hand in shaping Eliot's *The Waste Land*. But once published in the wake of World War I, *The Waste Land* (1922) took on a life of its own, gradually becoming the most influential twentieth-century poem in any language. Its devasted landscape, fragmented lines, and incomprehensible scraps from past and present cultures seemed to figure perfectly the postwar sensibility of utter collapse. If Darío had been iconoclastic in refashioning the Lord's Prayer as a hymn to Pan, what Eliot did in *The Waste Land* raises iconoclasm to a new level of demolishing force. Taking a hammer to all icons, pagan and Christian alike, Eliot smashes to barely recognizable bits every cultural artifact that had been counted on to provide humanity with meaning. Neither Christ nor Pan nor any other god or story is left standing amid the rubble of fragments from ancient archetypal myths.

With Imagism and with *The Waste Land,* modernism's characteristic literary unit became the isolated image, pulled from the wreckage of civilization's lost coherence. But World War I affected more than the literary scene. It brought modernism out of the cafés and literary journals into the general culture. The war's devastation made horribly relevant, even requisite, all the Symbolist stances: the disgust with authoritative tradition, the *fin de siècle* world-weariness, the disillusionment about ultimate meanings. "Cultural modernism" became a popular mode.[14]

Because modernism is in part a spiritual response—to the perceived loss of transcendent meaning—Jesus can figure naturally in modernist poetry as a main character. But his characteristic action on stage is the dropping of his uniquely salvific self. His divine robes slip to the floor, and he stands before us awkwardly human. Or he is dressed in the costumes of other gods, who collectively pantomime their shrunken significance. Romanticism could explore Jesus' human dimension without denying the divine, because it saw divinity residing in the very essence of the human; every person was Son of God. But for modernism the essence of the human is a loss of the divine, so a merely human Jesus is just that: merely human and nothing more.

The progressive church movement called modernist, we should note, also focused on the human Jesus, promoting especially his role as Teacher. This is a point at which the two modernisms of church and of literary culture do meet and undoubtedly feed into each other. But they meet only on the grounds of the human Jesus. The church movement then goes on its traditional way, carrying on its assumption that Jesus of Nazareth is Christ the Lord, whereas for literary modernism and its whole weltanschauung, this belief is now impossible. Their modernism nods yes to the Nietzschean proclamation that God is dead. It's a pained yes; modernism doesn't gloat cynically over God's corpse as postmodernism will do. And though modernism has moments of kicking up its heels with Darío's Pan to celebrate repressive religion's demise, those moments inevitably soften and turn sad. Modernism goes wistfully to the wake. "Weep for Jesus," writes Danish poet Ole Wivel in a poem mourning the loss of all divinity, not only the Christian, from our world.

WIVEL WAS ACTUALLY writing after World War II. So this is the place to take note of modernism's knack of reappearing when called for over the course of the twentieth century. Although as both literary aesthetic and as weltanschauung, modernism had particular dates of origin, it also remained hovering in the air over the whole century, materializing in one part of the globe or another as needed. What created the need was usually a traumatic social collapse. Wherever a culture's traditional cohesive social or political or moral structures ceased functioning and became discredited, intellectuals discovered modernism and urgently made it their own—as if it had been born that instant just for them. In one place, the French Symbolists would be eagerly appropriated. In another, Pound's Imagism or Eliot's fragmentation would be the inspirational model for local poets. The two world wars were naturally the impetus for most of modernism's reappearances. In much of Europe and North America, modernist poetry flourished in the aftermath of World War I. Elsewhere World War II was the breaking point. In Japan, for instance, it was after Hiroshima that intellectuals declared their country's military structure utterly discredited, and poets found in the French Symbolists the needed model for their own modernist voice. In the Arab Middle East (as we'll see in detail in chapter 6), the 1948 displacement of Palestinians at the creation of Israel was what moved poets to embrace *The Waste Land* vision as their own.

In the Scandinavian countries, World War II was modernism's defining moment. Symbolism had been represented in Denmark by a contemporary of Darío, Sophus Clausson (1865–1931), who, like Darío, sought a private poetic cognition that could pull together a universe otherwise in shambles; but modernism as a dominant aesthetic didn't take hold until after World War II. At this point, it merged in Scandinavian thought with the newly fashionable existentialism, to produce a sensibility that found meaning—if any were to be found at all—only in the isolated actions of the individual person. The Danish poet Ole Wivel (1921–), taking what action he felt he could in the face of postwar chaos, started publishing the literary magazine *Heretica,* which was influential in promoting art as society's only saving hope. Yet Wivel couldn't escape a sense of doom. In a grim poem called 'The Fish' (which we'll look at in another context), he shapes a figure of Jesus eerily silent—then shockingly dead at the Second Coming.

In Wivel's poem 'Weep for Balder—,' Jesus stands last in a line of gods who watch helplessly as their worlds go to Hell. The poem's three stanzas begin "Weep for Balder—," "Weep for Orpheus—," and "Weep for Jesus—," with the parallelism setting Jesus in his modernist relativized place. Balder, in Norse mythology, was a gentle and just god whose death was masterminded by the evil god Loki; Hel, goddess of the underworld, even then offered to spare Balder if all the world would weep for him, but Loki refused. So in the Wivel poem, Balder's stanza ends with the good god and his wife "Burning, bound for Hell their funeral ship." Orpheus's stanza narrates the descent of Eurydice to Hades after Orpheus's music has saved her but his anxious backward glance has lost her again; the stanza ends: "Hermes knew Eurydice was damned." Then comes Jesus:

> Weep for Jesus—he who only said:
> "Take your bed and go," and who commanded
> Waves to bear him safely to the boat.
> He was powerless like mortal men
> When he stood again in Galilee
> In their midst, and his disciples would

Not believe that it was he who spoke—
Would but see his bleeding hands and wounds.[15]

The poet has constructed an image of radical loss: a Gospel scene of Jesus' post-Resurrection appearance is drained of the Resurrection. And without the Resurrection, the Gospel story ends in death and disbelief. The figure who once commanded waves with supernatural power now stands "powerless like mortal men," shrunken from his divine stature to the merely human. Confronting this diminished figure, the disciples cannot joyously recognize "the Lord," as they do in the Gospels; all they can see is Jesus' "bleeding hands and wounds." A Gospel story ending without the disciples' belief in the Risen Lord has lost its possibility to go on and proclaim the Christian faith.

This is what Renan and the other Romantics believing in a divine humanity hadn't realized. With their exalted vision of "mortal men" as the very opposite of "powerless," as filled rather with divine inspiring strength, they could celebrate Jesus' sharing of human mortality and assert that Christianity lives on in the human spirit alone. But the more sober modernist vision takes mortality at its word: its root meaning of death. "We are souls bereaved," the Victorian Clough had written in 'Easter Day: Naples 1849,' staring an unrisen Jesus hard in the face. Clough and Arnold and Tennyson weren't fully modernist only because they still fought against giving in to the loss of religious faith. But I can imagine them reciting Wivel's poem with pained sympathy. They certainly shared the twentieth-century Danish poet's response to the sight of all salvific hope slipping from our world: he calls us to weep.

In the context of Wivel's use of the Balder story, weeping is a complex imperative. If we could genuinely weep for the loss of justice and beauty and healing power, if we genuinely longed for them, they would not disappear. But since chaos and disbelief have won the day, the poem suggests (as *In Memoriam* had too, at certain moments), we can only weep in mourning for our loss. Balder and Orpheus and Jesus become figures of a pained nostalgia.

Christ as nostalgia: again, as with Darío, we hear that characteristically modernist note. The next step, in which modernism moves toward a different, harsher tone, is to transfer the sense of loss to Jesus himself. This is what happens in an untitled poem by the Russian poet Vladimir Lvov (1926–1961). Quoted in full, it can serve here as both a final glimpse of the modernist Jesus and a preview of the postmodernist figure:

That yellowed body of the Lord
Hanging on the cross,
The face tormented with loss,
And we do not adore him
With his nails and small board.
The radiance of his scarlet blood,

The Crucifixion *(1911–12), by the Expressionist painter Emile Nolde (Germany, 1867–1956).
Taciturn and morose by nature, Nolde felt a lifelong mystic identification with Christ's Passion.
Though the Jesus of his paintings can express various moods and spiritual stances, here he is an
image of utter loss and defeat. Yellowed and gaunt, Jesus hangs at the center of a scene where
death reigns. All the figures except the one guard rolling dice (an image of smug scorn) look
drained of life, their angular bodies like jabs of hopelessness. © Nolde-Stiftung Seebüll. Printed
by permission of the Nolde-Foundation.*

> That worn-out, mournful face.
> We can only pity Christ today,
> So, of course, he's no longer great.
> Our earth loves the victorious.
> O, dear old God, forgive me,
> But when the cup runneth over,
> It's not quite decent to suffer.[16]

His body yellowed, his face worn out and mournful and tormented with loss, this Jesus is dried up and undignified. Whereas Darío and Wivel had mourned the loss of a divine Christ from their world, the mourning in Lvov's poem is done by Jesus. The poet's response, guardedly bland, is that of course "we do not adore" this merely suffering figure; "we can only pity Christ today." Lvov was writing in Stalinist Russia; little is known of his life except that he drowned in a Moscow swimming pool. It seems an appropriately sad and ignominious end for a person who saw that his world had reduced Christ to a pathetic figure. Like Wivel's Jesus, Lvov's is denied his Resurrection, and both poets seem to blame their contemporary world for the loss of a Risen Lord. But whereas the Danish poet's world is chaotic postwar Europe in which society's unifying structures have collapsed, Lvov's is a totalitarian society with too much unifying structure, a world that loves only "the victorious" and that has the power to keep victory and greatness for itself alone. A Christ denied his Resurrection is denied his victory; "so, of course, he's no longer great." The poet's tone borders on a cynicism that we'll hear more of in the next chapter. But "that yellowed body" remains an apt image with which to leave the modernist Jesus.

TO SEE ONLY JESUS' wasted mortal body, not to see him also as the embodiment of Eternal Life, is to look at the Gospel story without Christian faith. Modernism marks the end of the assumption that poetry on Jesus is Christian poetry. But, surprisingly, it doesn't at all mark the end of poetry on Jesus. One might expect that this particular body of poetry would yellow and dry up along with the body of Jesus that modernism sees. Yet the opposite was the case for the twentieth century. Freed from the requirement of belief, poets in historically Christian societies felt liberated to explore any personal attitude toward religion whatever: they could doubt it, scorn it, ignore it, test it out, even believe in it if they wished. (Novelists had a similar experience, as a study called *Fictional Transfigurations of Jesus* shows.)[17] This freedom gave an astonishing vitality to poetry in which Jesus figures. Poets, typical of their century, were energized by this sense of choice, so that when they did choose to treat the person of Jesus, there is often a remarkable freshness in the product.

At the same time, the Asian, Caribbean, and African postcolonial poets who spent the second half of the twentieth century freeing themselves from Western control brought to the figure of Christ—and to the whole Christian narrative—the fresh approaches of their native heritage. This is to say that, while twentieth-century literature did become unprecedentedly global in its embrace of modernism, it did not become uniform. Cultural uniformity may have been European colonialism's aim when, during the first half of the century, it spread Western intellectual movements around the world. But genuine local appropriation of Western thought and literature didn't come in most places until after World War II, as part of the independence movements that took place in the century's second half. In this liberating revolutionary atmosphere, poets freely transformed Western materials into native products. So throughout the non-Western world, the poetry of particular ethnic and religious cultures took over Christian stories and symbols, making them its own.

Also playing into non-Western poetic figurings of Jesus were the worldwide ecumenical and interfaith dialogues that are the major religious achievements of the twentieth century. The ecumenical movement (that is, dialogue among the various Christian churches) and the interfaith movement (that is, dialogue among Christian, Jewish, Muslim, Hindu, and Buddhist representatives) both began around the twentieth century's start. Early on, they inspired the casting of Jesus as "universal man" in poems by, for instance, the Bengali Nobel Prize-winner Rabindranath Tagore and the immensely popular Lebanese writer Kahlil Gibran.

World War II, that crashing midpoint of the century, divided ecumenical and interfaith developments as it divided so much else. For the first half of the century, these developments were dominated by the Western Christian world-view, a well-intentioned and (for the era) truly progressive domination, but domination nonetheless. World War II then broke open assumptions about Western superiority in every realm of sociopolitical life. The succeeding half century saw the birth pangs of the first genuinely multicultural world community, still far from being realized but at least on the way to being established as an ideal. As I write at the turn of the new century and millennium, I'd say the global multicultural community is in the dreadfully confused and self-destructive stage of early adolescence. I certainly don't want to gloss over the violence and anguish that accompany this process of creating a just and decent global society; indeed, my later chapters on African and on Arab poets set them in their all too painfully violent social context. Still, it's fair to say that the recent decades' multicultural ecumenical atmosphere has encouraged Christian poets of non-Western cultures to reimagine Jesus at home in their own towns. And, too, the century's interfaith ambience has inspired some Muslim and Hindu poets, as we'll see, to appropriate Jesus and the Gospels in fresh ways.

So a paradox of the twentieth century's religious as well as poetic theories and practices is that they were at once more universal and more culturally specific than ever before. Religion had a new universality in the sense that people of good faith, from whatever faith, sought an unprecedented common ground and common vision. But as the independence movements unfolded, people sought commonality through a deepening of their own culturally specific outlook rather than through the denial of value to that specificity that characterized the first half of the century. And local literary communities nearly everywhere, seeking to express in poetry their culture's particular crises, reached—with striking universality—for the Symbolist-modernist aesthetic that proved itself remarkably applicable to twentieth-century experience all over the world.

These terms make a grand sweep. For many readers' taste (including my own), they breeze too airily by the concrete life of the century. The rest of this book is rooted in the century's specifics: the particular poem coming from the particular poet configuring Jesus for a particular moment and place. Indeed, when we ask what happens to the figure of Jesus in twentieth-century poetry, we discover a plethora of new figures popping up practically all at once. With such a range of twentieth-century poetic responses to Christian material going on all over the globe each at their own pace, a chronological structure for this study would now be impossibly confusing; the clearest way to proceed seems to be by grouping these new figures. Accordingly, staying first in the West, the next chapter looks at Jesus as Antihero, a new figure shaped by a historically Christian culture that has lost—or thrown away—its identity as "Christian," defining itself as "secular" instead.

FOUR

Crisis of the Secularized West

Postmodernism's Jesus as Antihero

In 1906, Rainer Maria Rilke (1875–1926) wrote a poem, 'The Olive Garden,' picturing Jesus at Gethsemane. It begins:

> He climbed and, under the gray leaves, lost
> his gray self in a country of olive trees,
> and laid his dusty forehead deep
> in the dustiness of his hot hands.

> After it all was this. And this the end.
> Now I'm to go when I'm becoming blind,
> and why is it Your will that I must say
> You are, when I find you yourself no more.

> Find You no more. Not within me, no.
> Not in the others. Not within this rock.
> Find You no more. I am alone.

> I am alone with all the human grief
> I undertook, through You, to soothe,
> You, who are not. O shame unnameable.[1]

Here is a Jesus who, disillusioned, denies that God exists. Though still speaking to God, he addresses him as "You, who are not." I've tried to find you, Jesus complains, but I can't. Rilke has Jesus point to each of the places where a Romantic would have found God: within oneself, in the human community, in this rock (that is, in Nature). But the Romantic God is long gone, and with him any sense of connectedness to human and natural life. Annette Droste-Hülshoff's intensely Romantic Jesus at Gethsemane had passed through an anguished moment of feeling abandoned by God, but even then he was connected with the Nature that expressed his emotions. Rilke's Jesus feels connected with nothing; "I am alone." He's not anguished, but empty. And ashamed—because he feels cheated of the very purpose of his life. Since you "are not," he accuses the Being he can't even call "Father," I've taken on all this human grief for nothing.

About half a century later, in New Zealand, the poet R. A. K. Mason (1905–1971) fashioned a Jesus who likewise objects that God has betrayed him, has led him into a dead-end life. Speaking from the Cross in one poem ('Nails and a Cross'), Mason's Jesus protests:

God, I may say that I've been brave
    and it's led me—? Damned and deified
    here I spurt the blood from a riven side:
    blood, never revisit my heart again
    but suck the wisdom out of my brain
    I got in so many lonely days
    bruising my feet with flinty ways.[2]

Resentfully, this Jesus then recalls the comfortable childhood home he was "lured" away from "to follow the wild and lonely call." Both Rilke and Mason have their Jesus beat down repeatedly on the words "alone," "lonely," "solitary," to describe his state. Then Mason's Jesus concludes:

And I see, if I squint, my blood of death
    drip on the little harsh grass beneath
    and friend and foe and men long dead
    faint and reel in my whirling head:
    and while the troops divide up my cloak
    the mob fling dung and see the joke.

The bitter irony for this Jesus is that what draws him finally out of his loneliness is sharing with the mob the vulgar joke of his wasted life. Wasted indeed: worthy of nothing, he agrees, but to be covered with dung.

For readers, the shock in both these poems is hearing Jesus himself voice such scornful dismissal of the meaning of his suffering, of his very life. He has the same name as the central character on the Evangelists' stage, and the settings are familiar Gospel scenes (Gethsemane, Golgotha); yet his words would be inconceivable in the Evangelists' script. This twentieth-century Jesus is a parody of his Gospel self. He lives a nightmare even worse than the one that haunted Arthur Hugh Clough in the middle of the nineteenth century. Clough, as noted in chapter 3, feared that Christ, unrisen, was only "ashes to ashes, dust to dust." Rilke goes further in picturing Jesus reduced to dust: "his gray self" laying "his dusty forehead deep / in the dustiness of his hot hands." And then Rilke and Mason have Jesus himself voice the despair that Clough voiced for his contemporaries confronting the possibility that they were merely mortal, unredeemed by a risen Christ. For Clough in 'Easter Day: Naples, 1849,' if Christ is not risen, then we can only:

Eat, drink, and die, for we are men deceived,
Of all the creatures under heaven's wide cope
We are most hopeless who had once most hope,
We are most wretched that had most believed.

To which the Jesus of Rilke and Mason might say (*does* say, in different words): no, the most wretched is *I*, because the belief I was deceived in was belief in myself. Mason has another poem, 'Footnote to John ii:4,' in which Jesus could almost be continuing from these lines of Clough's, applying to himself their sense of disillusioned wretchedness. Speaking bitterly to his mother at Cana about the "work of doom" that, starting with this first miracle, he is being called on to do, he spits out this following self-portrait:

> I am a merciless cactus an uncouth
> wild goat a jagged old spear the grim tooth
> of a lone crag.

In two thousand years of poetry on Jesus, there is no moment before the twentieth century that could have produced this particular figure: this aggressively ugly collage-sculpture, a stuccoed compression of harsh flinty bits and pieces. Though the "lone crag" might have been cut from a Romantic landscape (that mountain peak where Jesus the Divinely Human Hero had proudly stood), this twentieth-century Jesus has been cut down to size. Cut down actually to less than size: chiseled down to the jagged point of a "grim tooth." A figure of Jesus as Antihero could hardly be more biting. He has hit rock bottom. With his life and death devoid of redemptive meaning—of any meaning at all—he is robbed of purpose.

Neither Mason nor Rilke was stuck with this single figure of Jesus, whom we might name Jesus Disillusioned. Mason, one of the first New Zealand poets to reject the sentimentality of the colony's popular literature, crafted a body of verse honestly responsive to the land's harshness. While his Jesus can be harshly cynical, in solidarity with all people who feel betrayed by life's false promises, Mason also put Jesus in some poems of fairly traditional faith-filled hope. Rilke, we'll see in a later chapter, went on to cast Jesus in other roles. But I've begun this chapter with their Jesus as an Antihero who is disillusioned and even cynical because he speaks for a crisis characteristic of the secularized twentieth-century West. For fourteen hundred years, Western culture had identified itself as Christian. Then, as we've seen, the eighteenth and nineteenth centuries increasingly called this identity into question. The twentieth-century West finally stopped questioning and said: clearly our culture is secular, post-Christian. That is, recognizing that it had changed utterly from a culture that could assume a communal religious belief, it claimed itself a culture presuming communal doubt.

What better figure to represent this secular stance than a Doubting Jesus? For Western Christian culture, Jesus had represented the fullness of meaning: as the Christ and the Logos, he was redemptive meaning itself, humankind's salvation, "the Way, the Truth and the Life" (as John's Gospel puts it). To imagine this figure of Meaning's Fullness now seeing his meaning emptied out, dissolved into dust—to picture him helplessly watching his own promise taken back—is the perfect representation of radical doubt. But doubt is not a ground on which a culture can really stand. A culture must make meaning for its members; a culture in fact *is,* by some definitions, the system of signs carrying meaning for a given society. The secularized West recognized itself in crisis because it had dispensed with its inherited belief system, yet had no other at hand to make sense of human existence.

The two predominant kinds of response to this crisis are generally differentiated as "modernism" and "postmodernism." In the previous chapter, we looked at modernism's characteristic response: to mourn the loss of inherited beliefs. And we noted there that the modernist tone of wistful nostalgia can be heard at points all through the twentieth century. Simultaneously, postmodernism's more hardened tone sounds throughout the century. That is, the two terms—modernism and postmodernism—don't designate a simple chronology, as their names suggest. Though the terms themselves did develop one after the other, they came to designate two ongoing tones toward the movement into a secular culture. Modernism, watching the culture's inherited faith disappear, feels a sense of loss; postmodernism loses the sense of loss. That double negative—the loss of loss—is right in postmodernism's mode. Postmodernism loves to play mind-games: to turn its own assertions on their head, to demonstrate that nothing has sure meaning, not even the concept of meaning.

Not all the poets to be presented in this chapter are postmodernists, but they're grouped together because they each craft a Jesus who is in some way or other a product of the postmodern worldview. Postmodernism can not invent heroes, only antiheroes; hence the subtitle of the chapter. A hero by definition does something significant, something of value; but postmodernism recognizes no value or significance, so all its characters are antiheroes, trying to make do in a world that undoes every gesture toward significant making. The characters of Thomas Pynchon's novels are classic examples. Jesus as Antihero in twentieth-century poetry takes on many forms, as we'll see. The Disillusioned Jesus of Rilke and Mason is only one.

R. A. K. MASON's Disillusioned Jesus, mocking himself as "a jagged old spear the grim tooth / of a lone crag," is a hardened figure. Other versions of a Stone-hard Jesus dot the postmodernist landscape. From Denmark comes a purposefully shocking one in a poem by Per Kirkeby (1938–), a well-known artist who has also written some poetry. Crafting a monotony of repeated phrases without syntactical bearings, to simulate the blank dullness of contemporary life devoid of meaning, Kirkeby describes a scene of "solitary rock formations" in which one building's supporting columns are sculpted as naked women wearing crucifixes:

with naked breasts on two naked women
somewhat smaller the naked Jesus
with drapings round the naked legs of
the naked Jesus who shows his perforated palms
behind the naked Jesus two naked women.[3]

This hammered-out nakedness is not erotic. It is mere emptiness in an utterly static world in which nothing is—either physically or emotionally—moved.

In a sense this isn't the first naked Jesus that we've seen. In the Jesus of modernism, we saw a figure who dropped the divine robes he had worn for nearly two millennia, to stand before us awkwardly human. Yet Kirkeby's Jesus is less than human; his nakedness is that of cold stone. Even this reduction to a diminutive stone figure fixed on naked stone breasts is not, however, the greatest indignity which the postmodernist Jesus on the Cross has suffered. With deliberate crudeness, Chilean poet Nicanor Parra (1914–), famous for his iconoclastic "antipoems" (more of these in the next chapter), trivializes 'The Cross' by turning it into a vulgar sexual object in his poem of that title. Beginning with an image that comes innocently enough out of the devotional tradition popular in Spanish culture since the late Middle Ages—"Sooner or later I shall come weeping / to the open arms of the cross"—Parra draws out the seductive implications of those open arms that invite an embrace, until the Cross lures him finally, outrageously, as "a woman with her legs open."[4]

The technique of twisting a traditional figure of Jesus into a perversion of its reverent meaning is useful for the shock value of declaring: this Jesus means less than nothing to us now. Danish poet Ole Wivel uses the technique in a poem taking its title, 'The Fish,' from the ancient symbol for Christ said to derive from the Greek word for "fish," *ichthys,* which can be formed by the first letters of the words of the Greek phrase for "Jesus Christ, Son of God, Savior." But Wivel's poem addresses a sinister Fish who, gliding silently through our world "with your unspeaking eyes," looks at first like an Antichrist:

It feels at first
As if you were men's enemy—
Your empty mouth
Will tell us only what is written
In the bubble's shimmering roundness
One second—but to burst.

Then an apocalyptic storm churns up the sea, and the poem ends with a shocking vision of the Second Coming: "You lie there bloody / In foam and tang— and are our Savior."[5]

I hear the poet uttering "Our Savior" with a cynical hiss. In the chapter on modernist figures of Jesus, we heard Wivel, in his poem 'Weep for Balder,' mourning the loss of gods from the postwar world. But I find Wivel's 'The Fish' more a postmodernist product because its tone isn't sorrowful but bitterly disillusioned, and its Jesus is even less than the mere powerless human of 'Weep for Balder'; its Jesus is dehumanized, the Incarnate God reduced to gory dead flesh of fish. Surely the nadir of Jesus as Antihero, Wivel's Fish ends up without even the status of Antichrist that it seemed to have "at first." It has nothing to say to us. With its "empty mouth" and "unspeaking eyes," it is a figure of Jesus Designified, image for the poet of the ultimate horror of meaninglessness at his near-millennial moment in history.

Less than Christ and even less than human, the antiheroes of Kirkeby and Parra and Wivel (and of many of their contemporaries whom I could just as easily cite) are a Jesus Trivialized, Dehumanized, even De-signified. A Jesus who resonates with all of these is the 'Dead Christ' of United States poet Andrew Hudgins (1951—). In the course of a productive poetic career that is still going strong, Hudgins has made much of the figure of Jesus, some of which we'll come to in the book's concluding chapter. But his 'Dead Christ' belongs here because of the elegance with which it plays off of other configurations of Jesus both from the poet's own postmodern era and from, interestingly enough, the Renaissance.

Hudgins's 'Dead Christ' is drawn from the painting of this title by Renaissance artist Andrea Mantegna. In a matter-of-fact tone, the poet describes this Christ as a man whose undeniable deadness, after his deposition from the Cross, is represented by every detail of the painting. Renaissance artists were eager to portray the fleshiness of Jesus, even his sexuality, as tribute to the wonder of the Incarnation. That is, Christ's divinity was so self-evident to them that vividly representing his humanity not only didn't threaten his divine status but honored its marvel. Hudgins, looking through late twentieth-century-eyes that he knows have lost this reading, focuses in on Mantegna's Jesus' sexual organs swelling under the funeral cloth "huge and useless" with death. The sexuality for Hudgins isn't at all a matter of trivializing Jesus, however, as it is for Kirkeby and Parra. Nor is Hudgins's Dead Christ the dehumanized one of Wivel. Hudgins's Jesus here is overhumanized. The painter carried out his era's Christian aesthetic so succesfully, suggests the poet, that maybe he went over the edge, making Christ so humanly dead that we're left with only "the empty corpse."[6]

Emptiness has been a feature of other configurations of Jesus that we've met in this chapter. The Jesus of Rilke and Mason is bitter at having been emptied of his salvific meaning, left as dust for Rilke, as dripping blood for Mason. Kirkeby's Jesus is immobilized in a stone-cold landscape empty of meaning. Wivel's Jesus emits bubbles from his "empty mouth." Yet for Hudgins, writing with the sophistication of someone who, at the end of a century's varieties of emptiness, is neither shocked nor cynical about its possibility but takes it in stride, Christ's "empty corpse" is an image not of radical doubt or dismissal but of recognition that meaninglessness is one possibility of meaning. Comfortable in the postmodern climate, the poet knows there are other options. 'Dead Christ' ends: "Most Christs return. / But this one's flesh. He isn't coming back." This particular Christ appears empty of salvific meaning; he's too dead to be resurrected, too far gone into flesh to come back as he does in the Gospel story. But there are other Christs, presumably not empty but full of meaning. Maybe even overfull.

TO BE EMPTY AND overfull of meaning are two sides of the postmodern coin—or, to use an image from within postmodernism's own vocabulary, two facing and mutually reflecting mirrors. Meaning's multiplicity is a favorite postmodern theme, couched always in suspicion of any claim that a particular meaning could be privileged or absolute. Since language for postmodernism is self-referential—a system of signs pointing to other signs, which point to other signs, ad infinitum—even the basic concepts of "meaning" and "understanding" are problematic. Jesus as the Word of God configures the problem conveniently for poets of this age, whether or not they are themselves postmodernists, because he represents an Absolute of language-as-meaning (that capitalized "Word") whose very status postmodernism denies. Poets of this era like to fashion a Jesus who resists the meanings pressed upon him, who baffles understanding, who is ultimately a figure of incomprehension.

I want to look at a cluster of four poems, from four of Western culture's different continents, in which the poet takes a Gospel moment and refocuses it through a twentieth-century lens onto a Jesus who baffles, who resists comprehension. Their figure of a Baffling or Misunderstood Jesus is in a sense ready-made in the Gospels. That is, a running motif of all the Evangelists is that the people around Jesus, including his disciples, didn't understand who he was or what he meant. But of course the Evangelists interpret Jesus Misunderstood quite differently from the way the poets of the postmodernist era do. For the Evangelists, he is a figure only of his earthly ministry; now that he has died and risen and sent his Spirit to enlighten them, he is in their own minds understood: as, most importantly, the Christ, the Son of God, and (for John's Gospel) the Word of God made flesh. For the four poets sampled here, what on earth this Word of God made flesh might mean is precisely the puzzle. They configure Jesus as Puzzle, as Word Problem or Image Game. In the poem 'Jesus,' by James McAuley (Australia, 1917–1976), Jesus is eager to give the clue to the puzzle, but people around him can't be bothered to listen; in 'Last Suppers,' by Mark Jarman (United States, 1952–), the people around threaten to obliterate Jesus in their violently self-reproducing scenes; in 'Unknown Letter,' by Tadeusz Różewicz (Poland, 1921–), Jesus himself blots out the main clue to his meaning; in 'John 1:14,' by Jorge Luis Borges (Argentina, 1899–1986), Jesus incarnates the word problem of self-reflexivity inherent in human language. All four are good, sharp poems by poets of fine craft. But I'll linger longest over Borges because he was formative in the very creation of postmodernist theory and literature, because he puts a great deal of his own essence as writer into his figure of Jesus, and because he leads us into some general issues linking postmodernism and Christianity.

Here first, in full, is McAuley's poem, 'Jesus'.

> Touching Ezekiel his workman's hand
> Kindled the thick and thorny characters;
> And seraphim that seemed a thousand eyes,
> Flying leopards, wheels and basilisks,
> Creatures of power and of judgment, soared
> From his finger-point, emblazoning the skies.
>
> Then turning from the book he rose and walked
> Among the stones and beasts and flowers of earth;
> They turned their muted faces to their Lord,
> Their real faces, seen by God alone;
> And people moved before him undisguised;
> He thrust his speech among them like a sword.
>
> And when a dove came to his hand he knew
> That hell was opening behind its wings.
> He thanked the messenger and let it go;
> Spoke to the dust, the fishes and the twelve
> As if they understood him equally,
> And told them nothing that they wished to know.[7]

McCauley, an adult convert to Catholicism, produced a large body of essays and poetry condemning the hedonistic emptiness of what he labeled modernity. To configure in this poem the problem of faith in a skeptical age, McCauley chooses a Gospel episode in which Jesus himself confronts this problem. The episode—where Jesus reads the Scripture in his hometown synagogue and preaches to incomprehending ears—is treated differently by each of the three Evangelists who include it (Mark 6:1–6; Matt. 13:54–58; Luke 4:16–30). So McAuley feels free to invent a slightly different version of his own. Instead of reading from Isaiah, as in Luke (the only Evangelist to identify the Scripture passage), McAuley's Jesus reads from Ezekiel—so that an apocalyptic vision can spark from his touch of the text. "Touching" is a significant first word for this poem, which is all about the Word made flesh, made tactile. Jewish readers in the synagogue do run their finger along the Hebrew text, to keep track, so this is a realistic detail. Yet the poet makes of it a marvelous symbol, much in the spirit of Jewish mysticism: as the "workman's hand" of Jesus touches the written word, the text blazes up to reveal in the skies his own ultimate meaning as

Word made flesh. Yet apparently only Jesus sees the apocalyptic vision. Stanza 2 has him turning away to walk through a mute world of stones, beasts, flowers, and people. He sees through them all, indeed pierces them with his speech; yet they are unresponsive, numb. Quietly, in stanza 3, he sees the consequences of their unresponsiveness to his being, his Word. Behind the messenger dove (descendent of Noah's dove, who brought the message that God had saved the world from its own sinfulness), Jesus sees for this world not salvation but damnation; the apocalyptic judgment of stanza 1 is upon the world, and it is hell. McAuley here is right in the spirit of John's Gospel (3:18): those who do not believe in Jesus are already condemned, *by* their very rejection of him. In the poem, Jesus tries once more to speak "to the dust, the fishes and the twelve," metonymic representatives of all his creation, inanimate, animate, and human. Yet they don't want to know what he says, what he is; so his speech is as "nothing."

For a poem all about speech, the whole is extraordinarily quiet. No spoken words are quoted, and this absence dramatizes the damning silence. All that happens is contained in a calmly paced, partly rhymed, iambic pentameter stanza form. Though the lines speak of an apocalyptic judgment on the world, the tone throughout is muted, calm—as if Jesus is resigned to being the Muted Word, the Word Unheard, the Word Not Understood. With great concision, the poem dramatizes a puzzle at the core of the secularized twentieth-century West: what can it mean to be the Word of God in a mute, incomprehending world?

The puzzle that propels Mark Jarman's 'Last Suppers' is similar though in a sense the reverse, since his Jesus is the mute center of a world that is decidedly noisy. 'Last Suppers' represents only one of the kinds of interaction between God and the world's meanings that Jarman, a prolific poet, continues to explore in his poetry. The meanings of 'Last Suppers' are signaled as multiple from the start, in the poem's plural title, which also announces its form: a cycle of eight sections, each looking anew at the scene of Leonardo da Vinci's famous painting. The painting itself strikes the poet with its qualities of dangerous, nearly violent deterioration, both in what it depicts and in its medium. In Leonardo's scene, Jarman sees the twelve apostles making such a mutually accusatory racket that their passions seem about to set the room ablaze, while at the center Christ, "the calm one," averts his eyes and "sadly" calls out "Fire!" The apostles' catastrophically deteriorating behavior is matched by the well-known decay of the very art work itself; because of Leonardo's failed experimental painting technique, the scene is inexorably disappearing from the monastery wall on which it was done. But Jarman's interest extends way beyond this doubly deteriorating scene of Leonardo's original in Milan. The other Last Suppers of the poem's title are reproductions of the scene that the poet has personally encountered: not only the ubiquitous copies hung in church annexes and family dining rooms, but also real scenes of tense family dinner-table violence that "reproduce" the painting, one even right under a gaudily lighted copy of Leonardo's work. The genius of

Jarman's poem—which I can't begin to do justice to in paraphrase—is the way he brings all these Last Supper "scenes" into interaction, so that paper copies and painted original and real-life representations all replicate one another's chaotic instability swirling around "the loneliness of God." So, for instance, "The tumult of the twelve thrusts out a snaking / Embrace to clutch us close and feel the pressure / Of our belief or nonbelief." But we in turn are impressed on Leonardo's twelve, in the poet's image of their scene as "a family's daily warfare."[8]

Many twentieth-century poems "on" Jesus are actually on paintings of his appearance in a Gospel scene. Such mediation of Jesus—through not only the Gospel narrative but again through a visual representation of the narrative—enacts well the postmodern sense of regressive or infinitely self-reflective meaning. Sometimes this mediation process is part of the poem's point, as we noted for the 'Dead Christ' of Andrew Hudgins, to whom 'Last Suppers' is dedicated. But Jarman took on in 'Last Suppers' the ambitious challenge of making of the mediation process a grand theme and variations. To me, a measure of the poem's success is that it manages to represent postmodernism's radical restlessness—in the instability and even irritability of meanings ready to self-destruct around Jesus—without itself becoming at all irritable or unstable. Jarman's prosodic determination is here, I dare say, his saving grace. The poem's eight sections are composed with absolute regularity: each is four stanzas of blank verse quatrains. Along with a steady tone of observant calm, this strict verse form holds in check the chaos that the poem everywhere signals. It also makes reasonable the vision with which 'Last Suppers' ends: an imagined scene of a family's peace if they would only allow themselves to be "touched for once by a deep tranquility," by that calm center who is nearly wiped out in the brutal, usually replicated din. The poem's Nearly Obliterated Jesus is for an instant pictured holding his own.

Obliteration is also the theme of Tadeusz Rózewicz's 'Unknown Letter.' This short poem is less ambitious than Jarman's and less dense than McAuley's, yet it invents a single sharp image that captures the figure of Jesus Incomprehensible. Like McAuley, Rózewicz imaginatively enters Jesus' mind in a Gospel moment: this one the scene, only in John, of the woman taken in adultery. What interests Rózewicz isn't the whole episode but just the line where John says that "Jesus bent down and wrote with his finger on the ground." The Evangelist doesn't say what Jesus wrote, and over the centuries many answers have been offered to this puzzle planted in the Gospel itself. Rózewicz's treatment of the puzzle has a new twentieth-century twist. Starting the poem with Jesus "bent over," writing on the earth, complaining (in his mind, addressing his Mother) that everyone around him persists in ignorance of his purpose and childishly demands repeated miracles, Rózewicz ends suddenly:

> When
> Matthew Mark Luke and John
> approached him

he covered the letters
and erased them
forever[9]

This final verse always gives me a shiver. Its electric-shock image says, with that single gesture of erasure, that the Gospels are based on an absence. The Word of God Erased is their central figure. Jesus is Unknowable, because we haven't known how to know him; and now it's too late.

Writing in the devasted aftermath of post–World War II Poland, Różewicz saw a world in which traditional values had become inaccessible—in effect, had been erased. He invents an Ultimately Unknowable Jesus to configure this sense. Jorge Luis Borges also plays with a figure of the Unknowable Word of God, but to a different purpose. Throughout his long and productive career, Borges was intrigued by the problem of the inadequacy of language, by its apparent inability to mean anything beyond itself. Not only is he, in this sense, appropriately classed as a postmodernist; he is universally recognized as one of postmodernist literature's formative writers. Most famous for his prose narrative *ficciones*, which invent worlds that turn out, teasingly, to be nothing but texts referring to other texts, Borges plays with language's self-reflexive nature in a large body of poetry as well. In 'John 1:14' (1969), he puzzles over the limits of language through the mouth of Jesus, the Incarnate Word.

Indeed, the whole point of the poem is the puzzle; its first words announce that the poem itself will be *un enigma*. At forty-eight lines, 'John 1:14' is too long to quote in full, but I'll try to touch on the key points. ("Touching" is the right metaphor for this poem in which, as in McAuley's 'Jesus,' the Word of God is decidedly tactile.) The Gospel verse to which the poem's title refers is one that encapsulates the Fourth Gospel's Christology: "And the Word became flesh and lived among us, and we have seen his glory, the glory as of a father's only son, full of grace and truth." Borges's speaker in the poem is this Word made flesh, whom Borges takes seriously as the preexistent Divine Word of the Fourth Gospel. Borges's audacious concept, though, is to make this speaker also the implied author of this very poem, with Borges in the role of scribe. The device allows him, writing the poem at the age of seventy, to meditate on his lifelong preoccupations *as* the preoccupations of the Gospel's Divine Word Incarnate: "I condescend again to human language, to the written word, / which is time in succession, an emblem."[10] It's a wonderfully Borgesian interpretation of the Eternal Word's sacrifice in becoming human. Obsessed all his life by time's inevitable passing, by the inability of language to hold time still, Borges sees the Incarnation as the Infinite's "condescension" to time and to the mere word, a wrenching diminishment from Eternity to mere reflections, signs, emblems. Yet there's something else going on here besides the infinitely self-reflecting signs and mirrors for which Borges is notorious. "My sacred books" and "this page" as well, the speaker says, are "dark mirrors of the Spirit," reflections of "I who

Sleeping Logos (The Way) *(1989), by Cho Kwang-ho (Korea, 1947–). A Benedictine priest whose art is widely exhibited in Germany and Seoul, Cho is fixated on the figure of the Unknowable Jesus. Cho has written of his art: "Ours is a world full of undecipherable codes, pregnant with innumerable messages rising like the mist on the sea of mystery. I become aphasic wandering in front of the gate of mystery, forever struggling for lucidness."* Sleeping Logos *is from the series of paintings called* Code for Logos-Mystery of Life. *By permission of the artist.*

am the Is, the Was and the Is To Come." In this identification of himself through the well-known line of the biblical book of Revelation, the speaker puts a stop to the infinite regress of words reflecting words reflecting words: a stop at the transcendent Infinite Word, beyond the merely verbal, which is all we can know in this human life.

The poem continues with Jesus telling the story of his Incarnation in Borgesian terms. To my ear, the long passage has the lilt and litheness of Wisdom's personification in The Wisdom of Solomon and in Proverbs, where she is with God from the beginning and then comes to play with creation. Borges's Jesus came among us because he wanted "to play with My children," to be close to their "mystery." He tells his story as if it were a fairy tale, full of "magic" and "enchantment." But when he mentions coming to know the "labyrinths of reason," we realize that all along Borges has been telling his own life story, too. And if we look back at his life's work in the terms he puts in the mouth of the Word made flesh, we can see that, yes, Borges always did have this awe at living in the flesh while sensing that his mind and spirit came from somewhere else. So when the poem's Jesus then shifts to a vividly concrete list of the tactile things that he "knew" as Word made flesh—"the taste of honey and apples, / . . . the weight of a piece of metal in the palm, / . . . the smell of the rain in Galilee"—we're meant to recall the sensuous tactility of Borges's early poems, where, under Rubén Darío's influence, he gloried in minute sense perceptions of the streets of Buenos Aires, while seeing them also mystically transformed by heaven's touch.

'John 1:14' returns in its closing lines to its initial preoccupation: Who is writing this poem and under what limitations? With sad resignation to the limits of human language, the speaker/Jesus/Borges laments that these written words will never be *lo que quiero decir*: the common Spanish phrase for both "what I want to say" and "what I mean" reaches handily for Borges into the crux of language and meaning. Like one of his favorite poets, Walt Whitman, he calls his words "signs" fallen from "My eternity." But whereas the Romantic Whitman could be exuberant about his role as scribe for the Divine Word, the postmodernist Borges has to belittle his own capability for the job. He has Jesus say that someone else, not the ordinary person writing here, should be acting as my scribe. The poem ends on a wistful note, with Jesus concluding: "I think with nostalgia, sometimes, / on the smell of that carpenter's shop." His nostalgia is for the immediacy of lived life, which language—always a mediation, even in such concrete images as those of this poem—can never grasp. There's a poignancy, as I hear it, to the whole poem. Reflecting on the meaning of his own time among us, Borges is saying: all that will remain of me is these writings, yet they can never be the reality of my life. Though 'John 1:14' is a metaphysical meditation, it is as far as can be from abstract metaphysics. It is autobiography, personal assessment—through the figure of Jesus as Ultimately Unknowable Word.

'John 1:14' was clearly important to Borges. He placed it first in the volume published to mark his seventieth year, *In Praise of Darkness* (*Elogio de la Sombra,* 1969), where it sets the tone of the book's autumnal reflections on death, immortality, and the mystery of writing, especially of poetry. I expect that many other readers are as surprised as I was to find Borges identifying so deeply and comfortably with the central figure of the Christian Gospels.[11] We North Americans first met Borges through his ficciones when, just translated into English in the 1960s, they were suddenly all the rage. In my giddily postmodernist graduate school community of the time, we were titillated by these inventive structures of infinite regress: texts that collapsed in on themselves when the narrator was revealed as the dream of another narrator who was someone else's dream; metafictions about fictions about fictions; invented worlds that might or might not be mirror reflections of our own. So it has been an eye-opener to get to know Borges better recently: to discover that he was a poet before, during, and after his prose experiments, to see that the mind-games of the ficciones weren't all for their own sake, but that behind them was a person genuinely searching for an ultimate ground of meaning. Indeed, in a poem written at the very time that Borges started crafting his ficciones, a poem that Borges once called the synthesis of all his poetry—'Conjectural Poem' ('Poema conjetural,' 1943)—the infinite regress of mirrors reflecting mirrors is stopped at an infinitely knowing God. The poem's speaker, a historically real person who was an ancestor of Borges, has just been shot in an ambush, and Borges imagines him joyfully discovering at this moment of death the meaning of his life:

> the missing letter, the perfect pattern
> that was known to God from the beginning.
> In this night's mirror I can comprehend
> my unsuspected true face.[12]

This was certainly not, however, Borges's last word on God. A man of remarkable verbal fluency (language streamed out of him, and he loved giving interviews), Borges tossed off through his life hundreds of mostly contradictory references to God, to Christianity, to his own engagement with religious faith. Raised by a pious Catholic mother and an adamantly atheistic father, he rejected both their extremes yet played at every possible position between them. In interviews, he calls himself a "happy agnostic" at one time, an "amateur Protestant" at another.[13] Systematized religion turned him off, yet he was drawn to religions' acknowledgment of the inherent mystery of existence. All his life, Borges enjoyed reading classic religious texts, especially Protestant theology, Swedenborg, and Jewish mysticism. He knew the Christian Gospels well, and though he doesn't make a lot of explicit use of them in his writing, he is comfortable drawing on them when he needs them. One of his prose fictions is an allegorized version of Mark's Gospel. Several poems besides 'John 1:14' play off of Gospel texts; they have titles like 'Matthew XXV:30,' 'Luke XXIII,' and 'From an Apocryphal Gospel' (which rewrites Jesus' Sermon on the Mount).

Borges's God is very much implicated in his labyrinthian universe, for good or for ill. Borges can imagine a perverse God, unconcerned about his creatures' pathetically futile attempts to solve eternal riddles. But he can also imagine a God who solves the riddle at the last minute, as in 'Conjectural Poem.' In a prose poem called 'A Prayer' (in *In Praise of Darkness*), Borges says that during his life he has recited the Lord's Prayer "thousands of times," without ever fully understanding it or ever expecting to. But who does understand it? Who does genuinely comprehend the God to whom this prayer is addressed? No one, certainly no true Christian; such at least would be the answer of one of the century's leading theologians, Karl Rahner. Speaking, for instance, in 1974 at Duquesne University in Pittsburgh, Rahner said:

> The Christian is the true and most radical sceptic. For if he really believes in the incomprehensibility of God, he is convinced that no individual truth is really true except in the process which necessarily belongs to its true essence, the process in which the truth becomes a question which remains unanswered because it is asking about God and His incomprehensibility.[14]

To call Borges a Christian based on this definition would be disingenuous. Yet Rahner's statement startles one into noticing that between the postmodernist and the Christian metaphysics of the twentieth century, there's no hard and fast line. Indeed, in the editor's introduction to an important recent anthology of contemporary Christian poets (*Upholding Mystery,* Oxford University Press, 1997), David Impastato makes a point of their surprising comfort in the postmodern intellectual climate. Though postmodernism insists on absence where Christianity sees presence, Impastato notes, both radically interrogate the world's wisdoms and power structures, and both privilege language. Christianity's sacred text is a language construct with all the elusiveness of a postmodernist narrative: the Bible (taken as "God's word") is a web of mixed genres and undatable revisions from the hands of unidentifiable authors. And Christianity has as its core figure—as Borges dramatizes in 'John 1:14'—the problematic Word.

But Christianity per se is not my subject in this chapter. Postmodernism's impact on poetic configurings of Jesus is. Though a few of the poets we've looked at would call themselves Christians, what brings together the poets in this chapter isn't their relation to Christian faith but their way of responding to the radical skepticism of their era. They make Jesus speak directly to—or speak for, or embody, or be silenced by—the crisis of radical doubt that characterizes the secular West. Whether their Jesus is Disillusioned, Hardened, Trivialized, Silenced, or Misunderstood, he is cast as an Antihero. That is, his meaningful role in his own story, the Christian story, is explicitly denied him. It's as if the adamantly secularized environment of the twentieth-century Western stage has closed in on the character who once—who indeed for most of the time since his birth—stood gloriously for the whole world's meaning. Instead of transforming the world, he is transformed by it. Closing in on him, the stage environment casts its dubious shadows over him. Closer still, it grabs him up, absorbs him. It turns him to dust, or to stone, or to mangled flesh. It makes him mute, or it bandies him about as a mind-game.

When we return later in the book to the Western stage, it will still be set, of course, as a secular environment. That setting didn't basically change during the century. But we won't see Jesus cast as the Antihero he has played in the poems of this chapter; even in a secular world that presumes communal doubt, Western poets have come up with lots of other roles for him. Now, though, we move to some other twentieth-century cultures to see what their poets have made of the figure of Jesus.

FIVE

Crucified Africa

The Politicized Jesus of Africa and Beyond

Lord Jesus, at the end of this book, which I offer You
As a ciborium of sufferings
At the beginning of the Great Year, in the sunlight
Of Your peace on the snowy roofs of Paris
—Yet I know that my brothers' blood will once more redden
The yellow Orient on the shores of the Pacific
Ravaged by storms and hatred
I know that this blood is the spring libation
The Great Tax Collectors have used for seventy years
To fatten the Empire's lands
Lord, at the foot of this cross—and it is no longer You
Tree of sorrow but, above the Old and New Worlds,
Crucified Africa.

These are the opening lines of Léopold Senghor's 'Prayer for Peace,' written in Paris in January 1945.[1] Born in 1906 in French colonial Senegal, where he was raised Catholic and trained as a priest, Senghor had gone to France to complete his university studies—as was customary for the French colonial African elite. In the intellectual excitement of Paris in the 1930s, Senghor discovered his true vocation as teacher and poet. (Later he would add that of politician, becoming the first president of Senegal at its independence in 1960.) But his priestly formation helped shape his consciousness. 'Prayer for Peace,' for instance, is a sustained petition to "Lord Jesus," and the book of poems that it concludes is called, with reference to the communion hosts of Mass, *Black Hosts* (*Hosties noires*). Like many of his black compatriots, Senghor had been drafted into the French military during World War II. Captured by the Germans, he spent nearly two years in a German prison camp, where most of *Black Hosts* was composed. These poems rage at France for making sacrificial victims of Senegalese soldiers, not only in this war but during seventy years of shedding their blood as a "spring libation . . . to fatten the Empire's lands." So Senghor offers the poems "as a ciborium of sufferings," an offering plate full of black bodies, which will become Christ's body at the sacrifice of Mass. And seeing that these black hosts will "once more" be sacrificed to European interests as the war spreads to the Pacific, Senghor painfully envisions his whole continent as Christ on the Cross: "Crucified Africa."

Yet Senghor writes, he says, "in the sunlight / Of Your peace on the snowy roofs of Paris." 'Prayer for Peace' is a long poem of many moods and moments. Because, remarkably, it moves through many of the tones and stances that would be taken by African literature for the next half century, and because its author is a major poet who also became a major politician in post-colonial Africa, I'm going to open the poem up, so to speak, to allow it to structure this chapter's material. Modern African poetry—that is, poetry written in European languages and shaped by the colonial experience—is highly politicized; where Jesus appears, it is within the drama of African people's recent history. The passages I'll quote from 'Prayer for Peace' will serve as headings for the principal roles that African poets have called on Jesus to play.

> Crucified Africa
> And her right arm stretches over my land
> And her left side shades America
> And her heart is precious Haiti, Haiti who dared
> Proclaim Man before the Tyrant. ('Prayer for Peace,' ll.13–17)

PLACING THE HEART OF Crucified Africa in Haiti, Senghor must be picturing the early stirrings there of the movement that came to be known as negritude: an effort by black intellectuals of the African diaspora to throw off the "Tyrant" European culture and "proclaim" with pride their common African heritage. Actually, as Senghor's cosmic crucifixion image suggests, "America" in general was a site of this newly awakening black consciousness. Though negritude wasn't named as such until the mid-1940s, it's considered to have begun with the Harlem Renaissance poets of the 1920s. One of their number, Langston Hughes, put their common purpose this way: "We younger Negro artists who create now intend to express our individual dark-skinned selves without fear or shame."[2] In Haiti there was similar ferment. A group of young intellectuals, including the poet Jacques Roumain, founded in 1927 the literary journal La Revue indigène (The Native Review), dedicated to exploring their African roots. Their inspiration was the Haitian physician and elder statesman Jean Price Mars, who had returned from Europe stimulated by German and French anthropologists' reevaluation of traditional Africa as a culture of great richness. "Our only chance to be ourselves," Price Mars declared, "is to repudiate no part of the ancestral heritage."[3]

It's hard now to realize how revolutionary it was in the 1920s for blacks to proclaim their full humanity. Certainly racism is far from erased from human consciousness, but we've come a long way. A people's pride in their ethnic heritage is something we now assume—thanks precisely to efforts such as these of the negritude movement. Senghor himself was an influential force in the movement. In 1948, the year he published Hosties noires, he also published in Paris a collection of the new work of African francophone poets titled Anthologie de la *nouvelle poésie nègre et malgache.* Senghor had a talent for promotion; through this anthology, negritude coalesced as a cause, complete with a name, a theoretical grounding, and a motto. The name negritude had actually been coined by the Martinican poet Aimé Césaire in a book-length poem published the year before, but it was from the *Anthologie*'s excerpt of that poem that the term took off. For theoretical grounding, Senghor got Jean-Paul Sartre to write a preface, which turned out to be the book's main selling point; controversial as always, Sartre validated the concept of black identity in newly fashionable existentialist terms, crafting philosophical nuggets like a neo-Cartesian *je suis nègre donc je suis* (I am black, therefore I am). And as negritude's motto, readers of the *Anthologie* spontaneously picked up the last eight lines of Haitian poet Jacques Roumain's militant 'New Negro Sermon.' Throwing Christianity in the face of white hypocrite Christians whose "church bells shower death on hungry multitudes," the poem ends with a rallying cry: "We'll no longer sing the sad, despairing spirituals" but will march forth under "red flags" stained by our brothers' blood, "standing tall, the legions of the hungry!"[4]

It might have been this very poem that Senghor had in mind for the "heart" of crucified Africa: *"Haiti who dared / Proclaim Man before the Tyrant."* 'New Negro Sermon' definitely and defiantly proclaims the black person as Man— and that Man as the person of Jesus. Christ in the poem is a "poor nigger" hauling cotton; conversely, the black race victimized by injustice is the suffering Christ. In so appropriating the figure of Jesus for its revolutionary cause, the poem stands out among negritude works. Naturally negritude had to free itself from the Christian baggage that was part and parcel of imperialist European culture. But most negritude poets expressed their freedom by heaving the whole parcel into the sea; they just ignored Christian stuff and dug instead into their ancestral African religious treasures. Roumain, too, threw out the institutional Christian baggage, but not before opening it, lifting out the figure of Jesus, and saying: look, he is ours, he is us.

Roumain's contemporaries did look, because the poet was preaching what he himself had practiced—and had suffered for. A member of Haiti's educated class, dynamic and charismatic, Roumain (1907–1944) was the chosen leader of his generation of intellectuals. And like intellectuals the world over in the 1930s, he was moved to put ideals of universal human dignity into action and moved particularly by the communist program for acting on behalf of the impoverished masses. Giving up the comforts of his social class, Roumain formed the Haitian Communist Party in 1934, thereafter suffering beatings and imprisonment by his government for his bold stands against the state, capitalism, and the Church. He had earned the right, in 'New Negro Sermon,' to claim the "hungry multitudes" as "brothers, comrades," and to draw Jesus into their ranks as communist hero: "They spit on Your black face, / Lord, our friend, our comrade."

Yes, it is true, Lord, that for four centuries of enlightenment
[White Europe] has thrown her spit and her baying watchdogs on my lands.
('Prayer for Peace,' ll. 22–3)

JESUS BEING SPIT ON by government soldiers (Matt. 26:67) is a natural image for a colonized people whose human dignity has been systematically denied. Yet in Africa the image remained tragically apt even after "white Europe" withdrew from political control. Many of the nations that gained their independence from Europe during the 1960s and 1970s soon fell prey to military coups, dictatorships, and civil wars. Crucified Africa was still stalked by "baying watchdogs," but now they were as black as the people around whom they prowled. Poets, whose freedom of thought is by definition a threat to dictatorships, felt hounded. Indeed, in some countries of the continent the problem of corrupt, repressive governments remains. Imprisonment or forced exile is an almost inevitable experience of the African poet writing since the 1960s. So poets have continued to be drawn to images of Jesus spit on, bound, mocked—and betrayed.

Jack Mapanje, for instance, a Malawian poet (1944–) detained for years without charge or trial, writes of another political prisoner in 'The Tale of a Dzeleka Prison Hard-Core Hero': "Your garments are like Jesus', except that / Like the other thief you have indeed robbed"—robbed, that is, the authorities.[5] And Wole Soyinka (1934–), writing during his imprisonment by the Nigerian government from 1967 to 1969, sets a crown of thorns on his lonely inspired figure of 'The Dreamer,' the contemporary African martyred for his political ideals. But these are isolated poems in oeuvres where Jesus makes only a passing appearance. A poet for whom Jesus hounded and betrayed is a central figure, even a personal obsession, is Sierra Leonian Syl Cheney-Coker (1945–). Forced into exile by an intolerant government, Cheney-Coker spent the 1970s in restless travel in the United States and South America. His poems collected in 1980 in *The Graveyard Also Has Teeth* record a frantic spiritual as well as geographical journey attuned to the tumultuous spirit of those times. Cheney-Coker was wrestling with his identity: a Creole Christian, he belonged to a privileged minority community in his own country, from which he was now alienated; identifying with Christ the outcast, he also rages against a Christ whose commandments now strike him as "lies." Christ seems irrelevant in the face of the world's multiple injustices, hence now a Judas himself, betraying all he stood for. The poet's self-disgust as much as his anger at the world and its lost ideals makes him feel that "my soul was made porous following a deluded Christ."

Also feeling betrayed both by and along with Christ is the Congolese poet Tchicaya U'Tam'si. But U'Tam'si's treatment of Christ transcends the personal. Tangling with a crucified figure whose complex of meanings is tied to the poet's whole country and continent, U'Tam'si brings us back to Senghor's Crucified Africa.

> *and it is no longer You*
> *Tree of sorrow but, above the Old and New Worlds,*
> *Crucified Africa. (Prayer for Peace, ll.11–13)*

U'TAM'SI WAS BORN in 1931 in the French colony of Moyen Congo, but in 1946 he moved to France with his father, who had been elected (along with Senghor) for Africa's first delegation to the French National Assembly. After completing his education at French lycées, U'Tam'si kept France as his lifetime home, though Africa remained his poetic preoccupation. Like that of Senghor, U'Tam'si's poetry focuses on the tensions of self-imposed exile in Europe, on the African roots he is both nourished by and cut off from. But U'Tam'si is of the next generation, coming of age as a poet in the postcolonial period, so his political and literary worlds couldn't be Senghor's. The difference was dramatized with U'Tam'si's publication of his third collection of poems, *Epitomé,* in 1962: Senghor hailed it as a great negritude achievement, but actually the poems go much beyond negritude's sense of how poetic language should be engaged in the political world.[6]

For negritude, as for the literature of oppression generally, language had been a rallying cry. In an empire that repressed direct political action, poetry was the means of both practicing and pushing for freedom. The cause of black identity and the force of white rule repressing it were both clearly defined. So poetic language could be clear, indeed black and white; an external enemy always simplifies the world. But for postcolonial Africa of the 1950s and 1960s, the internal political chaos within newly independent countries, with its black on black violence and interfactional betrayals, made such clarity impossible. U'Tam'si led the way, at least among the francophone writers, in crafting a new poetic language capable of capturing the tortured complexities of the chaotic new world. Surrealistic images linked up, split apart to find new partners, turned upside down, and sometimes met again; as in modern music, moods continually shifted, sometimes soft, more often clashing with sharp wit. One image cluster that is treated this way in *Epitomé* is that of Christ in his Passion.

Epitomé is subtitled *Headings for the Summary of a Passion.* The Passion is that of the poet and his country during the 1960 Congolese Civil War. U'Tam'si spent August to October of that disastrous year in Léopoldville, where he'd been invited to edit the new daily newspaper; the violence and corruption he witnessed tore him apart. One poem sequence from this period, 'The Scorner,' tries to make sense of his own anguish and his country's by addressing Christ. This stanza quoted in full conveys some of the poem's feel:

> Christ I laugh at your sadness
> oh my sweet Christ
> Thorn for thorn
> we have a common crown of thorns

I will be converted because you tempt me
Joseph comes to me
I suck already the breast of the virgin your mother
I count more than your one Judas on my fingers
My eyes lie to my soul
Where the world is a lamb your pascal lamb—Christ
I will waltz to the tune of your slow sadness[7]

Through the course of the poem, several of these lines are then picked up to dance with others, though not always to waltz. A clashing war-dance is just as likely. And where one minute "I laugh at your sadness," at another "I suffer with joy," and at another "Christ I spit at your joy / The sun is black with suffering negroes"—while on the next page the poet bemoans "the false negroes" of the Congo and the continent. Nothing can be counted on in this world of opportunism and shifting loyalties, which the poet scorns in himself as much as anywhere else. Constancy is a joke.

That taunting "Christ I spit at your joy" is interesting to put next to Roumain's image of just a generation before: "They spit on Your black face, / Lord, our friend, our comrade." The colonial poet Roumain could simply identify with Jesus mocked by their common imperial enemy; the postcolonial poet U'Tam'si must, in all honesty, identify with both roles, spitting on Christ while also sharing with him "a common crown of thorns." For the previous generation, that is, white Europe was crucifying Africa; now Africa was crucifying itself. That didn't mean that white Europe was now absolved of its imperialist sins. Far from it. Postcolonial intellectuals continued to see the former imperialist powers implicated in Africa's ongoing civil chaos. But what's intriguing for the study of how Jesus figures in the poetic sensibility of a particular time and place is that even poets dedicated to freeing Africa from colonial culture have held on to the image of Christ Crucified. For U'Tam'si, with one foot in each continent and each culture, this isn't surprising. It's remarkable, however, that for postcolonial African poets without close ties to Christianity or to Europe, the figure of Christ Crucified, drawn from the very Western culture they're rejecting, has continued to be a privileged image for the suffering of their particular country or tribe.

No other archetype of sacrificial suffering, apparently, has the universally recognized power of Christ's Cross. So a poet like Wole Soyinka, who otherwise rarely draws on the Gospels, chooses crucifixion images to construct his lone figure of the contemporary political martyr in 'The Dreamer' and other poems. South Africa's Oswald Mbuyiseni Mtshali (1945–), too, in his poem 'Ride upon the Death Chariot,' identifies the suffocation of three black vicims of apartheid as "their Golgotha." And even for a writer whose life work has been devoted to recovering native religion and culture lost under colonialism, Nigeria's Chinua Achebe (1930–), the Passion can still be the chosen image for his people's suffering in the Nigerian Civil War:

We are the men of soul
men of song we measure out
our joys and agonies
too, our long, long passion week
in paces of the dance. We have
come to know from surfeit of suffering
that even the Cross need not be
a dead end nor total loss
if we should go to it striding
the dirge of the soulful abia drums.[8]

This passage from Achebe's poem 'Beware Soul Brother' brings us to another characteristically African use of the figure of Christ. Besides finding an arche-typal Christ Crucified useful to represent their communal suffering, modern African writers sometimes dramatize their sense of conflict between native and European cultures as a tension between native gods and a Christ set down in their midst. Achebe himself takes the tension in stride here; his African "men of soul" aren't afraid to incorporate the colonial religion's symbols (the passion, the Cross) into the paces of their tribal dance. Achebe is Nigeria's most cele-brated novelist, author of the already classic *Things Fall Apart* (1958). With the nuanced and sympathetic understanding of human nature that marks a fine novelist, Achebe explores his Igbo people's turbulent twentieth-century history without demonizing any of the protagonists. His own Christian upbringing isn't something he wants to discard; rather, he has said, it actually enriches his sense of Igbo religion. Christ and Christian ritual can—not completely, but to a large extent—figure in the Igbo dance.

Primarily a novelist, Achebe turned to poetry only during the disruptive years of the Nigerian Civil War. For other poetic representations of Christ in the midst of native gods, we can return first, again, to Senghor.

And they [Christians] have burned intangible forests like
    hunting grounds,
Dragging out Ancestors and spirits by their peaceful beards.
    ('Prayer for Peace,' ll. 30–31)
Bless this nation that brought me Your Good News, Lord,
And opened my heavy-lidded eyes to the light of faith. ('Prayer
    for Peace,' ll. 81–82)

SENGHOR FELT IN HIS SOUL the conflict on his native soil between European Christianity and African religions. In 'Prayer for Peace,' one way he deals with the conflict is by presenting the bad and good of the colonial religion separately, as in these passages, at different moments in the poem: white Europe *both* burned our ancestral shrines *and* brought me my faith. Other poets have found their own ways of dealing with the both/and. Ghana's Kofi Awooner (1935–), for instance, in his poem 'Easter Dawn' dramatizes a single moment in which the risen Christ and native gods contend within the poet's being. As a child, Awooner was educated in a Christian mission school but also went regularly with his mother to her ancestral shrine. In 'Easter Dawn' the two religious practices seem to pull at the poet with nearly equal strength. He hears the native gods bemoaning their abandonment by the Christian dawn marchers "singing their way towards Gethsemane"; yet "the resurrection hymns come to me from afar touching my insides."[9] More recently, Awooner has said, the ancestral shrine has won out in his soul and heart: it's there that he finds real "communion" with God and with the continuity of his people.[10]

A poet who lived the tension between colonial and native religion every bit as intensely as Awooner or Senghor, though he expressed it in a very different poetic idiom, was Nigeria's Christopher Okigbo (1932–1967). No contemporary poet has gripped his fellow African writers' imaginations quite like Okigbo. Partly this is due to his early death as a partisan in the Nigerian Civil War; whether he should have sacrificed his great poetic gifts to politics so utterly is a matter of anguished debate. But the gifts themselves, and the way Okigbo developed them, are what most stimulate other writers. Okigbo's single theme, developed in poem sequences that he published under the collective title *Labyrinths,* is his ongoing quest for his identity as an Igbo, Nigerian, Christian, Anglophone, twentieth-century poet. Every term of this series carries weight for Okigbo; he deeply identified with all these characteristics of his being. And he found a poetic medium through which he could explore how these multiple identities both made him up and also pulled him apart. It was an imagist poetry influenced by T. S. Eliot. Multivalent images from a range of cultural myths and customs slide into and out of each other in Okigbo's verse, making it as charged with multiple significance (and as difficult to read) as *The Waste Land.* For instance, images from Okigbo's childhood Catholicism turn up next to those of Igbo tribal practice, sometimes in apparent harmony, sometimes in conflict. The figure of Christ can appear at one point as Isaiah's Messiah; at another as the poet's personal rival, conflated with the rival brother in the Gilgamesh myth; at another as tragic protagonist representing the slain Patrice Lumumba, sacrificed (in Okigbo's view) to narrow fanatical interests. In a scene in *Labyrinths* recalling the all too common historical occurrence of Christian missionaries burning down a pagan shrine—as in Senghor's lines, "dragging out Ancestors and spirits by their peaceful beards"—, Okigbo sets down a Jesus whose character comes straight from the Gospels. "Man out of innocence" offering salvation to a people who scorn him, Okigbo's Christ merges in the scene with the god of the burnt shrine, with an ancient Sumerian deity, and with the poet himself.[11]

The fluidity of meanings borne by the figure of Christ—often melted into figures from other religions or societies—is a mark of the open reach of

Okigbo's mind. Though the poet's own quest for identity naturally takes place in the context of his particular society, to make sense of that quest—and of the drama of contemporary African history—he draws on all the cultural myths and histories he can get hold of, refusing to restrict any to one-dimensionality or stereotype. In Okigbo's introduction to *Labyrinths,* he mentions among his sources the Orpheus myth, Gerard Manley Hopkins, Debussy's "Nocturne," Melville's letters, Rabindranath Tagore, the *Aeneid,* and more, while likening the book's opening poem sequence to the Christian Stations of the Cross.

Okigbo's multidimensional way of looking at the world exemplifies, according to Nigerian writer Ben Okri, a particularly "African aesthetic." "It's the aesthetic of possibilities, of labyrinths, of riddles—we love riddles—of paradoxes," Okri said in a 1990 interview.[12] It's not bound to one tribe or nation; "it's more fluid and more interesting than that." For Chinua Achebe, what is most inspiring about Okigbo's constantly searching openness to the complexities of human experience, wherever in the world he finds them, is its integrity and true artistic commitment. "Commitment" is a vexed term in African intellectual discourse. Partisans have co-opted it for narrow political causes; and, indeed, in all societies where political exigencies press in on the intellectual community, the temptation to make artistic "commitment" a matter of limited political advocacy is strong. But Achebe insists on a concept of commitment such as he finds in Okigbo: "not commitment to a narrow definition of the world, to a narrow perception of reality, to a narrow view of politics or economics or anything, religion, race." Artistic commitment is to something "bigger, something of infinitely greater value."[13]

Though Okigbo never plays down the cultural tensions at the root of his personal and Africa's communal experience, he has a fundamentally reconciling spirit. The poetic medium through which he envisions tensions dissolving may be unique in his continent's literature, but the urge toward reconciliation is not. Nor is the use of Jesus as a reconciling figure. After having seen how Jesus enters into African poetry as archetype of sacrificial suffering, as well as representative of European culture in contention with native gods, we can now, to conclude, focus on his reconciling roles. Senghor, again, can be the keynote.

Lord God, forgive white Europe! ('Prayer for Peace,' l. 21)

Sicut et nos dimittimus debitoribus nostris *('Prayer for Peace,' epigraph from the Vulgate Latin: "as we also have forgiven our debtors")*

FORGIVE US OUR DEBTS, as we also have forgiven our debtors. This line of the Lord's Prayer, from which Senghor draws his epigraph, is a favorite allusion in poetry by Western imperialism's victims, because it puts a special power in the victim's hands. Jesus on the Cross appeared powerless, victim par excellence. Yet in petitioning God for pardon of his persecutors—"Father, forgive them; for they know not what they do" (Luke 23:34)—he exerted what Christianity has interpreted as the great liberating power we all have over others. When we forgive those who have harmed us, we are granting them a fresh start. We're saying: no matter how evil your past, the future holds hope for you. Conversely, when we deny forgiveness, we condemn our debtors to hopeless imprisonment in debt. We hold them bound in their sinfulness.

To hold them bound can be a bittersweet revenge. Jacques Roumain, in his 'New Negro Sermon,' quoted earlier, twists Jesus' line on the Cross into a whip against his people's white oppressors: "We do not pardon them because they know what they do." Roumain is lashing out not against Jesus—who is the black victims' friend, "our comrade"—but against an oppressive, hypocritical Christianity that has betrayed Jesus himself. Similarly, Roumain's fellow Haitian poet René Depestre (1926–) castigates white Christian capitalism for betraying its own "tender Jesus." In an angry poem sequence, 'Epiphanies of the Voodoo Gods,' published in the 1967 collection *A Rainbow for the Christian West,* Depestre has various Haitian folk gods pass scathing judgment on Christianity. The god Agoué-Taroyo, for instance, hearing a mythical white Alabama woman tearfully plea "Oh! Papa-Taroyo! . . . Forgive us our errors, pardon our sins," responds with disdain: "No I tell her I am a Negro without forgiveness / . . . You have dried up the last drop of dew / That glistened at the end of my forgiveness."[14] Alluding to the Lord's Prayer throughout the poem, Depestre knows full well that by refusing to forgive his white debtors, he is forfeiting God's forgiveness of his own debts. *Forgive us our debts, as we also have forgiven our debtors.* And that's the bitter point. In effect, he's saying: you've ruined your God for me; I couldn't care less whether such a god forgives my debts or not; I'll stick to my own gods, thank you. The rejection is not simply of a single line spoken by Jesus. The rejection is of Christianity's core message and meaning, since the purpose of Jesus' taking on our humanity and sacrificing himself for our sakes was (as it is put in one of the main biblical metaphors) to pay off the debt incurred by our sins, thereby reconciling us to one another and to God.

In the context of such embittered rejections of Christianity's core reconciling message, voiced both before and long after Senghor's 'Prayer for Peace,' his "Lord God, forgive white Europe" becomes a bold political statement. The whole poem actually dramatizes the black African poet's difficulty in being able to forgive "our debtors." Detailing France's sins against the Senegalese, picturing each brutality inflicted and each indignity suffered, Senghor is repeatedly tempted to hate. The refrain "Yes, Lord, forgive France" is not easily won.

As difficult as Christian forgiveness was for Senghor—and it's the thrust behind much of his poetry—for the next African generation, the task was even more complicated. Suffering now not only from the colonial heritage but from home-grown violence as well, Africans confronted a daunting nexus of evils. After his 1960 experience with the Congolese Civil War, Tchicaya U'Tam'si wrote a twelve-part poem, 'Viaticum,' wrestling with the complexities of forgiveness in a country where neither the French nor the native Congolese had clean hands. The title refers to the rite of Holy Communion for a person about to pass into death and beyond; *viaticum* is the Latin word meaning "food for a journey." The poem's journey is that of the poet's country in danger of death. Because his country can't survive without reconciliation, the poet seizes on the dimension of forgiveness implicit in any communion rite. Moving metaphorically down the Congo River, into which washes the country's history of succeeding horrors, the poem at first mocks Christian humility and forgiveness as debasing: "turning the other cheek," the poet gives up "all my dignity . . . / My cheeks like two hills / where the tree of my laughter had sprung." But during the course of reflecting on the horrors floating down with him through his country's experience, he comes to see this "night strange sacrament" as the only hope, not only for his own land but for all people's suffering of injustice. So, in the final verse "I forget to be negro so as to forgive / I will see no more my blood upon their hands / the world will repay me for my mercy."[15]

In 'Viaticum,' a Gospel saying ("turn the other cheek") and a Christian sacrament are the poetic vehicles for reconciliation in the political realm. In another long poem—'African Easter,' by Sierra Leone's Abioseh Nicol (1924–)—Jesus himself appears in his reconciling role. Like so much modern African writing, 'African Easter' charts the poet's quest for identity as an intellectual in a contentiously multicultural, multireligious society. To structure his quest, Nicol chooses the poetic genre of dramatic monologue, set into the ritual drama of Easter weekend. The poem's first part, called 'Good Friday,' is spoken by a figure called the Wounded Christ; the second part, 'Easter Eve,' is spoken by the African Priest; and the final part, 'Easter Morning,' by the African Intellectual.

The Wounded Christ begins by saying straight off to the poet:

> I am not your God
> If you have not denied me once, twice,
> If I have not heard you complaining,
> Or doubting my existence.[16]

Plunging right into forgiveness of religious doubts that have evidently been plaguing the poet, Christ goes on to make, almost casually, a key theological point: "For what then am I worth to you / If you are always sinless." Our sins have made him the Wounded Christ, yes; but they have also permitted him to lavish his pardoning love, healing at once our wounds and his. He goes on to acknowledge the junk that his missionaries dumped on the African continent, and in effect asks the poet to pardon it, to "bury" it all. Then the African Priest enters, sitting by the grey Niger River. As elsewhere in African poetry, the flowing river symbolizes the continent's muddied course through recent history. The Priest calls on God to come closer, to be better seen:

What are you, Negro, Lebanese or Jew,
Flemish, Italian, Indian, Greek?
I know within my heart exactly what you are—
What we would like to be, but never are.

The poet sees in Christ, that is, another reconciling image: that the racial and political identities that so obsess us dissolve in God's identity, which is also our own ideal self. Yet another dissolution of images follows: recalling Christ's scourging, the African Priest sees "our salty tears of brown remorse" changed into Christ's flowing blood, which—blending with the River Niger—becomes "your new sacrificial wine," which "I . . . will sip, / With my thick lips." There's nothing like liquids for the metaphorical vision of total merging. The Priest's eucharistic wine is the tears of his continent's tormented course, sacramental-ized by—and as—Christ's sacrifice. *Crucified Africa.*

But then the poem moves on to Easter morning. The African Intellectual speaks. In the midst of the muezzin's cry and the pagan drums and an English nursery rhyme scrap from the colonial past, he is called by church bells to re-view his chosen identity as an African for whom "Christ is risen." Identifying with the crucified, buried, and risen Christ, the Intellectual becomes (as we'll see again in modern Arabic poetry, though under strikingly different literary and religious circumstances) an image of his society reborn after crushing political deaths. The poem ends by returning to the river, that deep flow of African his-tory, which seems almost to reach for Christ (now the rising sun) as the conti-nent's hope for restorative love:

The great muddy river Niger,
Picks up the rising equatorial sun,
Changing itself by slow degrees
Into thick flowing molten gold.

It's a rare postcolonial image of Africa taking in Christ and being thereby richly transformed. Crucified Africa moves, for a moment, into a Resurrection expe-rience.

WHEN SENGHOR HIMSELF saw crucified Africa moving past suffering to re-demption, his vision was of the continent playing a salvific role for all hu-mankind. In a 1978 essay, Senghor wrote: "Still on the benches of the Cours sec-ondaire in Dakar, I lived the essential myth of Africa. On one hand [*sic*], Africa, crucified, like Christ, for five centuries by the Slave Trade and colonization, but Africa redeemed and, by its sufferings, ransoming the world, coming back to life to bear its contribution to the germination of a panhuman civilization."[17] Others have observed, without relying on terms from the Christian narrative, that Africa's current gift to human civilization can come especially through its

Living Word (1997), by Luvon Sheppard (United States, 1940–). Drawing on his African heritage, Sheppard has done a series, Kinship, of paintings that express his vision that "people of
every race and tongue" are washed as one in "the river of the water of life" flowing from the
Word of God (Rev. 5:9, 22:1). Here, in representing Christ as the water washing over an African
dancer joyously waving his feather overhead, Sheppard envisions—with Chinua Achebe and
Abioseh Nicol—how Christ can indeed figure in the native dance. Sheppard's dancer is left exuberantly free in his tribal identity yet also immersed in the universally cleansing identity of God's
living Word. By permission of the artist.

art, as long as that "art" is broadly conceived. "All art is propaganda, though not all propaganda is art," Chinua Achebe has said. Quoting this line in a 1981 collection of critical essays, *The African Experience in Literature and Ideology,* University of Ibadan Professor Abiola Irele elaborates: "Our relation to the Western world, which has crossed our historical path and modified the realities of our life" necessarily grounds modern African literature. But, he goes on, "true art" has a "larger human import," and now "our need is less to press our claim . . . to an original difference, than to begin to restate our common involvement with the rest of humanity. It is precisely in this perspective that our modern literature will derive its enduring interest."[18] My impression as an outsider reading the best of modern African poets is that their inescapable relation to the Western world is in fact what has made possible their special contribution to "the rest of humanity." Brought to written (as opposed to oral) literature through the colonizers' culture—that is, within radically foreign social, political, religious, and literary institutions—modern African writers can't help but engage questions that are political in the broadest sense. The best have turned their given context into an opportunity to explore universal human concerns. Unavoidably living two deeply conflicting cultures, they wrestle with what a "universal" human nature might be. Inheriting a recent history of foreign dominance as well as a present of ongoing domestic chaos and persecution, they know firsthand the suffering that human collectivities can cause. The protests for which Wole Soyinka has been jailed, for instance, are as much against the universal human capacity for evil as against the particular evils perpetrated by his government at the moment. As the world moves into the twenty-first century, issues of multicultural relations and identity, of power's insidious ways, of human dignity and the forces that threaten it, are very much on the agenda. The African writers who are committed, in Achebe's sense, to probing the complexities of our human experience as political beings are an invaluable resource for us all.

THIS IS WHY I'VE chosen Africa as the place to focus on how the figure of Jesus is politicized in modern poetry. But of course elsewhere in the world, as well, poets freely make Jesus a political figure. The political roles he is called on to play are too various to summarize neatly, but some samples can suggest their range. In 'The Abduction of Saints,' by the African-American poet Alice Walker (1944–), Jesus is cast as a rebel whose own followers inadvertently betray him simply by reducing him to a harmless image hanging on the wall, rendering his true wild message tame. Walker's point for the contemporary political scene is that "as it was with Christ, so it is with Malcolm / and with King . . . the body / was stolen away." Another African-American poet, Gwendolyn Brooks (1917–), in 'Riot,' sets Jesus Crucified into the unlikely body of a Southern white bigot being murdered by a black mob. Daringly, Brooks gives to the dying man Jesus' pardoning words—"Lord! /

Forgive these nigguhs that know not what they do"—when the irony is of course that they know full well what they do, and that the bigot, unlike the real Jesus, deserves it.

One common socially engaged role that poets cast Jesus in is as activist in the cause of the poor. In this role he can turn up in places as far afield as the Depression-era United States, Sandinista Nicaragua, New Zealand of the 1960s, and Pinochet's Chile. A historically interesting United States appearance is Sarah Cleghorn's poem 'Comrade Jesus,' where Jesus stands up at a workers' meeting speaking Gospel lines of solidarity with the poor. Cleghorn (1876–1959), an activist famous for her impassioned poems on such topics as poverty and child labor, enlists Jesus (as did Jacques Roumain) in the Communist Party. Though quaint to us today, her poem was bold in its time. Proudly giving Jesus his red card, the poet implores: "Ah, let no Local him refuse! / Comrade Jesus hath paid his dues."[19]

Jesus is a Communist hero for Nicaraguan priest and poet Ernesto Cardenal as well. Cardenal (1925–), an early advocate of liberation theology, was minister of culture in Nicaragua's Sandinista government. In his long (four hundred eighty page) poem *Cosmic Canticle* (1993), he envisions a Jesus who ranges the universe preaching "nothing else but the Kingdom of Heaven" as a Communist utopia. Cardenal's wildly expansive and all-embracing vision—a late-twentieth-century version of the Cosmic Christ first sketched in the New Testament Pauline epistles, then filled in a millennium later in medieval cosmological detail—includes the teaching of Buddha, the Tao, Darwin's evolutionary theory, and Einstein's relativity, among other scientific/philosophic theories and wisdom traditions old and new.

More down to earth but still with a cosmic dimension is the activist Jesus who turns up in 'The Maori Jesus' by James K. Baxter, a New Zealand poet. After his conversion to Catholicism, Baxter (1926–1972) had heard a voice in a dream say "Go to Jerusalem," the name of a village of the indigenous Maori people. Leaving a comfortable life with only one change of clothes and a Bible in Maori, Baxter went to settle in the village, where he turned out a large body of fine taut verse in the Hebrew prophetic spirit. In 'The Maori Jesus,' Baxter casts Jesus as an indigenous outcast who wears dungarees and smells of filth. Baxter's purpose in the poem is to condemn the contemporary world's blindness to God in its midst, so he focuses on the authorities' treatment of this unsettling figure who calls his disciples from among the local down and out, and who, speaking the language of the sixties, declares simply and happily: "Man, / From now on the sun will shine." In seven days that reverse God's creation, the authorities first arrest the Maori Jesus for being unemployed, then beat him, then send him to an asylum "for telling a screw the sun would stop rising," and finally have him lobotomized for saying "I am the Light in the Void." With God's brain thus "cut in half," the earth is left in the Void, the sun doesn't rise, and the poem ends in a chillingly "civilized darkness."[20]

Modern Migration of the Spirit *(1932–34), by José Clemente Orozco (Mexico, 1883–1949).
Orozco's Jesus strikes a militantly engaged pose in this culminating panel of the monumental
Dartmouth College mural,* Epic of American Civilization. *Preceding panels of the mural trace
the continent's checkered history: Orozco depicts both the indigenous and European masters
bringing a mix of good and evil. But at this moment in the 1930s, in Orozco's view, the evils of
dehumanizing industrialization and war prevail. From this background, Christ aggressively rises
from the dead civilization as Savior. Shattering his Cross and turning his back on the junkheap of
outmoded religions and self-destructive modern wars, he glares challengingly ahead, personifying
the spiritual energy that Orozco insists humankind will need to create a new life-enhancing future. Commissioned by the Trustees of Dartmouth College, Hanover, New Hampshire. © Estate
of José Clemente Orozco/ SOMAAP, Mexico City/ Licensed by VAGA, New York, NY. By permission of Instituto Nacional de Bellas Artes, Mexico.*

Another ragtag Jesus appears from among the poor in Chile, preaching a whole book of offbeat poems published in 1977 as *Sermons and Homilies of the Christ of Elqui,* written by the iconoclastic poet Nicanor Parra (1914–).[21] The figure of the Christ of Elqui wasn't Parra's invention; during the 1920s and 1930s, a former construction worker named Domingo Zárate Vega had wandered through Chile engagingly preaching contradictory prophetic messages and not disputing popular claims that he was a reincarnated Christ. When Parra was looking during the 1970s for a poetic vehicle to undermine the oppressive Pinochet régime, he decided to put his satiric verse in the mouth of Zárate. Parra's Christ of Elqui is outrageously irreverent, mocking everyone including himself, but basically affirming his solidarity with the poor. "I've always been taught," he says in one sermon poem, "that neither the Father nor the Son was rich /—I assume the Holy Spirit wouldn't be either— / . . . but that didn't stop them from being God / quite the opposite, isn't it?" The sardonic Parra has no illusions, however, that a mere change of government can cure social ills. In another poem the Christ of Elqui prophesies that "the left will overcome" but that their leader "will commit suicide / once he finds himself betrayed and alone."

It's interesting to note that Jesus can be called on as political activist in a range of poetic genres. Cleghorn and Roumain write an engaged, exhortatory verse; Baxter's mode is prophetic social critique; Parra's is satire; Cardenal's is mythic vision, closer to Teilhard de Chardin than to any traditional poetic form. Nor does a poet need to be a Christian believer in order to engage Jesus for a political cause. A Communist Jesus would most likely come from an atheist pen (Cardenal being an exception). And we saw, in connection with African use of the Crucifixion archetype, that even poets with little fondness for Christianity can choose Jesus on the Cross as figure of the contemporary political martyr. In this company one could add Russia's Anna Akhmatova (1889–1966). Her poetry's wide range of reference hardly touches at all on the Gospels; yet the 'Crucifixion' section of her poem 'Requiem,' on her son's political imprisonment under Soviet rule, has him speak Jesus' words on the Cross and has the poet herself respond as Mary.

Perhaps an even more surprising place where a politicized Jesus appears is the poetry of certain Arab Muslim poets; but their story, inseparable from a unique political context involving Muslim and Christian poets together in an Arab cause, requires a chapter to itself.

SIX

Archetypal Christ

Arabic Poetry and Other Wastelands

In a lecture, "Modern Arabic Literature and the West," given at several British universities in 1968, Palestinian poet Jabrā Ibrāhīm Jabrā explained the revolution in Arabic poetry of the 1950s. "Most important of all was 'The Waste Land,'" he bluntly said.[1]

The assertion might apply to twentieth-century poetry worldwide. Probably no other single poem did more to create an aesthetic adequate to the century's recurrent experience of civilization in ruins. Writing the poem in 1922, T. S. Eliot himself was reacting to the wreckage of Europe after World War I. Disillusionment was the spirit of the time; the war had destroyed not only millions of lives but also confidence in traditional values as a source of meaning. In Eliot's method of breaking the literature of the past into fragments, then reconnecting them through myth, he found a way, in his words, "of controlling, of ordering, of giving a shape and a significance to the immense panorama of futility and anarchy which is contemporary history."[2] The idea of myth as a unifying structure across eras and cultures came to Eliot from a new book that was generating much excitement at the time: *The Golden Bough,* by anthropologist James Frazer. And the specific myth cluster he took from Frazer to figure a wasted world longing for renewal was the ancient Eastern Mediterranean harvest myth of the dead land thirsting for rain, finally fertilized and restored to life by the blood of a god—named usually Tammuz or Adonis.

As dislocations succeeded one another over the decades and over the globe—the economic collapse of the Great Depression, the destructive horrors of World War II, the internal clashes in many non-Western countries as they wrenched themselves from colonial rule—poets of various cultures kept discovering *The Waste Land* anew, seizing on its fragmented method to represent their own broken societies. For Arab poets, the devastating experience that drew them to the poem was what they uniformly refer to as the Palestinian *disaster* or *debacle*. The formation of Israel in 1948 displaced masses of Palestinians; the failure of other Arab states to restore Palestine and relieve the refugees' suffering generated cynicism among Arab intellectuals, about the good will not only of the West but also of their own often tyrannical governments. *The Waste Land* seemed to have been written out of their precise situation. Parched land longing for rain was naturally an age-old literary image in this desert region, which was, moreover, the original home of the Babylonian Tammuz myth. Jabrā himself did an Arabic translation of the Adonis section of *The Golden Bough,* other writers translated Eliot's poems and essays; and the wasteland motif gripped the Arab poetic imagination.

Indeed, reading through the rich body of Arab verse of the 1950s, one can't help being struck by the ubiquity of wasteland image clusters: sterility/rock/barren land; blood/sacrifice/Tammuz/the Cross; water/rain/fertility; flower buds/new sprouts of grain/bread/resurrection/the Phoenix. A collective symbol system such as this would have been inconceivable among poets in the twentieth-century West, with its prime value of individualism; a Western counterpart might be the typology of medieval Europe. Also striking is the intense energy of the poems. Partly this comes from a new-found prosodic freedom, a determination to break with strict classical Arabic verse forms so as to find meters commensurate with anguished commitment to the issues of the day. And this social commitment is the other source of the poems' intensity. T. S. Eliot had certainly cared about the collapse of civilization, but fundamentally his purpose was to envision it rather than to intervene. *The Waste Land* is, one might say, a philosophical poem, whereas Arab poetry of the 1950s was essentially political. It was a call to resist internal repression and external aggression alike, and a good bit of the poetry's charged energy comes from how much the poet personally risked in making the call. Here is another difference from most modern Western societies, in which—poetry lovers must concede—poetry really isn't considered to matter all that much. In the Arab world, poetry had long been heard as the voice of society's soul. When that voice began to condemn the society's rulers, the poet was bound to be in danger. So a call for the god's sacrificial blood to fertilize and renew the land was more than metaphor. Real blood was being spilled. The ritual death in the Tammuz/Adonis myth was, it seemed, being horribly reenacted in the place of its origin. The barren land was the poet's own country, deprived of life by tyrannical rule. To free the land from death, sacrifice would be necessary, with the poet and people playing the sacrificial part. One major poet, Syria's 'Ali Ahmad Sa'id, so identified personally with the myth that he took the pen name Adonis.

The myth's urgency for Arab poets made them—as Jabrā points out in his lecture—use it more explicitly than Eliot had done. In *The Waste Land* the myth is infrastructure. In Arab poetry it is landscape and buildings, characters and plot. The difference from Eliot is most noticeable with respect to the Tammuz/Christ identification, unmentioned in *The Waste Land* but quite explicit for the Arabs. Jabrā explains that he and his fellow poets of the 1950s reached for the figure of Christ out of their agonized hope that a resurrection of their society would come of their sacrificial love. For these poets, he writes:

> [L]ove and sacrifice shall bring fertility to the land, though they may both come
> in lightning and thunder that rend the temple's veil. The Cross thus came into
> Arabic poetry as a symbol of great immediacy, and Christ and Tammuz were

made one, and the poet was identified with them, as seen in the poetry of Badr al-Sayyāb, Salah 'Abd al-Sabur, Yūsuf al-Khāl, Khalīl Hāwī, Adonis, Tawfiq Sāyigh and a few others.

Jabrā's list includes both Muslims and Christians, who equally used the Christ/Tammuz conflation for political purposes. In Islam, Jesus is not "Christ" in the sacrificial messianic sense that Christians understand the title; Jesus is, rather, a great prophet in the line beginning with Abraham and Moses and culminating with Muhammad. But, as we've seen in poetry the world over, poetic language often stretches the boundaries of religious orthodoxies, and for Muslim poets, the conflation of Christ with Adonis and Tammuz in the sacrificial fertility myth was useful for couching a subversive political message. The Iraqi Muslim Badr Shākir al-Sayyāb (1926–1964) said outright in a 1963 newspaper interview that his motive in employing myths in the 1950s had been political: "When I wanted to resist the royal Sa'idi regime with poetry, I used myths to veil my intentions. . . . I also used them for the same purpose in the regime of Qasim."[3] He goes on to mention 'City of Sinbad' as one poem in which "I satirized Qasim and his regime severely" without their recognizing it. 'City of Sinbad' is a good sample in which to get a feel for how this generation of Arab poets was treating the figure of Christ, especially as al-Sayyāb, considered among the greatest contemporary Arab poets, was the first to use the fertility myth skillfully (in a famous poem 'Song of Rain') and made Christ a recurrent figure throughout his work.[4]

A long poem of five parts, 'City of Sinbad' opens in a winter wasteland, which is al-Sayyāb's image of his country under the autocratic rule of Nuri al-Sa'id's in the mid-1950s. The poet calls for rain to renew the soil: "Bestir, o rain, / The bed of bones and snow and particles of dust, / Make the seed grow, let the flowers open."[5] The rain comes. Yet it is "Blood in the form of rain"—that is, the bloody 1958 military revolution led by General Qasim. This rain indeed brings new life, but it's a life of such horror that the resurrected bones cry out:

> alas, o rain,
> We should like to sleep again
> We should like to die again . . .
> We wish the god would take us back
> To the heart of his deep, many-layered mystery.

Representing the Iraqi people by a Gospel figure to hide his meaning, al-Sayyāb has the bones ask: "Who awakened Lazarus from his long sleep? / Who is this that gave us to drink from a mirage, / And concealed the plague in the rain?"

Much of the poem continues in the form of questions about who this god can be who claims to be Adonis or Christ but brings death instead of rebirth. Al-Sayyāb explained in the 1963 interview why he wouldn't call the god by his locally known name: "When I wanted to depict the failure of the original aims of the July (*Tammuz*) revolution, I replaced the Babylonian name of Tammuz by the Greek name of Adonis." The poem's questions are posed in wasteland terms:

> Is this Adonis, this emptiness?
> And this pallor, this dryness?
> Is this Adonis? Where is the glow?
> And where is the harvest?
> The sickles are not reaping,
> The flowers are not blooming,
> The black fields have no water!

Qasim's Communist tyranny is then symbolized by the Tatars, who murder justice and all religious values, represented by the linked figures of Muhammad and Christ: "They have bound up Muhammad . . . / Tomorrow, Christ will be crucified/ In Iraq." Because the Communists have betrayed the cause of good, the poem elsewhere calls them "red-robed Judas."

Christ is linked also with the goddess Ishtar (Astarte) from the Adonis myth, to figure the poet's desperate longing for a real spring of political freedom:

> Then will it seem to the hungry that Ishtar,
> The goddess of flowers, has brought back the captive
> To mankind, and crowned his lush forehead with fruit?
> Then will it seem to the hungry that the shoulder
> Of Christ has rolled back the stone from the tomb
> Has set out to resurrect life from the grave
> And cure the leper or make the blind to see?

Yet for now death reigns: "Women are aborting in slaughterhouses / And the flame is dancing along the threshing floors, / And Christ will perish before Lazarus." That is, the spirit of political rebirth will die, the poet fears, before it can recall the Iraqi people to genuine freedom.[6]

This use of Christ as a death/resurrection archetype to configure a country's political suffering and hope isn't unique to Arab poets. Postcolonial African poetry, we've seen, draws on the Cross as archetype of sacrificial suffering, to represent a postcolonial people's political experience. Conflation with pagan gods in the wasteland myth is, however, special to the Arabs. Also common in Arab poetry of the time, as Jabrā mentions, is for the poet to identify personally with the god who takes on suffering for his people's salvation. Al-Sayyāb plays with the identification in many poems, but the place where he develops it most fully is his famous poem 'The Messiah after the Crucifixion.' The poem begins startlingly, with the poet speaking as Christ from his tomb:

> When they brought me down I heard the winds
> In long lamentation weaving the leaves of palm-trees,
> And footsteps receding far, far away. So the wounds
> And the Cross to which I have been nailed all through the afternoon
> Have not killed me.[7]

In the Qur'an, it's unclear whether or not Jesus actually died on the Cross, and the question has always been unresolved in Islam. So for a Muslim poet, there is a tradition for imagining Christ buried alive. But the contemporary political application that the poem goes on to make is of course not only untraditional but dangerously subversive. The poet imagines his own sacrificial blood soaking the soil of his native village, Jaikur, to fertilize and redeem it:

> When Jaikur spreads out to the limits of fantasy . . .
>
> . . . .
>
> Warmth touches my heart and my blood flows into its earth
> My heart is the sun when the sun throbs with light
> My heart is the earth throbbing with wheat, blossom and sweet water
> My heart is the water; it is the ear of corn
> Whose death is resurrection . . .
>
> . . . .
>
> I died so that bread might be eaten in my name,
> That they might sow me at the right season.

Identification with the key Gospel image of the redeemer as the bread of life could hardly be stronger. And throughout, the poem couches the Iraqi political situation in Gospel terms. As in 'City of Sinbad,' Judas again represents the tyrannical government. The soldiers' rifle-fire "dreams of my crucifixion." And, most moving for the poet, his compatriots share his crucifixion. The poem ends with the poet looking out across the plain from his cross: "In place of every target there was a cross and a grieved mother. / Blessed be the Lord! / These are the pangs of the city in labour."

IT'S NATURAL TO ask whether al-Sayyāb's fellow Arab poets who are Christian relate to the figure of Christ any differently. Certainly in the poetry of, say, Tawfiq Sāyigh, there's a quest for how his Christian faith might overcome his desolation over the loss of Palestine; in chapter 7, I'll consider his work in the context of other poetic searches for an elusive God. Staying with wasteland settings, we can take as an example of Arab poetry's Cross motif in a

Christian key 'The Eternal Dialogue,' by Yūsuf al-Khāl (1917–1987), the son of a Lebanese Protestant minister. Al-Khāl made his name first not as a Christian poet but as a leader of the free verse movement; his mission in the 1950s and 1960s was to renew Arab poetry, and he founded the influential journal *Shi'r* to promote avant-garde verse. Yet he never hid his religious identity, and 'The Eternal Dialogue' is one poem where a particularly Christian spiritual pain is the central theme.

The poem is a meditation on human sinfulness. Clinging as if for dear life to the repeated insistence that "God's cross is still raised on the hill of time," the poet surrounds this salvific hope with images of human evil that make him agonize over whether "our sins, made with our own hands" are so great as to be beyond redemption. Sand blows through the poem, always threatening to bury us, not alive, but already (spiritually) dead:

> Are we dead
> On the road and don't know it, I wonder?
> We are hidden from sight by shrouds
> Of sand, of dust diffused by hoofs
> In the arena of the sun.

The poet longs to trust that we, like Moses striking the rock at God's command, can "strike / The brow of dawn with our hands, and bring forth / From the rock gushing water that carries the sand / To the sea." Yet instead, he fears, "[modern man] has emptied the sea / Into his eyes, and hidden his head in the sand." He has quenched "his thirst for conquest" by killing a dragon and letting "its blood run in the earth." The poem strains to hope yet can't keep from wondering: "This naked creeping being—is he a man, / Is he a man in the image of God?"

THE DESPAIRING question is not at all unique to Arabs. Here is the twentieth-century Filipino poet Ricaredo Demetillo (1911–):

> I mourn man, man diminished, unfulfilled,
> Whose shadow drags the darkness of his night
> Across the endless dreariness of days,
> Where no oasis greens the sand-choked waste.
> I mourn for man, my brother crucified. . . .
> In rooms where locusts crunch the dog-eared crop,
> Despair bisecting thought in fields of blight . . .
>
> . . . .
>
> His cries croak down the echoes of my heart
> Though often I would spurn his rattled knock.
> Is he not neighbor to my creaking bed?[8]

Demetillo's "sand-choked waste" probably owes nothing specifically to T. S. Eliot. It's simply the landscape that spreads itself out before the imagination of a poet trying to picture what the twentieth century looks like. The texture and verse form of Demetillo's poem are very different from those of al-Khāl, yet half a world away from each other they share a nightmare view of the human condition in their time. As we enter the twenty-first century, celebration of how far our species has come in two thousand years is inevitable, and certainly justified to an extent. Yet it is sobering to recall that a dominant experience of the final century of the second millennium was of sociopolitical disaster: of brutal wars, genocides, nuclear terror and attendant collective moral collapse. And in response, a dominant mood—in all the arts, not only poetry—one of near despair. In the next chapter I'll present even more poetry that engages this disastrous experience of the second millennium's close. Here the focus is only on poems that engage it through the wasteland image cluster. This grim vision of a wasted world perhaps too evil to be redeemed transcended cultural boundaries to a remarkable extent.

In poetry, the Crucified Christ can figure in this view either as practically powerless to redeem so fallen a world (as in al-Khāl's 'The Eternal Dialogue') or as pathetically representative of our scraggly human condition (Demetillo's title is 'The Scare-Crow Christ'). The Christ figured in these ways is still basically an archetype: an image now of universal defeat, impotence, waste. To picture this Christ as redemptive takes an extraordinary act of imagination. And of faith, too, one would have to say, looking for instance at the effort in a grimly powerful poem called 'Do You Love Man?' by Danish poet Nis Petersen (1897–1941).[9] The title question is thrust repeatedly at the poem's speaker while the disgusting figure of slimy, morally decaying Man comes toward him, "dragging" and "creeping" like the modern humankind of both al-Khāl and Demetillo. Revolted by the "stench growing / From the thousand diseases of lying" as Man inches closer, the speaker keeps shrieking "no!" to the question challenging him to love. But then the Man reveals himself as the Crucified Christ:

> he stretched his hand toward me,
> And lo! the nail-prints flowered red—
> Up to the shoulders his naked arms
> Were covered with black wounds of sin—
> And then smiled:
> God so loved . . . !

The speaker needs no more than these three words to recognize the core Gospel message: "God so loved the world that he gave his only Son" (John 3:16). All at once, he can cry out "Man—I love you!" but at this cost: "And my mouth was full of blood, / Of human blood." To love this human creature requires of the speaker precisely the sacrificial death of Christ.

Peterson's Christ taking into himself the evil of modern humanity is very much a New Testament figure: the Christ preached by Paul and by John as crucified for human salvation. This Christ becomes human, but at the archetypal level of the sin/redemption crux of the Christian narrative. Another poetic strategy for confronting evil's grip on the world is to take the figure of Jesus, not as archetype but as Gospel character during his public ministry, and set him into our contemporary moral wasteland. A chilling instance is 'Stones and Bread,' by the Hungarian poet György Rónay (1913–1978), editor of the Catholic literary journal *Vigilia,* which boldly encouraged religious writing under Communist rule. In a terrifying scene blending the Gospel healings with the Temptation, the poem dramatizes the mob psychosis of people in evil's grasp. In a pounding rush of words that imitates the way we sinners clamor for healing yet shrink from sacrifice, the poet gives a startling new meaning to Satan's challenge to Jesus to turn stones into bread: the stones are the hard hearts of the throngs whom Jesus has healed but who, when he asks that they share in "just one of the thorns which tear my forehead ragged," all slink away. Satan taunts Jesus: "Behold . . . the blessed / people your people! . . . hearts stone only stone no hearts . . . so change the stones to bread!" But Jesus, though grieved at humanity's utter desertion of him, resists the temptation to force us to goodness:

> No
>
> said Jesus wearily
>
> What for
>
> said Jesus discouraged
>
> Depart from me Satan
>
> said Jesus sadly
>
> *I will not change*
> *the stones to bread.*[10]

The Greek poet Ángelos Sikelianos (1884–1951) takes even further liberties with the Gospels in order to place Jesus in the midst of modern corruption. Sikelianos invents a wholly new episode for Jesus, announcing the fiction in the poem's title, 'Agraphon' ('Unrecorded'), yet otherwise appearing simply to retell a Gospel story:

> A little beyond the walls of Zion walking
> one day somewhat before the set of sun,
> Jesus and his disciples came by chance
> to that place where for years the town had cast
> its rubbish: burnt mattresses of the diseased,
> rags, broken crockery, refuse and filth.
> And there upon the highest mound of all,
> bloated, its legs turned upward toward the sky,

Menorah *(1993)*, by Roger Wagner *(England, 1957–)*. *The artist's shocking visual conflations force us to ponder where God might be in the wasted twentieth-century landscape. Scattered Hasidic survivors disconsolately mourn their dead on a field flooded by nuclear power cooling towers whose sinister smoke evokes the Auschwitz crematoria; yet the six towers and their central chimney also form a giant menorah, Jewish symbol of God's presence. God is present, too, unexpectedly, as the naked crucified Jesus, sharing human vulnerability in the face of great evil. As Elie Wiesel wrote of watching a boy horribly hung at Auschwitz: "Where is God now? . . . He is here. He is hanging there on the gallows." By permission of the artist.*

> the carcass of a dog lay stretched, from which
> at once, as vultures thickly piled on it
> took fright at steps approaching, so foul a stench
> broke forth, that the disciples as one man,
> holding their breath within their hands, drew back.[11]

The stinking garbage heap is the world "from the one end to the other" (the poem later says outright) in the winter of 1941, with the war having trashed civilization. The dog's carcass tossed on top is Greece, whose people that winter were literally starving to death. Here again, as in Demetillo, is a wasteland vision that had no need of T. S. Eliot; the poet had only to look out of his own window, so to speak, to see his land as decaying waste.

But the poem doesn't see only corruption. It also sees—or at least searches for—hope. In the next verses, Jesus calls his disciples' attention to "how in the sun the teeth of this dog shine, / now like the hailstone, now like the lily, far / beyond the decay." Greece, that is, still has within its corpse something that can be "reflection of the Eternal."

The Jesus set by poets into our wasted world can have a range of responses. Rónay has him painfully saddened by our self-protective hardness; humanity's *desertion* of him is the *desert* of his Temptation. Sikelianos has Jesus point to a glimmer of hope within the decaying corpse of our collective being. The Welsh poet R. S. Thomas (1913–), in one of his most well-known poems, 'The Coming,' pictures a different response—which is actually closest to Jesus' character in the Gospels yet is envisioned in starkly modern terms. The poem is set in that pre-Incarnational scene that poets like to invent, imagining the heavenly Father and Son viewing fallen humankind and considering the desperate need for some salvific intervention. Thomas's version in 'The Coming' has Jesus look down at the scorched earth, see wasted humanity reaching beseechingly toward a bare tree, and decide to come save them. He knows the cost. For "a vanished April to return" to the tree's "crossed boughs," he'll have to give it his own life. He'll have to hang, himself, on the tree.

An April in this context has to recall Eliot's *The Waste Land,* where April is so famously "the cruellest month." Thomas is taking his century's overwhelming sense of barrenness back to the Christian redemption story. In fact, what's so powerful about this short poem is that in only eighty-eight words it presents the basic Gospel story—of helpless human emptiness filled by the sacrificial gift of divine life—in terms that merge major metaphors from either end of two millennia of poetry's reimaginings of the Gospels' meaning. Picking up the Cross as Tree of Life, a persistent Christian symbol since the second century, the poem plants it in the twentieth-century landscape of a despairing wasted world. Here is 'The Coming' in full:

> And God held in his hand
> A small globe. Look, he said.
> The son looked. Far off,
> As through water, he saw
> A scorched land of fierce
> Colour. The light burned
> There; crusted buildings
> Cast their shadows; a bright
> Serpent, a river
> Uncoiled itself, radiant
> With slime.
>   On a bare
> Hill a bare tree saddened
> The sky. Many people
> Held out their thin arms

To it, as though waiting
For a vanished April
To return to its crossed
Boughs. The son watched
Them. Let me go there, he said.[12]

SEVEN

Jesus Absent

The stage set of Samuel Beckett's mid-century play *Waiting for Godot* is nothing but a barren tree. It is the same setting as R. S. Thomas's 'The Coming,' and the entire play is a succession of darkly comic music-hall routines that could be an acting out of the poem's lines "Many people / Held out their thin arms / To it, as though waiting / For a vanished April / to return to its crossed / Boughs." *Godot* was written a couple of decades before 'The Coming,' but I'm not suggesting any direct influence between the two works. I juxtapose them because both writers see in the lone barren tree, around which scraggly people helplessly wait to be saved, an image of the twentieth-century human situation. This stark version of the Tree as Cross loomed large in Thomas's poetic imagination; at the end of this chapter I return to other ways it figures in his work. But here I want to stay briefly with Beckett's use of this Christian archetype, because *Waiting for Godot* is considered, deservedly, the classic representation of the era's overwhelming sense of God's absence from the human scene.

Beckett was born on Good Friday, and all his life he pondered how his fate might be tied to that crucial event. He was especially intrigued by the account in Luke's Gospel of the two thieves crucified on either side of Jesus; one of *Waiting for Godot*'s protagonists, Vladimir, identifies with these thieves and hence anxiously fusses over why one would have been saved and the other damned. Vladimir and his sidekick Estragon are spending the play—a free-floating time period teasingly suggestive of the century's first fifty years—hanging around the barren tree by which the mysteriously absent Godot has told them to wait. Their situation is as if humankind were stuck on the Saturday between Good Friday and Easter: Vladimir and Estragon know that "our Saviour" has been crucified, and they've vaguely heard of his promise to return, but meanwhile they're frozen in comically meaningless repetitive words and gestures. A more sinister tone enters as well, in the form of two other characters, Pozzo and Lucky, whose sadomasochistic relation alludes to the century's penchant for oppressive brutality in sociopolitical relations. Vladimir and Estragon sense that something is wrong here; yet with no moral bearings, they have no ability to judge, let alone to intervene. They can't manage to accomplish any action at all. Occasionally they idly consider hanging themselves on the tree just to pass the time, but they can't marshall the energy of concentration to do it. Their refrain is that if Godot comes, "we'll be saved." But he doesn't, so they just wait.

When the play was first produced in the 1950s, it became an instant international hit. People everywhere saw in it the mirror image of their era's situation: humanity bumbling along meaninglessly and even murderously in the absence of God. The post–World War II sense of upheaval that disposed societies to see themselves on Beckett's stage covered most of the globe, as we noted in the previous two chapters. But in this chapter, I want to return mainly to the West, because there the Absent God became a major theme—to the point of obsession—in the century's philosophy, theology, and literature. It's easy to see why if we pick up where we left Western society at the end of the last chapter and, previously, in Chapter Four's "Crisis of the Secularized West." The radical doubt that was secularism's intellectual stance seemed both cause and effect of the corrupting evil that exploded with World War II and then slipped seamlessly into the collective insanity of the nuclear arms race. In such conditions of crass unconcern for the fate of the earth and its inhabitants, even many believers had trouble finding God. Yet in the confusion, it wasn't obvious why God was gone. Whether humanity had dismissed God from the scene or whether God had up and gone for his own good reasons was a question, as we'll see, that exercised theologians and some poets as well.

As Christianity's Incarnate God, Jesus necessarily figured prominently in the whole matter of God's absence from the human scene. It might sound odd to talk of an Absent Jesus figuring at all, so I need to clarify the focus of this chapter's poetry. By the title "Jesus Absent," I don't mean any poem whatever in which Jesus doesn't appear. That would bring in the bulk of the century's poetry. I'm talking about poems that evoke his absence where his presence would be expected, or where (as in *Godot*) the poet's point is that his presence is missed.

This missing figure of Jesus actually exerted a powerful force on the twentieth-century imagination as represented in poetry. In fact, he makes so many varied "appearances"—if I can use the word for a figure defined by his not appearing—that I'm going to group them around the work of three major poets: Rainer Maria Rilke, Czeslaw Milosz, and R. S. Thomas. There is much that these poets *don't* have in common. It's a long way, for instance, from Rilke's confident dismissal of Jesus from the stage, to Milosz's dark scenes from which a forgotten Jesus has dropped out, to Thomas's fixed stare at the untenanted Cross in a silent church. But these poets serve to anchor this chapter because each makes a point of the Absent Jesus as a hollow core of the human condition. And each articulates a vision representative of a prevalent outlook of the twentieth-century West.

I'll also glance here at a few poems that treat Jesus Absent in other characteristic ways. Through all the poetry in this chapter, the settings that configure his absence are remarkably varied; an empty stage with lone barren tree is far from the only symbolic environment that poets have devised. What the settings have in common is that Jesus is conspicuously not there. Rilke, actually, did keep

Jesus on the scene—though at the edge of it—during one phase of his long poetic career, so this is where I begin.

RILKE AT MID-CAREER, the period of about 1904 to 1913, was firmly anti-Christian. He had been raised by an obsessively pious Catholic mother whose notion of religion he had come to reject. Humankind, Rilke insisted, had no need of a Mediator, because God is the very stuff of life itself. And since life is already redeemed, joyous and full, neither was there any need of a Redeemer. The concept of sin and especially sexual guilt, Rilke was convinced, was a Church plot to keep people fearfully subservient.

Nietzsche's influence here is clear, and the way this influence first came to Rilke is remarkable, since it was through the woman loved, in turn, by both men. Lou Andreas-Salomé, to whom Nietzsche (unsuccessfully) proposed marriage in 1882, was Rilke's mistress some sixteen years later, when he was in his twenties and she was a married woman fourteen years his senior. An intellectually and emotionally strong person, Lou remained Rilke's mentor even after their sexual relation ended. But Rilke was someone who chose his influences deliberately. In 1902, determined to rid himself of any vestige of Romantic subjectivity, he moved to Paris to apprentice himself to Rodin, eager to learn from the sculptor how to see things in their own "thingness" (*Dinglichkeit* was Rilke's term). And while in Paris, he sought out Baudelaire's poetry for its unflinching gaze at the horrible. Yet, more like Nietzsche than like Baudelaire, Rilke came to see life's terror as the very essence of its beauty. So, with Nietzsche—and the parallel became less a matter of influence than of compatible worldviews—Rilke pointed to the Christian martyrs as models of how to take life-endangering risks for the sake of meaning, while scorning their displacing of meaning onto a beyond.[1] Both Nietzsche and Rilke had contempt for what they branded Christianity's otherworldliness, and both saw it as a religion that could now do nothing but harm. As Rilke wrote to Lou from Toledo in 1912, speaking of Spanish Christianity, "[t]he fruit is sucked dry,—all that is left for us is, speaking crudely, to spit out the rind."

Yet at just this time, Rilke was composing a good bit of poetry drawing on Jesus and Gospel scenes. During this 1904–1913 period, he wrote 'The Olive Garden,' 'The Last Supper,' 'The Arisen,' 'Pietà,' 'Crucifixion,' 'Emmaus,' 'The Harrowing of Hell,' and 'The Raising of Lazarus,' along with most of the thirteen poems in his cycle *The Life of Mary*. This is a surprising list coming from a poet who repeatedly asserted that he was not writing as a Christian, for whom Christianity was indeed distasteful. We might reasonably wonder, then, what Jesus is doing at all in Rilke's poems. We saw in chapter 4 that what Jesus is doing in 'The Olive Garden' is voicing disillusionment about his own destiny. But except for that poem, Rilke's Jesus is not the voice of cynicism that we might expect from so anti-Christian a poet.

To see what does attract Rilke to the other Gospel episodes, it's best to engage one of the poems. 'On the Marriage at Cana,' from *The Life of Mary* (1913), is a good one: a fine poem in itself and good for our purpose. The poem looks at the Cana story from Mary's point of view. In the opening three stanzas she is recalling her early wonder at her son, during the years before this fateful wedding. She remembers her "amazed" sense of his youthful "glory," which had led her to "follow him with astonishment." Until that moment at Cana, however, she had restrained her pride, holding herself back from any public "display of her delight in him." Then, in the poem's middle stanza, comes the turning point (as Rilke sees it) of their relationship and their linked destiny:

> But at that wedding-feast, there when
> unexpectedly the wine ran out,—
> she begged him for a gesture with her look
> and didn't grasp that he resisted her.
>
> And then he did it.[2]

That is, he performed his first miracle: changing the water into wine. Rilke's stanza continues:

> Later she understood
> how she had pressured him into his course:
> for now he really was a wonder-worker,
> and the whole sacrifice was now ordained,
>
> irrevocably. Yes, it was written.
> But had it, at the time, as yet been readied?
> She: she had driven it forth
> in the blindness of her vanity.

Rilke's implication about why Jesus resisted his mother's request for more wine is consistent with John's Gospel: because Jesus knew the requested miracle would place him irrevocably on the road to his sacrificial death. What is not in the Gospel is the motivation Rilke gives to Mary: vanity, the natural desire finally to show off her son. Rilke makes a point of Mary's delayed awareness of her own role in pushing her son onto his course. At the wedding she "didn't grasp" his resistance; "later" she understood that she had, in effect, sacrificed her son to her blind vanity. Her pain at this realization, Rilke imagines in the next and final stanza, is grasped at Cana by her body, though her mind is still ignorant of what she has already made come to pass:

> At the table piled with fruits and vegetables,
> she shared everybody's joy and didn't know
> that the water of her own tear ducts
> had turned to blood with this wine.

Like her agonized son's sweat at Gethsemane, her tears at his suffering become blood. With this miracle, concurrent with his changing the water to wine, her body partakes of his fate.

The poem is so gripping that we need to pry ourselves away to note that Jesus scarcely figures in it. And that neither he nor his mother are named: they are "he" and "she" throughout the poem. This is a clue that Rilke's subject is not so much either of the characters as their relationship. He has used the Cana story as a figure of how two people can be implicated in one another's destinies—how we work miracles, for good or ill, on one another. The Marriage at Cana of the poem's title is actually the union of these two people's fates.

Rilke was fascinated by the power of love (his own love life was intensely complicated) as well as by how little we understand the invisible forces that move us. His other poems on Gospel characters' encounters with Jesus tend, like 'On the Marriage at Cana,' to push Jesus to the margins of his own story in order to focus on how others react to this mysterious figure impinging on their lives. So the Gospels' post-Resurrection stories naturally attracted Rilke, since there Jesus is both in the world and out of it. In a poem called 'The Arisen,' Rilke takes the scene of Jesus' appearance to Mary Magdalene in the garden outside his tomb (John 20:11–18). It's another "he/she" poem, without anyone named; the he/she relation this time is specifically that of lovers. As in John's Gospel, the point of view is Mary's, but her concern is utterly foreign to the Gospel: in the poem, Jesus' words to her in the garden teach her what she hadn't understood before, that only in physical separation can their souls embrace. This idea that love can be fulfilled only in separation was dear to Rilke, who had his closest relations with women (including his wife) when they were physically apart, linked only by their correspondence in letters. In the poem, liberated by Jesus' strange new distance, Mary herself is "transported" and "swept up" beyond the reach of his voice. 'The Arisen' of the title turns out to be "she" as well as "he." As in 'On the Marriage at Cana,' a title commonly applied to a Gospel event belonging to Jesus is shifted to apply to another person in relationship with him.

The vexed question of whether or not Jesus was divine doesn't trouble Rilke in these poems. At the very time that modernists were bemoaning the loss of belief in a divine Christ, Rilke took this for granted and turned the loss to his gain. Jesus could still carry the mythic meaning of immanent transcendence, and this was useful to Rilke. He was already playing with the idea that became the grand theme of his late work: that humankind can only truly live when it lets its "visible" dimension open up to its deep being, which is "the invisible." So in 'The Last Supper' (1904), ostensibly describing Leonardo da Vinci's fresco, Rilke's Jesus (as, again, only "he") represents a serene center that agitates "them" (the disciples, or any of us) because they can't get hold of it. They "flutter" anxiously around him, "astounded, bewildered": Rilke's motif of our not understanding life's forces is here, too. It's a point of his poem 'Emmaus' (1913) as well, where "they" (here, Jesus' companions in Luke's post-Resurrection story) get "flurried" as they sense, without recognizing it, the invisible breaking into their lives. Terrified as "his" unexpected presence bursts their limited world and "convulses them into vast relation," they finally "know" and as a result are "rapt into intenser living."

At this phase of his career, Rilke was still comfortable using Jesus to configure the invisible that convulses us "into vast relation." But these are the last poems he wrote that make explicit use of the Christian story. In his later, major works—the *Duino Elegies* (composed 1912–22) and the *Sonnets to Orpheus* (1922)—he dropped Jesus and the Gospel stories in favor of the pagan Orpheus and an angel figure that Rilke himself invented. In a famous 1925 letter to his Polish translator explaining his purpose in the *Elegies* and the *Sonnets*, Rilke vehemently insists that his angel "has nothing to do with the angel of the Christian heaven." Rather, it is "that creature in whom the transformation of the visible into the invisible, which we are accomplishing, appears already consummated."[3]

"The transformation . . . which we are accomplishing": this is Rilke's key point, underscoring the "we." Creation depends on us to release it from its apparently time-bound nature. We humans must plunge "into the whole," Rilke continues in this letter, though "*not in the Christian sense* (from which I am more and more passionately moving away)" (his italics). To his mind, as to Nietzsche's, Christianity fatally erred in denying the earthly, the sensual. For Rilke, it is *in* "a blissfully earthly consciousness" that we touch the "deep being" of transcience. Hence "it is our task to imprint this provisional, perishable earth so deeply, so patiently and passionately in ourselves that its reality shall arise in us again 'invisibly.' . . . The earth has no way out other than to become invisible: *in* us, who with a part of our natures partake of the invisible . . . *we are these transformers of the earth.*"

Thinking back to chapter 4, where we looked at the crisis of the secularized West as it dispensed with its Christian inheritance but had no other belief system to put in its place, we can see Rilke here responding to this crisis. The responses we focused on in chapter 4 were the negative ones: skepticism, nihilism, cynicism. Rilke did voice such radical doubt in his poem 'The Olive Garden.' But he moved on in his poetry, as summarized in this 1925 letter, to an energetically positive alternative. In effect, he jubilantly shouts to the bygone Christian belief system: good riddance, now we're free to make our own meaning! Rilke wasn't alone in this enthusiastic stance. Many of his contemporaries (Virginia Woolf comes to mind) were also working to craft a spiritual substitute for the collapse, as they saw it, of the Christian vision. They had confidence that art could achieve a new synthesis, a new wholeness of life and death, better than that of Christianity. Though Christianity was discredited, transcendence was not. Rilke's Orpheus and his angel are both figures of the poet himself, prophet and synthesizer of a new self-creating age.

Affirmations of life as the work of our own transformation resounded through the twentieth century. This was the century, after all, that at midpoint produced existentialism: philosophy's version of the confidence in making one's own meaning anew in each moment of choice and action. Human powers of self-creation then took a pop psychology form in North American culture's human potential movements in the sixties and seventies. More generally, a popular outlook of what was called secular humanism prevailed. Heir of the Englightenment, secular humanism dismissed the very notion of divine revelation, insisting that human intelligence on its own could find the values that give our life meaning. Though Rilke didn't go so far in tossing out transcendent values, he was firmly convinced that the world finds its transcendence through "us alone." This is why Rilke continued to speak to the century for seventy years after his death. Offering a positive alternative to Christianity, he gave voice and poetic vision to secular humanism's most constructive thrust: "we are these transformers of the earth."

RILKE'S LINE READS now almost as a manifesto for the poetry that followed it. All through the century, poets emerged who, whether inspired directly by Rilke or not, celebrated humanity's self-transforming powers. The poems I turn to next dramatize the belief that "we are these transformers of the earth" through an ingenious device: they take a Gospel episode and remove Jesus from the scene, displacing his miraculous powers onto the people who act on stage. Going one step further than Rilke, who pushed Jesus to the edge of the stage in Gospel scenes where other characters are moved by his mysterious force, these poems push Jesus completely off stage. Banished from his very own Gospel episodes, he is, one can surely say, a Jesus conspicuously Absent.

Scenes of Jesus' miracles work well for this purpose, and the Raising of Lazarus is especially popular. The Belgian-American poet May Sarton (1912–1995) wrote a marvelous poem simply called 'Lazarus,' which finds hope in human creativity as the force that can triumph over death in our "heavy world."[4] Yet the triumph doesn't come easily. The poem, in two parts, begins with the poet standing before a stone Lazarus at Chichester Cathedral that was sculpted around the year 1000. This Lazarus, as she sees him, is lifted from the rock by the anonymous sculptor, "carved out of sleep" but only to awake to our world of stoney death. It is the wasteland world we encountered in chapter 6, heavy with the evil that is death to the human heart. It is also the desperate modernist world bereft of redeeming faith, peopled by those who numbly "wish to pray but have no prayer." Staring at this world of the very death from which he thought he'd just emerged, Lazarus has a (nicely punned) "grave" look, and he "relearns despair." Sarton's masterful metrics convey the heaviness of our human situation: a weighty tetrameter line hammers out the repeated endrhymes of deep/keep/sleep; bear/stare/despair. Suddenly, with part 2, the meter lightens up and loosens, as the poet shifts to her own present moment back at home writing this poem. At first she feels overwhelmed, inadequate to the task of creating anything at all. Then, in the silence, she hears Lazarus "calling me by name," enabling her "buried self" to break through as she "lift[s] the poem free." Images of weightless dancing that follow celebrate the creative act as a resurrection experience.

With its movement down through the concrete weight of the material world and out to the uplifting power of poetry itself, this poem could almost have been composed to illustrate Rilke's proclamation that "our task is so deeply and so passionately to impress upon ourselves this provisional and perishable earth, that its essential being will arise again 'invisibly' in us." Rilke would have liked that it is a *sculpted* Lazarus—the creation of another artist a millennium before—that calls forth the creative act in Sarton's poem.

Jesus is utterly absent from Sarton's 'Lazarus.' And she is far from alone in putting Lazarus in a poem where he returns from death without the aid of Jesus. Though the focus of this chapter is on poetry of the West, I can't help briefly glancing beyond, to other cultures of the twentieth century's second half, because a satellite view would show Lazarus coming forth as a death-resurrection figure in poetry all over the globe. In Nigeria, he sprouts from Wole Soyinka's 'Seed,' one of Soyinka's prison poems meditating on injustice but waiting in hope for the natural power of human regeneration to exert its force.[5] In India, Lazarus emerges from the tomb, in Jasbir Sing Ahluwalia's poem 'Autobiography of Mr. X,' as the common man outwitting socio-political forces that contrive to crush him to death.[6] And in Iraq, in Badr Shākir al-Sayyāb's 'City of Sinbad,' as already shown in the previous chapter, Lazarus represents the Iraqi people released from a deadening autocratic regime only to be awakened to a false life; since the bloody revolution has betrayed their hopes, Lazarus is revived into a city of death. From a range of particular sociopolitical contexts where forces of evil seem to prevail, in all these examples Lazarus is called on by the poet to figure his compatriots' potential for rebirth, the *human* possibility of renewal from death back into life. In no case does Jesus call Lazarus forth.

Lazarus isn't the only Gospel character whom poets have taken to configure the life-giving powers that in the Gospels belong to Jesus. Returning to the West, I want to look at one more poem in which Jesus' powers are displaced from him onto the human actors on stage. In a 1920s poem called 'Magdalene,' by the Greek Marxist poet Kóstas Várnalis (1884–1974), this displacement is the explicit point. In richly sensuous images, the poet traces the course of salvation history on Magdalene's body. She is the poem's speaker, recalling first how "in the four kingdoms of Judea, I was the Fountain: / the unwithering and musk-fragrant citrons of my breasts," yet "darkness lay within me, stretches of vast, dry sand." Then she addresses Jesus, recalling how his cleansing message gradually sank into her whole being, until "I longed impetuously to cast myself at your feet" and then did "follow in your footsteps," shedding "my diamonds, silver, gardens, palaces, and silks." And though "you never said anything new"— Várnalis saw Jesus as only one of many heroic forerunners of the modern proletarian spirit—what you gave me, she continues, was your "power to hear the silence of the heavens" even to "the heart of God." Raising her rhetoric to that of a rally to the masses, she proclaims in a rousing conclusion that *because* of her fleshliness "only I, who once was whore and mud, have felt / how mortal you were, Christ! And I shall resurrect you!"[7]

The Gospel story is useful to Várnalis because he can take its resurrection narrative and turn it on its head: yes resurrection is real, but it is humankind who in the end will resurrect the divine spirit. The truly hopeful Marxist vision of the 1920s has the confidence that humankind, in its very bodiliness, can transform reality for the good. Precisely because Magdalene embraces her material essence, because she has lived mortality to its fullest, she can embody the power of re-creation; she can represent what Rilke proclaimed in the same decade, that "we are these transformers of the earth." Half a century later, Czeslaw Milosz (Lithuania, 1911–) articulated the twentieth century's sense of human empowerment in a way Várnalis would have understood. The value that in our time we oppose to "evil Matter," Milosz said (he had in mind particularly death, the ultimate evil Matter), is "value no longer flowing from a divine source and now excusively human."[8]

MILOSZ HAD ALSO experienced Marxism, though as its victim rather than its champion, and he considered its Soviet Communist manifestation one of the great evils of our day. Evil is a dominant force in Milosz's writing, more of a presence than the Incarnate God. A poem Milosz wrote on the Gospels, 'Readings,' makes a useful introduction to his particular sense of Jesus Absent. Though Jesus is conspicuously missing from this poem, it's not for the same purpose as in the poems just presented. Far from being displaced onto humankind, Jesus' divine powers are entirely upstaged in the poem by the devil's wiles.

"You asked me what is the good of reading the Gospels in Greek," the poem begins, in the conversationally analytic style that Milosz crafts in much of his verse. The rest of the poem develops the poet's initial reply: that immediate engagement with those "enduring" words forces our attention onto the shocking closeness between the Gospels' epoch and our own. "It is the same eon," the poet asserts, illustrating with a list of things that are "the same": "fear and desire . . . oil and wine and bread . . . the fickleness of the throng." By way of example, he then moves into the story of the Gadarene swine in Matthew 8:28–33. In the Gospel, Jesus heals two *daimonizomenoi* (the poem does use Matthew's Greek word) by ordering the demons who possess them to leave the people and enter instead into a herd of swine, which then promptly rushes into the nearby sea and drowns. Milosz recounts these details, but absent Jesus. His interest is rather in the demons: in the mastering force they continue to exert after "twenty centuries." Still today they

> may enter swine,
> Which, exasperated by such a sudden clash

The Last Supper *(1961), by Bernard Buffet (France, 1928–). At this grim Last Supper, Jesus as the life-giving God is absent. His body is there; but with a skull for a head, he is the image of death in the middle of his disciples. What seems to have knocked the life out of him is the evil personified by Judas; as the only figure with a semblance of motion, Judas takes the foreground as he goes off to his act of betrayal, leaving Jesus and his disciples alike in despair. Scala/Art Resource, NY, and © 1999 Artists Rights Society (ARS), New York/ADAGP, Paris.*

> Between two natures, theirs and the Luciferic,
> Jump into water and drown (which occurs repeatedly).[9]

In a series of interviews published as the book *Conversations,* Milosz explains that he labels the diabolical power here "Luciferic" because Lucifer is the devil's form as pure and haughty spirit. Self-proclaimed purity combined with pride, Milosz continues, are the deadly afflictions both of the Nietzschean artist and of the political ideologues "who wanted to improve humanity in our century."[10]

Milosz knew firsthand the evil that political purists could do. His native Lithuania, absorbed into Poland after World War I, had suffered the devastating Nazi occupation followed by the demoralizing communist regime. Though Milosz defected to the United States in 1960, these back-to-back totalitarian horrors shaped his entire life's work. His poetry is always political, though not in the sense of protest. It is a poetry of moral and philosophical reflection, concerned with the individual person as imposed on by a harsh and lying history. No wonder, once settled in California, he had little patience for the self-indulgent introspection of much American poetry. And no wonder we in the United

States started to listen, our breaths held, to the calmly wise turns of his verse, especially after the 1980 Nobel Prize for Literature spread his name. For the same reason we treasured, during those last two decades of the century, every word from the mouth or pen of Václav Havel. The Eastern European experience of "the demonic doings of history," as Milosz put it in his Nobel Prize lecture, had produced in these two men a commitment to the language of truth, in the service of a vision of public good, that we sorely needed. Surrounded in our country by a frantic politics of distraction that seemed unable even to conceive of a genuine political morality, we gratefully found in Havel and Milosz a wisdom rooted in the special Eastern European sensibility that could stare the century's evil in the face without losing compassion or hope.

Milosz has said that his own sense of hope, in the face of all the historical realities that would argue against it, came from his religious faith. A lifelong practicing Catholic, he talks about God throughout his voluminous writings—poetry, essays, fiction—with a comfort born of regular liturgical worship and prayer. There is none of the angst or searching that is the dominant tone of relations to God in the twentieth-century West. Questions about God's relation to the world do abound in Milosz, but they are probed with a constant, classic, calm. The overriding question in all his work is the primary one that the twentieth century by its end had to pose: where *is* God in our world so overrun by horrors that humankind seems to be frankly suicidal, to be—as in 'Readings'—the biblical herd of swine that, possessed by Lucifer, "repeatedly" plunges into the water and drowns?

In the poem that Milosz placed right after 'Readings' in his 1974 volume *From the Rising of the Sun,* he addresses this implicit question with which 'Readings' ends. This next poem, called 'Oeconomia Divina,' opens: "I did not expect to live in such an unusual moment." The line could be referring to the "bedeviled" time of 'Readings,' though it also functions as topic sentence of its own poem. Milosz wants the Latin title, he explains in *Conversations,* to evoke its old meaning in Christian moral theology, "divine pedagogy," which refers to the way God educates the world through his involvement with it. God's current pedagogical device, as Milosz sees it, is set out at the start of the poem:

> I did not expect to live in such an unusual moment.
> When the God of thunders and of rocky heights,
> the Lord of hosts, Kyrios Sabaoth,
> would humble people to the quick,
> allowing them to act whatever way they wished,
> leaving to them conclusions, saying nothing.

The divine educational method of the moment is this: God has left us on our own, to see how we'll handle it. It's as if God is giving us an Outward Bound experience: leaving us to discover how we'll manage without a divine parent stepping in to reward and punish our actions. Milosz doesn't pretend to have invented this scenario. As he says in his discussion of this poem in *Conversations,* the notion that "God has decided to withdraw, to become Deus absconditus," is "a recurrent motif in the twentieth century." As examples he mentions Heidegger, Rózewicz (whose poem on Jesus erasing his words we looked at in chapter 4), and *Waiting for Godot.*

'Oeconomia Divina' continues by describing the "spectacle" that met the poet's eyes as he gazed at our world, from which God has withdrawn. The details of his vision are (as in *Waiting for Godot*) at once comic and terrifying. Objects, without God to ground them, lose their bearings and their very being: whole cities, the poet reports, "ran short of their essence and disintegrated"; "materiality escaped" from lemons on the table; "letters in books turned silver-pale, wobbled, and faded." People, entering into the wacky spirit of this metaphysical tragicomedy, "were throwing off their clothes on the piazzas." Since this poem was written in Berkeley in the hippie days of the early 1970s, Milosz wasn't imagining this particular detail. But his analysis of it is his own: the poem ends by seeing the naked people bare of any sense of their own being.

> But in vain they were longing after horror, pity, and anger.
> Neither work nor leisure
> was justified,
> nor the face, nor the hair nor the loins
> nor any existence.

This loss of people's sense of their own ontological value as human individuals, Milosz believes, is precisely the emptiness on which the century's totalitarian terror fed.

In poems where Milosz brings Jesus into this world from which God has apparently absconded, it is—as we'd expect—only to dramatize that he has no role here. In a couple of poems written during roughly the same middle period of Milosz's career as were the ones we've just looked at, Jesus enters as a figure forgotten, unknown even to himself, without even a name. In 'How It Was' (1968), Jesus steps into a scene of spiritual absence and feels so out of place that he doesn't know who he is or why he's here. The poem is set on a mountaintop from which the poet, surveying the contemporary landscape, reports: "I saw absence." Listing the signs of divinity that are missing, beginning with Native American religious figures no longer in evidence, the poet goes on:

> God the Father didn't walk about any longer tending the new shoots of a
>   cedar, no longer did man hear his rushing spirit.

> His son did not know his sonship and turned his eyes away when passing
>   by a neon cross flat as a movie screen showing a striptease.

This time it was really the end of the Old and the New Testament.

The poem 'Counsels' (1959) also pictures the end of the Old and New Testament through an image of a Jesus forgotten: God, the poet observes,

> has been hiding so long that it has been forgotten
> how he revealed himself in the burning bush
> in the breast of a young Jew
> ready to suffer for all who were and will be.

Unnamed, the young Jew could be Moses, to whom God spoke in the burning bush, but he is also clearly Jesus. Both the burning bush and Jesus function here as what I will call the Forgotten Revelation.

The image of Jesus averting his eyes from "a neon cross flat as a movie screen showing a striptease" seems so specifically a satire of American vulgarity that Milosz made a point in *Conversations* of clarifying that he had in mind here the whole world. And I wonder if by "the world" he might have meant not only the contemporary situation but the human condition in general, its metaphysical status in relation to an absent God. The very next line in 'Counsels' mentions Ananke, the Greek figure of Necessity who stands ready to rule whenever God withdraws. And this *whenever*, according to one of Milosz's favorite philosophers, Simone Weil, is all the time. "God is not in time," Weil writes; by his very act of creating the universe, "God has left us abandoned in time." This is Weil's theory of "creative renunciation": that "God causes this universe to exist, but he consents not to command it, although he has the power to do so. Instead he leaves two other forces to rule in his place": "the blind necessity attaching to matter" and "the autonomy essential to thinking persons." Blind necessity is the world's evil that God leaves us exposed to; but he also leaves us free to turn to him in love. And our turning, even if it's only a turn upward of our eyes, is precisely what God waits for eternally, in silence. "Time," Weil writes, "is God's waiting as a beggar for our love." Weil often jolts us like this, mixing her stern abstractions with startling images. And mixing, as well, the contradictory assertions that we are at once utterly abandoned by God yet absolutely in his presence.[11]

"I am indebted to her for an understanding of contradiction," Milosz said in *Conversations*. He does enjoy constructing a poem around two frankly contradictory metaphysical or theological positions, and a couple of his late poems of this sort concern themselves specifically with the Jesus of Christian faith. 'Either/Or,' from Milosz's 1991 collection called *Provinces*, begins "If God incarnated himself in man, died and rose from the dead," and then draws out the implications of either accepting or rejecting this proposition as true. Finally, though, the poet calls a halt to this line of thought with an outright: "Why either-or?" People have always lived as if gods did matter but were also a mystery, he says, and this is all we can expect. Such a conclusion sounds potentially cynical, but Milosz's tone is quite the opposite. He's not at all the cavalier postmodernist, lightly shrugging off the impossibility of grasping sure meanings. Rather, he's the supportive spiritual counselor. The poem ends with advice on how to live as moral beings whose ultimate questions can't be answered: "Trying to do good within our limits, / Forgiving the mortals their imperfection. Amen." Similarly, number 5 of his 'Six Lectures in Verse,' written in the mid 1980s, presents sympathetically our muddled human situation "on the mute earth," where neither theologians nor philosophers have anything useful to tell us and where even Christian believers must confess "I don't know" to the question "Has[Christ] risen?" Yet despite this indecision, and even "after the great wars," he concludes, "we plod on with hope."

But I don't want to leave the impression that Milosz's world is unrelievedly dark. He always insisted that, no matter how grim reality in fact was, the poet could imagine the world as it should be. And especially in his late poems of the 1980s and 1990s, he enjoys evoking colorful images of paradise and claiming beauty's power as a force for good over evil. God may have withdrawn, Jesus might be the Forgotten Revelation; yet a late poem called 'On Prayer,' starting in Milosz's typical topic sentence fashion—"you ask me how to pray to someone who is not"—continues with an extended metaphor of prayer as an aerial bridge over golden landscapes. It's a marvelous vision of our human condition as a collective tightrope walk: risky but elegantly balanced.

MILOSZ ISN'T THE only twentieth-century poet to evoke a Jesus Forgotten. As one would expect in a century that identifies itself as secular, Jesus is a Forgotten character in poetry fairly often. The effects of his being Forgotten range widely from Milosz's, and I want to look now at just a few poems that suggest the range. I've chosen them from poets of varying nationalities—from a Native American, an Israeli, and a Russian—to illustrate how the twentieth-century poets' Jesus seems to be Forgotten all over the place. Consistent with the evocation of a Forgotten character, in none of these poems is Jesus named. Each sets a scene where his Absence is noted: where the fading memory of his life, of his meaning, is the point.

N. Scott Momaday (1934–), considered the dean of Native American writers, sets his scene in his poem's title: 'Before an Old Painting of the Crucifixion: Carmel Mission, June, 1960.' The painting, we learn during the poem, is a fading mural near the sea. Pondering it leads the poet to reflect on time, death, and the "silence" that seems the only message left from a mural that is (in a word also used by Milosz) "mute." It seems to the poet, musing here, that "The Passion wanes into oblivion" and "The void / Is calendared in stone." And in this void, he continues, "the human act, / Outrageous, is in vain." That "the" has a crafted ambiguity: is it the outrageous act of Christ's Passion, or is it any "human act"? Jean-Paul Sartre's existentialism, popular at the time this poem was composed, did posit that, without a grounding in transcendence, humankind could no longer count on any act's having meaning apart from the meaning it made for itself at that moment. "The human act," *any* act, was "in vain." Whether or not Momaday read Sartre doesn't matter; this was a sensibility in the air, across the seas, in the 1960s.[12]

Toward the end of the century, across other seas, the Israeli poet Natan Zach (1930–) wrote a poem actually entitled 'Recalled and Forgotten' (1996), which begins: "He turned walking on water into a kind of art."[13] In the tone of light-hearted detachment that was a popular end-of-the-millennium poetic style (Milosz cultivated it, too), Zach retells the Gospel story as if from the point of view of the small-town gossip of Jesus' contemporaries to whom nothing much seems at stake. People would make jokes about this man's walking on water; some "suggested he take up / water-skiing." But "after a while he was forgotten." Some old folks continued to recall his exploits of walking on water, but "his name they no longer knew. Nor did they know, and perhaps hadn't known / from the start, why he did what he'd done." In Zach's poem the unnamed Jesus ends up "in several travel books / under the heading Folklore." It's curious that both Momaday's and Zach's Forgotten Jesus are composed in relation to water. I wouldn't want to make much of what might be a coincidence of only two poems. Yet the natural symbolism of a large body of water, representing a constancy that's as close as the visible world gets to the eternal, makes a nice environment to set off the forgetting of the figure who was once supposed to be eternity's representative on earth.

But who has forgotten whom? The leading avant-garde Russian poet of his time, Nikolai Gumilyov (1886–1921), in his poem 'The Progeny of Cain,' plays with a possibility that also intrigued Milosz: that it is *God* who has forgotten *us*.[14] An outspoken monarchist even after the Russian Revolution, Gumilyov took part in an anti-Soviet conspiracy that cost him his life; he was executed by a Bolshevik firing squad. His poetry celebrates heroic gestures and a life force like that which his contemporary Rilke also exalted. In 'The Progeny of Cain,' people see themselves with unlimited creative power, as if they were acting out Rilke's dictate that "we are the transformers of the earth." Yet for Gumilyov in this poem, humanity's sense of its transformative power has a sinister overtone, coming directly from Lucifer's promise in the Garden that "you will be as gods" if you simply "taste the fruit." Gumilyov does make a point of identifying the tempter as Lucifer, exactly as Milosz would later do in 'Readings.' Responding to Soviet Communism at very different stages of its development, both poets saw it as the height—or nadir—of humankind's tendency to give itself over to Luciferic pride. 'The Progeny of Cain' goes on to suggest, cautiously, in the form of a wry question, what might be missing from a world given over to dreams of human omnipotence. If we are truly as gods, the poem asks, "why, then, do we stoop in impotence, / Feeling, perhaps, that Some One has forgotten us, / Seeing, perhaps, the horror of that first temptation, / Whenever any hand unites / Two sticks, two blades of grass, two poles, / Into a casual, momentary cross?" All the poet can do in his dangerous political situation is merely hint that something—or Some One—is missing from a world where human dreams of absolute power seem to come true. Gumilyov evokes a Jesus Forgotten who is "perhaps" also Jesus Forgetting. In either case, he is suggestively also a Jesus Missed.

The Syrian poet Tawfiq Sāyigh (1923–1971) also constructs a character of Jesus Missed, but with Sāyigh we move away from Jesus Forgotten. Sāyigh, a Christian who agonized over the relevance of his faith to the Arab political struggles that we looked at in the previous chapter, sometimes wished that he *could* simply forget Jesus. But he felt, all his life, both pursued by Jesus' love and pursuing it, unable to rest in it as long as Palestine was lost. Sayigh's intensely personal poem 'The Sermon on the Mount' dramatizes his restless engagement with the Gospel character who shifts between Absence and Presence in the poet's life.[15]

Throughout the course of the poem, the poet/speaker is the only constant in the scene. He sets himself on the hillside of the Gospel narrative, one of the multitude whom Jesus feeds and preaches to, while "he" (unnamed, as in so many of our poems configuring a Jesus Absent) moves in and out of the picture. Words that recur like a refrain enact the poet's waiting: "Alone I lay upon the hill . . . / Alone I lay, waiting for his return." When "he" does come, he engages the poet so intensely that "I thought he talked only to me." Sometimes Jesus seems not to do the miracles claimed for him in the Gospels; at other times the miracles do work, though not on the poet himself. ("Water-turned-to-wine / tasted water to my lips.") Yet still "On the hill I lie . . . / I know he will return, and wait for him." Sāyigh's Jesus, when Absent, is Waited For and Missed.

THE MAJOR twentieth-century poet of *waiting* for the Absent God is indisputably R. S. Thomas. Because Thomas spent his entire working life as an Episcopal priest in the Church of Wales, his configuring of Jesus Absent is especially interesting. Here is a person who remained faithful to the daily duties of a Christian calling, while producing a steady output of poems circling around the core of God's utter silence.

Not that there isn't change over the half-century course of Thomas's poetic career. His early collections of poems, basically from the 1940s and 1950s, are steeped in the rural Welsh life whose bleakness overwhelmed him when he stepped into it as a young parish priest in 1942. Though himself born in Wales, Thomas had grown up in the city, so—as he described the experience in a 1972 BBC film made about him—"this muck and blood and hardness, the rain and the spittle and the phlegm of farm life was, of course, a shock."[16] It all seemed to embody the grim despair of Welsh history, with its battlefield defeats at the hands of the English that left an impoverished, embittered people robbed of even their language. Thomas's first poems mostly stare at a solitary, hardened peasant working the resistant soil and wonder how these people have endured. His poetry of the 1960s then starts wondering how he himself can endure: endure not only the stark landscape and passively suffering, unresponsive congregation to whom preaches, but also his own growing question of where divine love can be in this apparently God-forsaken place. More and more he sees humanity obsessed by a primitive bloodlust, reduced to the bestial.[17] And here enters his first major image of Jesus Absent.

The image is an "untenanted" Cross. Two poems from the 1966 collection *Pietà* use this adjective: the title poem and one called 'In Church.' The short poem 'Pietà' presents itself as a landscape painting: a "still scene" with only the hills as "remote witnesses":

> And in the foreground
> The tall Cross,
> Sombre, untenanted,
> Aches for the Body
> That is back in the cradle
> Of a maid's arms.[18]

The empty Cross "aches" for its tenant because, as surrounding poems suggest, only the sacrifice of God's own Body can satisfy the primitive human lust for blood. 'In Church,' as the title implies, moves the untenanted Cross inside, to a scene that is in fact a recurrent tableau throughout Thomas's poetic career: the speaker/poet/priest alone in an empty church. "Often I try," the poem begins,

> To analyse the quality
> Of its silences. Is this where God hides
> From my searching? I have stopped to listen,
> After the few people have gone.

Where, he goes on to ask, is there life in this church? Its ancient stone walls are "hard ribs / Of a body that our prayers have failed / To animate." Only the advancing shadows seem alive, and some bats, and the tensely listening poet, "Breathing, testing his faith / On emptiness, nailing his questions / One by one to an untenanted cross." Christianity's central icon, the Cross, is empty of meaning. Jesus is Absent from the place where Christianity has put him as answer to the central needs of human existence, and in his body's place what is "nailed" (a recurrent verb for Thomas) is the poet's questioning of this very absence.

So the poet remains, alone with his questions, in the empty church where, as the early poem 'In a Country Church' put it, "the dry whisper of unseen wings" is the sound of "bats not angels" in the roof. In this earlier poem, the poet/parson is "kneeling," a position he holds through the succeeding decades of poems of waiting in God's silence. But something does dramatically change, in the works of the 1970s, in Thomas's encounter—if we can call it such—with God's persistent absence. All at once with the collection *H'm* (1972), Thomas yanks

God to center stage in his poetic imagination, rips down the Welsh countryside backdrops, and replaces them with mythic creation-story gardens blown up to cosmic scale, with giant hands crafting destructive machinery, all churning inside the gaping bloody wound cut in Christ's side on the Cross. My violent language is intended to give the feel of this important period of Thomas's work, from which comes his fame as "poet of the hidden God." His God in these poems isn't always precisely hidden, but when he appears, he's imagined with such brutality that we might wish he'd stayed behind the scenes. It's as if Thomas, determined to wrestle with this elusive God once and for all, realizes that the stage must be properly set for this ultimate showdown. The scene must be transformed from the specific empty church and bare hills of God-forsaken Wales to the mythopoeic stage of God's creation and redemption of the world. Here the poet will throw his imagination—at all costs—into the biblical moments that might give him a grip on what God is about.

So in 'Cain,' for instance, he focuses on Abel's blood, which the poem's Cain accuses God of thirsting for. God doesn't deny the charge, and even elaborates it to make Christ's crucifixion result necessarily from this mythically first bloodshed. God says of Abel:

> The lamb was torn
> From my own side. The limp head,
> The slow fall of red tears—they
> Were like a mirror to me in which I beheld
> My reflection. I anointed myself
> In readiness for the journey
> To the doomed tree you were at work upon.

Planting the "doomed tree" of Christ's Cross back in Eden is traditional Christian mythography, so Thomas's setting it just outside the Garden, in the story of Cain and Abel, isn't far afield. But the other conflations in this dense passage are his own: the bleeding Abel as Christ who is the lamb torn as in a cesarean birth from God's side, which is however Christ's own wounded side on the Cross.

During the poems of this period, Thomas returns again and again to the wound in Christ's side. It is the biblical image through which, more than any other, he seems to hope to get a handle on the elusive God. As if becoming that other Thomas—the biblical Doubting one to whom Jesus said: "Reach out your hand and put it in my side" (John 20:27)—the poet probes the wound with other images, practically crawling inside it to live in his imagination. The "tree" itself, Thomas's other recurrent Crucifixion image, even grows out of the wound at one point. In this cluster of poems, the wound swells to a startlingly cosmic-sized Jesus Absent, a gaping hole at the center of the created and sacrificially redeemed universe, as in the much-quoted poem 'Via Negativa':

Why no! I never thought other than
That God is that great absence
In our lives, the empty silence
Within, the place where we go
Seeking, not in hope to
Arrive or find. He keeps the interstices
In our knowledge, the darkness
Between stars. His are the echoes
We follow, the footprints he has just
Left. We put our hands in
His side hoping to find
It warm. We look at people
and places as though he had looked
At them, too; but miss the reflection.

The poem's title situates it in the classic mystical tradition called the "negative way": the idea that we come to God by emptying our minds of all that is not God, including all words and images that we think are "about" God. The negative way is Thomas's main way throughout his poetry; in silence, in absence, is where he senses God must be. Yet for the traditional mystic and the poet alike, the paradox in the negative way is that it can be spoken of only through language, and a running motif through Thomas's entire poetic career is precisely this tension between needing to use words as his medium and distrusting their capacity to mediate what truly matters. In 'Via Negativa' he deals with the paradox by frankly listing metaphors of absence. God is the site of our "seeking"; "interstices" and "darkness between stars" give the site a cosmic scale; "echoes" and "footprints" picture an absence that leave a trace; God's side opened by his wound on the Cross embodies an absence that invites us in. This is a God who wants to be sought, so much so that he offers in his crucified body the measureless hole that makes room for our search and invites in our hands, as he did the hand of the biblical Doubting Thomas.

It's fascinating that this is actually an image of the Cosmic Christ, major figure on the stage of the medieval imagination. Here in the twentieth-century West, where Jesus has been not only brought down to earth but has been reduced to a yellowing corpse and then to dust, he can reappear as the Cosmic Christ—who is now also Jesus Absent. This new configuration is not of Jesus' resurrected body (as it was in Dante's celestial vision of the Cross as dazzling light), nor even really of his crucified body, but of the *hole* in his crucified body. It seems grotesque, in a sense, to be imaginatively inside a gaping wound. Yet what a powerful image for the cosmic pain and emptiness at the center of human existence, into which we enter as into a God who gives himself as this pain, this wound, this sacrifice. Thomas's mythic imagination has been able to reconceive the Cosmic Christ for his era as a figure of Jesus Absent, by making the hole in his side the site of our search for "that great absence / In our lives" that is God.

Commentators tend to bring in Simone Weil when explicating Thomas's great poems of God's absence. Her theory of creation as God's self-emptying, which I noted in connection with Czeslaw Milosz, is indeed akin to Thomas's poetic vision, as is her tough anti-Romantic stance that distrusts the human imagination's tendency to push material of its own fancy into the holes God has left. Also akin to Thomas's worldview is a dominant theme of twentieth-century Christian theology, that God can be present in creation only through absence. Karl Rahner, for instance, writes: "The term of transcendence [Rahner is hesitant even to name it here as "God"] . . . presents itself to us in the mode of withdrawal, of silence, of distance, of being always inexpressible, so that speaking of it, if it is to make sense, always requires listening to its silence."[19] When I'm reading Rahner and Thomas together, I feel that both these writers are probing horizonless spaces that would make many of us woozy. Not afraid to float free of the illusion that their words are attached to God's reality, they keep stretching their language toward transcendence, knowing that they'll never actually reach that limitless horizon and yet that to be human means to keep hanging in the air, always reaching.

This is a very different sense of God's absence than that of secular humanism, which firmly doubts God's existence, confident that we humans are just fine on our own. The twentieth-century Christian theology of God's absence says quite the opposite: that our own very existence is radically dependent on God. But it is a God beyond our mind's grasp, a God always over the horizon of our intellectual reach, so that the sense of God's absence is a sense of distance, not of doubt. The Swiss Protestant theologian Karl Barth started the century off with a bang by shooting the Christian concept of God out into this distance. Barth was reacting against the nineteenth-century theological developments that we saw in chapter 2 as a breath of fresh air for their time but that had led, in Barth's view, to a stifling overdomestication of God: Schleiermacher moving theology's ground inside our own religious feelings; historical criticism reducing Jesus to a sensitive person strolling the Galilean hills. *No!* Barth boomed in his magisterial works; God is totally Other, and any knowledge we have of God starts from God's own initiative. Even our apparent "self-knowledge" is God's revelation of us to ourselves. Kierkegaard's and Heidegger's existentialist terminology then offered theology, continuing from Barth, a way to speak of God as the "ultimate ground of being" (in Paul Tillich's famous phrase), a ground we humans are necessarily estranged from in order that we can become "actual" in our free choice for God. And when we have that free choice, but its ultimate ground has disappeared? The despair that must result was detailed, interestingly enough, by a genuine atheist, Jean-Paul Sartre. With the courage of his conviction that there in fact was no ultimate ground of being, Sartre invented a parable to show how the world remains a ground now marked by the absence of its transcendent ground. As paraphrased by Dennis O'Brien in *God and the New Haven Railway,* a delightful book that makes these basic twentieth-century philosophical and theological themes not only accessible (which they are far from being in their originals) but even fun, Sartre's illustrative story is as follows. "I go to the café to meet Pierre. He is not there. I search across the crowd of faces for my friend. But he is not there. The café becomes the ground on which the figure of Pierre does not emerge. So, for Sartre, the world is the ground on which the figure of God does not appear for all that we search for him—believing, in fact and spirit, that we had a prearranged appointment." And here we are again on the stage of *Waiting for Godot.*

I offer this brief digression into the century's philosophy and theology of absence not because it influenced Thomas but because it helps explain his widespread appeal. Thomas did read (and write some poems about) Kierkegaard, but the strongest influence on his spirituality of emptiness wasn't theology but his personal experience of bleak Welsh rural life. In his poetry, readers find the contemporary search for a distant God more vividly realized than in dense theological and philosophical writings. Furthermore, Thomas is so attractive, I think, because his poetry is also taking account of other senses of God's absence looming large in the secular century. He writes much, for instance, of the sinister triumph of the "machine," his symbol for technology's control of human freedom. He even engages the celebratory sense of good riddance to all things Christian that appeared in Nietzsche and Rilke, though the version Thomas dialogues with is Yeats's theory that the two-thousand-year Christian era has passed through its twenty-eight moonlike "phases" and a new cycle with unforeseeable consequences is about to begin. Indeed, in Thomas's popular poem 'The Moon in Lleyn,' (1975) he directly engages this Yeatsian sense of a Jesus who is Absent because his historical phase is drawing to a close. The poem is worth pausing over, not only because it presents another configuration of Jesus Absent, set now not in a mythopoeic world but in the more immediately experienced world of elemental natural forces, but also because it's one of the rare poems in which Thomas mentions Jesus by name.

"The last quarter of the moon / of Jesus gives way / to the dark; the serpent / digests the egg." This is how the poem starts, frankly adopting Yeats's images. The poet/speaker, from his characteristic position on his knees in an empty stone church, watches other natural forces erase the remaining traces of Christian belief: "the tide laps / at the Bible" and the congregation is nothing but "shadows and the sea's / sound." "Yeats was right," he concludes; "Religion is over, and / what will emerge from the body / of the new moon, no one / can say." Yet it's a conclusion at only the midpoint of the poem. What follows, with a new paragraph, is a startling event in Thomas's poetic life of waiting in silent churches for God to speak: "a voice sounds in my ear: Why so fast, mortal?" The wording, as well as the succeeding images of elemental nature receiving the divine spirit, recalls the Lord's promptings to Ezekiel in the valley of dry bones: "Mortal, can these bones live? . . . Prophesy to these bones [that] I will cause breath to enter you, and you shall live" (Ezekiel 37:3– 5). The comparable voice in Thomas's poem speaks of Christian life manifesting its own force in hidden but effective ways over the pagan world: "these very seas are baptized," pilgrims are finding their way to worship "in their own spirits," and so:

> You must remain
> Kneeling. Even as this moon
> making its way through earth's
> cumbersome shadow, prayer, too,
> has its phases.

The moon of Jesus will emerge, the symbols imply, from this dark phase in the spiritual life of the modern world and of the poet personally, and the only exhortation to the poet himself is that "You must remain / Kneeling."

In a poet of a more comic temperament, it might be seen as a joke that when he finally hears a voice in prayer, it tells him to keep doing what he has been doing for decades of silence. The poet *had* remained kneeling, and he would continue to, sometimes in the silent twilight sensing "The Presence" or hearing "The Answer," but also continuing in "The Absence" and "Waiting" (all titles of later poems). So on his knees is a good way for us to leave him. And the poem I'll leave him kneeling in, called in fact 'Kneeling' (1968), can bring us back to *Waiting for Godot*. Not only the poem's theme of waiting for God's message but also its central metaphor of the actor on stage invite comparison to Beckett's play.

> Moments of great calm,
> Kneeling before an altar
> Of wood in a stone church
> In summer, waiting for the God
> To speak; the air a staircase
> For silence; the sun's light
> Ringing me, as though I acted
> A great role. And the audiences
> Still; all that close throng
> Of spirits waiting, as I,
> For the message.
>   Prompt me, God;
> But not yet. When I speak,
> Though it be you who speak
> Through me, something is lost.
> The meaning is in the waiting.

In this poem from before Thomas's mythopoeic period, the scene is realistically set in his parish church, where his congregation waits for his sermon to begin. And "waiting" is the poem's entire action. The priest is "waiting," like an actor, to be prompted in his lines; his audience is "waiting" as well in the silence; finally, "the meaning is in the waiting." Since for Beckett's play, too, the meaning is in the waiting—and in both cases the waiting is for a message from an absent God—it's instructive to compare the "meanings." For each, the meaning comes through the particular manner of waiting. One waits in the mystic's calm silence, surrounded by a stillness packed full of the throng of expectant spirits. The other waits in noisy music-hall chatter and frantic repetitive activity, to ward off fear of the void. Both wait as if on Holy Saturday, the day between the Crucifixion and the Resurrection; as noted at the start of the chapter, the situation of *Waiting for Godot* is sometimes described this way. Yet one work waits out the day in the secular century's doubt, the other in a faith ripened for two thousand years. Thomas, that is, has faith that God will speak, indeed that God has already come and spoken. This is precisely what his poem 'The Coming,' quoted at the end of the previous chapter, dramatizes: that, moved by the pathetic sight of scrawny people reaching desparately toward the bare tree, the son watching from heaven says "Let me go there." And the Christian story is that he does go, does come. Beckett's story can't end with any such movement, because it's a story of paralysis at the loss of the Christian story. The one signficant change that could have moved Beckett's protagonists is lost on them: at the start of the play's second half, the stage directions say that the lone tree has sprouted "four or five leaves." The protagonists notice the leaves—"Everything's dead but the tree," Vladimir comments a few lines before the final curtain—but, having forgotten how to read archetypal symbols, they have no confidence that this could be a sign of hope. So they respond by repeating their routine of lethargically considering using the tree to hang themselves, then repeat their banter that if Godot comes tomorrow "we'll be saved," then end the play deciding "let's go" but remaining immobile on the stage. Thomas's absent God will enter the scene as Jesus Present, hanging on the tree; Beckett's will stay absent, the tree untenanted and useless.

IN ANNIE DILLARD's essay 'Teaching a Stone to Talk,' a tree stands for the silence of our world. Dillard's mythic vision in the essay is that we humans banished God when, as the Israelites terrified by God's actual voice at Sinai, we begged God not to speak again, and he agreed. But in silencing God, she reasons, we silenced all of nature. It won't speak a word to us now, even though we try to call God back. To dramatize our human situation in this mute world, Dillard takes us at the end of the essay to the Galápagos Islands, where she sees in their characteristic tree, the palo santo (literally, "holy stick"), a symbol of silent witness. "Thin, pale, wispy," the palo santos appear "leafless, paralyzed, and mute," though like *Godot*'s dead-looking tree, they do sprout a "few meager deciduous leaves." Watching silently over a landscape she calls "godfor-saken," as unresponsive as Thomas's Welsh countryside, the palo santos become for Dillard "emblems" of our own muteness in the face of the mute world we've made. "I see us all as *palo santo* trees, holy sticks, together watching all that we watch, and growing in silence."

The final paragraph of her essay picks up language from Genesis and Revelation, the first and last books of the Bible, to identify the silence both with the world before creation and with "the alpha and the omega" who is Christ. And she ends with Paul's imperative from 1 Thessalonians 5:15, which in the context of the poets I've been considering seems to merge Thomas on his knees with Czeslaw Milosz concluding that all we can do "on the mute earth" is to "plod on with hope."

> The silence is all there is. It is the alpha and the omega. It is God's brooding over the face of the waters; it is the blended note of the ten thousand things, the whine of wings. You take a step in the right direction to pray to this silence, and even to address the prayer to "World." Distinctions blur. Quit your tents. Pray without ceasing.[20]

EIGHT

Between Absence and Presence

Playing Around with Jesus

Song for Holy Saturday

When His tears ran down like blood
I was sleeping in my clothes

When they struck Him with a reed
I cracked a very clever joke

When they gave Him a shirt of blood
I praised the colour of her dress

All the way up the hill
We were laughing fit to kill

When they were driving in the nails
I listened to the steel guitar

When they gave Him gall to drink
We were sipping the same glass

When He cried aloud in pain
We were playing Judases

When the ground began to shake
We pulled up the coverlet

Clean confessed and comforted
To the midnight mass I come

You who died in pain alone
Break my heart break my heart
Deus sine termino.[1]

This 1958 poem by New Zealander James K. Baxter jabs its stabbing couplets at our modern distractedness, perhaps the prime spiritual problem of our time. In 'The Maori Jesus,' discussed in chapter 5, Baxter mocks the contemporary world's blindness to God in its midst. Here in 'Song for Holy Saturday,' he puts himself right at dead center of the target he's shooting darts at. The poem works well as keynote for one of the ways that poets see us playing around with Jesus: while Jesus is very much present, they find, it is we who are absent, fooling around to keep from paying attention to what his presence means. Later in the chapter, I look at another sort of playfulness, in poems where Jesus himself is the jokester who pops up to surprise us in unexpected places. The keynote poem there is one in which Jesus is cast as a comedian.

This chapter might be seen as a comic interlude between Jesus Absent and Jesus Present. Not that play between absence and presence is confined to the few poems I'll touch on here. For instance, R. S. Thomas, great poet of the absent God, has a powerful sense of God's presence as well. But in the poems of this chapter, the interplay between absence and presence takes on a tone that in one sense or another is comic, though as Baxter's 'Song' already shows, the comedy can be quite dark.

It's fascinating to find two of Baxter's metaphors for our inattention—sleeping and playing games at the foot of the Cross—also in a Russian poem of about the same time. Yevgeny Vinokurov (1925–) in his poem 'In the Dresden Gallery,' puts himself in a painting of Golgotha in which the spectators doze through the Crucifixion and awake to a circus scene turning "as if on a carousel," while "Sadducees, / Quibbling about good and evil, pass by."[2] Our ironically twisted preoccupations in the face of the Cross are Baxter's point, too. His stinging wordplay lashes each couplet like a whip at our follies: we crack jokes as the reed strikes His back; the steel guitar's music diverts us from the crucifying nails; and so on.

But the major twentieth-century poet of our absence to Jesus' presence is W. H. Auden (1907–1973), who is also, not coincidentally, modern English poetry's master of dry wit. In Auden's two extended sacred works, his poem cycles *For the Time Being* (1941–42) and *Horae Canonicae* (1949–54), he exposes the games we play to keep from attending to what truly matters. In *For the Time Being*, subtitled *A Christmas Oratorio*, what matters is the Incarnation; in *Horae Canonicae*, it's the Crucifixion. These two events, the works insist, aren't just historical realities of a bygone time. The Incarnated and Crucified God is present in every moment of our individual and collective being. But, as Auden had put it in his still popular poem 'Musée des Beaux Arts' (1938), we merely cast an indifferent glance at "the miraculous birth" and "the dreadful martyrdom" as we go about our daily business.[3]

For the Time Being actually dramatizes many more responses to the miraculous birth than inattention. In a tour de force of play with contemporary sociopolitical, moral, and philosophical discourses, Auden transposes the Gospel Nativity story to Europe on the eve of World War II, turning the Shepherds, for example, into factory workers brainwashed by Marx, and Herod into a mimic of both Marcus Aurelius and the modern bureaucrat smoothly rationalizing his Slaughter of the Innocents. Since I can't pause here over each of the oratorio's movements, as a guide through their brilliance I highly recommend Anthony Hecht's chapter on *For the Time Being* in his analytical book on Auden's poetry, *The Hidden Law*. The one speech I do want to settle briefly into is the Narrator's concluding reflection, where Auden himself settles into the voice, in Hecht's terms, "of the beleaguered believer . . . who is thought to be an eccentric and a freak by the vast body of secular society."[4] This was the role Auden cast himself in at this time. He had recently returned to the Anglican Church at the age of thirty-two, after losing interest in it as an adolescent, though his childhood church experience had been happy. *For the Time Being* was his public announcement of himself as a religious poet, and he uses the Narrator's final speech to draw out some implications of being a believer in a secular age.

"Well, so that is that," the Narrator begins his conclusion to the Christmas story, already suggesting in this tone of shrugging sigh that the miraculous birth won't have made much of a difference. We haven't even been able to love all our relatives who came to Christmas dinner, he sardonically notes. We pack up the decorations, aware that

> Once again
> As in previous years we have seen the actual Vision and failed
> To do more than entertain it as an agreeable
> Possibility, once again we have sent Him away,
> Begging though to remain His disobedient servant,
> The promising child who cannot keep His word for long.

"Once again we have sent Him away." Other Christian poets around the same time were composing variations on this theme. Most famously, T. S. Eliot's Magi and Simeon had in effect "sent Him away," though decidedly not as an "agreeable" possibility. As many readers have noted, Eliot's 'Journey of the Magi' (1927) and 'A Song for Simeon' (1928) are striking for the pall they cast over the Nativity. Their speakers see mainly death in this birth. Eliot has his Magi find the Incarnation disagreeable because, as they rightly see, it will require them to die, themselves, to their own comfortably sensual lives, a self-sacrifice they'd rather not make. As for Simeon, he is sad because he won't live to see the full vision promised by Christ's birth, though what prevents his fulfillment, Eliot implies, is his own inadequacy. Apprehensive and depressed, Eliot's Simeon represents a twentieth-century mode of shrinking from the Christian vision out of fear of not being able to live up to it. A less well-known instance of how "Once again we have sent Him away" is the poem 'Jesus Leaves Nazareth Forever' by Hungarian poet Istvan Sinka (1897–1967). Conflating various Gospel scenes where Jesus is rejected by his own countrymen, Sinka presents the villagers as too weighed down by their copper dishes and Persian rugs to be able to do more than glance with amazement as Jesus' "otherworldly radiance" moves past them, driven out of town by their stubborn indifference.[5]

Auden's sense that "we have sent Him away" has a touch of each of these attitudes, but his Narrator's taut wordplay weaves in more. The pun in our merely "entertaining" the possibility of the Vision mocks the lightness with which we act out the role of believer—and Auden's "we" does implicate us all—without committing ourselves to its consequences. Our ambivalence is further exposed in the jokes on our begging "to remain His *dis*obedient servant" and in our being the punningly "promising child": the child who shows promise (has potential) yet can't keep its promise (we can't keep our word). The wordplay doubles and redoubles in the rest of the line, practically rolling over itself with further teasing, as the promise we can't keep turns out to be not *our* word at all, but "His word," biblical shorthand, of course, for Jesus, the Word of God made flesh in the Incarnation. Continuing beyond the passage quoted, the Narrator elaborates on what keeps us from keeping His word. In the stable, Auden writes, borrowing from Martin Buber, "for once in our lives / Everything became a You and nothing was an It." But we're pulled away from that ideal relation by forces whose entanglement Auden dramatizes by toying with the language of the oratorio's title. The title phrase slips in first by way of an idiom so common that we scarcely notice it (which is Auden's point): "But, for the time being, here we all are." The tone of this "for the time being" is the same shrug as the Narrator's opening "so that is that." And where we all are is the ambiance of the secular city: "Of darning and the Eight-fifteen, where Euclid's geometry / and Newton's mechanics would account for our experience." It's the rationalist world which presumes to explain everything quite well, thank you, without the archaic inconveniences of religious belief. Entangling the believer further to pull him away from "the actual Vision" are his own inevitable doubts and sense of inadequacy, exacerbated by routine daily distractions ("bills to be paid, machines to keep in repair"), in the midst of which a "Time Being" startles us. Capitalized twice within twenty lines, the title phrase now makes us do a double take. Right there, in the idiom that had entered the poem as a casual shrug, is the transcendent meaning that we can't seem to attend to: "the Time Being to redeem / From insignificance." So the oratorio's title becomes a dedication: the poem is *for* the Time Being, for the very Being that gives meaning to Time. Yet the idiomatic usage remains in tension with the transcendent: our distractedness from the already redeemed Time is what makes it necessary for the Time to be redeemed anew from insignificance each instant.

Redeeming the Time is of course also the theme of Eliot's *Four Quartets,* which were just being published as Auden was composing *For the Time Being.* So Auden would have been consciously playing his own sense of Time against Eliot's. For our subject of poetic configurations of Jesus, what's noteworthy in the comparison is how Eliot keeps Jesus almost completely out of his poem. For this reason I don't discuss *Four Quartets* here. Though considered the twentieth century's preeminent Christian poem in English, it takes its inspiration not from the Gospels or their central character but from Dante, from the Anglican liturgy (most notably in Jesus' sole appearance, in 'East Coker,' as wounded surgeon who becomes Holy Communion), and from the Christian and Hindu mystical

Detail, Last Call (At the Shepherd Park Go Go Club) *(1983–88), by Fred Folsom (United States, 1945–). In his colossal* Last Call, *six feet high and eighteen feet across, Folsom creates a world teeming with the raucous self-absorption of ninety distinctly realized individuals. But like poets Baxter and Auden, Folsom sees Jesus offering his redemptive presence in the midst of our distractedness. Here in the painting's lower right corner—where a policeman shines his flashlight onto evidence, just outside the frame, of a crime that appears to be the Crucifixion—Christ's wounded hand raises the cup of his blood into the scene. It is the punned "last call" at the night club: a call for the saving drink, always available for those who choose to heed it. By permission of the artist.*

tradition. Eliot's vision is really that of classical mysticism, where the meaning of life lies in dying to self. Since such self-surrender can happen only in particular moments—in a particular place and time where, paradoxically, eternity breaks in—the intersection of timelessness and time is Eliot's motif. It is Auden's, too, though this common way of referring to the theme of *Four Quartets* doesn't quite fit for Auden, whose interest is much more in the horizontal plane of each redeemed moment. I'm thinking here of the sociopolitical dimension of Auden's work: his lifelong concern with the interaction between public and private worlds, his sharp analysis of the self-delusion that weaves through both. Much taken (with many of his generation) by Freud, Auden saw early that Freudian terms like "neurosis" had a social application. He became a master at poetic devices for exposing our personal complicity in what ails society at large. The famous Audenesque ironic turns of phrase, the syntactical convolutions, the brilliant array of ultrasophisticated rationalizing voices: all are in top form in his other major work on what we do with the time that has been redeemed for us, *Horae Canonicae*.

The redeemed time that marks our daily moments is right in the cycle's title, as it was in a different way in *For the Time Being*. The *Horae Canonicae* are the seven canonical hours of the Western Church, which Auden takes as the names of his individual poems: Prime, Terce, Sext, Nones, Vespers, Compline, and Lauds. Auden follows the tradition of placing Prime at 6 A.M, with the succeeding poems set at three-hour intervals, so that Sext at noon and Nones at 3 P.M. span the time of the Crucifixion in the Gospel accounts. Auden's 'Nones,' at the hour of Jesus' death, calls attention particularly to "the blood / Of our sacrifice . . . already / Dry on the grass," but calls attention to it in order, really, to call attention to our inattention, our tangled awareness and denial of our complicity in its violence.

A personal experience of shocked recognition of our human capacity for violence had been the immediate impetus for Auden's return to the Church, so he wasn't merely theorizing in this poem. The recognition had come at a Manhattan movie theater in November, 1939, during a scene from a Nazi propaganda film showing the invasion of Poland. At the sight of Poles on the screen, some of the audience shouted "Kill them!"—and Auden was overcome by despair at the depth of our human depravity. His spiritual response was to resume going to church, sensing that the only force powerful enough to overcome such human evil—in his own unconscious as in everyone's—was Christian atonement and forgiveness.[6] His literary response included the poem 'Nones,' first published along with 'Prime' in his 1951 collection *Nones,* a book he dedicated to his new like-minded friends, Reinhold and Ursula Niebuhr. Adding the other hours to complete the *Horae Canonicae,* Auden filled out his meditation on our human propensity for violence that makes us, in effect, recrucify Christ every day.

But though the Crucified God is the motivating Presence in the poem sequence, Auden can't directly look either at the Crucifixion or at his personal relation to it. He comments in his prose collection *The Dyer's Hand* that confessional poetry in the mode of Donne or Hopkins makes him uneasy. This doesn't mean that Auden doesn't acknowledge his own guilt. Quite the contrary. "[M]y name / Stands for my historical share of care / For a lying self-made city," says the speaker in 'Prime.' But Auden felt that a religious witness in our time must be indirect. So, for instance, the speaker of 'Prime' is only one of *Horae Canonicae's* narrative voices, which shift between "I," "we," and "he," in a typically Audenesque interlacing of the personal and the public. And in another device of indirection, Auden avoids actually naming Jesus or Christ. This deliberate omission isn't, however, a sign of Jesus' Absence, as it was for the poets discussed in the previous chapter. Rather, for Auden, it's a sign of *our* Absence to his Presence: we can't bear to look at, to name, the need for and means of our redemption. So throughout the poems of *Horae Canonicae,* the Crucified Jesus is Present as this unnamed fixed point of reference, the "victim" whom we, in the ordinary round of doings in the modern city, kill daily without letting ourselves acknowledge what in fact we have done "between noon and three." A nice late-afternoon siesta wipes out our memory of shouting with the crowd for his death; waking refreshed, "we have time / To misrepresent, excuse, deny, / Mythify, use this event / While, under a hotel bed, in prison, / Down wrong turnings, its meaning / Waits for our lives."

So Auden has us, as Baxter puts it in 'Song for Holy Saturday,' cracking clever jokes and playing self-deluding games at the foot of the cross, or just "pull[ing] up the coverlet" to escape into our dream worlds. In their images of sleeping and of joking around as versions of absence, both poets (Auden more ambitiously, linking the societal dimension to the personal) are putting their fingers, in the form of their darkly comic lines, on the contemporary West's major spiritual problem of distractedness. In an early review of *For the Time Being* and *The Sea and the Mirror* (Auden's verse exploration of a Christian concept of art), Louise Bogan offered terms that would apply later to *Horae Canonicae* as well: "The two poems, taken together, constitute the most minute dissection of the spiritual illness of our day that any modern poet, not excluding Eliot, has given us."[7] Bogan wrote this more than a half-century ago, but I think her terms fit our own time, because our modes of communal distraction have multiplied and internetted so all-absorbingly that our daily round gets tied up in the illusion of total worldwide connectedness, while our personal schedules keep us dashing from meeting to meeting, car phones at one ear, radio chatter (which Auden was appalled by from its inception) in the other. As remedy for our own frenzy of distractedness at the millennium's turn, more and more people, at least in the United States, are discovering the sanity of contemplative monasteries (sometimes, in a nice irony, through the monasteries' Web sites). Of the many recent books recounting such finds, Kathleen Norris's *Dakota: A Spiritual Geography* (1993) stands out for its surprise bestseller status, a clear indication that Norris is speaking to a larger cultural need. Indeed, all these years after its publication, every copy of *Dakota* in my city's library system continues to be charged out. Norris (1947–) was raised a Presbyterian, but when she stumbled across St. John's Abbey in Collegeville, Minnesota, her life and her poetry were transformed. During two nine-month stays at the abbey, she absorbed the tranquilly bubbling joy of the Benedictine routine, which is paced—as Auden would have appreciated—by communal prayer of the canonical hours. I single out Norris's discovery of this antidote to modern distractedness, because her poem 'Luke 14: A Commentary' is my keynote for this chapter's second half: playing with Jesus where he is the jokester, popping up to surprise us.

Luke 14: A Commentary

He is there, like Clouseau,
at the odd moment,
just right: when he climbs
out of the fish pond
into which he has spectacularly
fallen, and says condescendingly
to his hosts, the owners
of the estate: "I fail
where others succeed." You know
this is truth. You know
he'll solve the mystery,

unprepossessing
as he is, the last
of the great detectives.
He'll blend again into the scenery, and
more than once, be taken
for the gardener. "Come

now," he says, taking us
for all we're worth: "sit
in the low place."
Why not? we ask, so easy
to fall for a man
who makes us laugh. "Invite those
you do not know, people

you'd hardly notice." He puts
us on, we put him on; another
of his jokes. "There's
room," he says. The meal is
good, absurdly
salty, but delicious. Charlie

Chaplin put it this way: "I want to play
the role of Jesus. I look the part.
I'm a Jew.
And I'm a comedian."[8]

I have to confess that I can't read this poem without smiling. Though I've
read it literally dozens of times, each reading delights me anew. Norris has managed, at least to my mind, to give her readers the very experience she's talking
about: of being gloriously surprised by a Jesus who entertains us by saving us
and saves us by entertaining us. She does this, first, by catching us off guard with
her opening simile: "He is there, like Clouseau." This Jesus is unquestionably
Present, but in a guise we'd never have guessed: as a film comedian who plays
the role of bumbling detective. From then on, the poem tumbles through line
after line of wordplay that is at once fun and profound, teasing theological
depths out of everyday idioms in such a disarmingly bright way that we can only
gasp out a laughing "Wow!" by the end—which is precisely the experience
Norris wants to give us of Jesus.

I won't try to point to every one of Norris's jokes. But I'll note a few that open
our eyes to dimensions of Jesus' character that are in Scripture and traditional
Christology but which, Norris is showing, we don't appreciate the wonder of.
Casting Jesus as comic detective, she can say he does indeed "solve the mystery"
of the meaning of our lives; he can be billed, Alpha and Omega that he is, as "the
last of the great detectives"; he could apply the comic twist "I fail where others
succeed" to all his apparent failures in the Gospel narratives, culminating in the
scandalous failure of the Cross. Among the idioms that Norris turns into theological puns, there is Jesus' "taking us / for all we're worth," and there is our
"fall[ing] for a man / who makes us laugh" by falling, himself, into the fish pond
of humanity. It's a splashing Incarnation that wins over our hearts. And there is
the multiple punning of "He puts / us on, we put him on," which reminds me of
Ephrem's fourth-century wordplay with the paradoxes of the Incarnation: in the
idiom for teasing as "putting someone on," Norris uncovers both the classic formulation that Jesus has put on our humanity and St. Paul's imperative that we put
on (clothe ourselves in) Christ. Norris has also slipped some Gospel allusions, clev-
erly, like clues, into the film set of a backyard garden party by the pool. Merged
with the wedding party scene of the poem's title, where Jesus advises us to take
the low place, are some of his other surprising sayings that turn conventions upside down: the wedding parable at which people are pulled in off the street; the
promise of room for all in his Father's mansion. And wrapping it all up, as in the
best farce, is the layering of roles and disguises: Jesus is Clouseau playing a detective who is taken for the gardener who is (in the post-Resurrection appearance to
Mary Magdalene) Jesus himself, who—finally—Charlie Chaplin wants to play.

To my knowledge, 'Luke 14: A Commentary' is Norris's most extensive poetic treatment of Jesus. Her poetry has increasingly focused on spiritual figures,

especially since her stays during the early 1990s at St. John's Abbey, where many of her poems of this period take place. But figures like Mary, Eve, Wisdom, angels, and the saints populate her poems more than the person of Jesus does. And Jesus' appearances tend to be oblique. Typical is the way he enters in 'True Love,' the final poem of Norris's cycle called 'Mysteries of the Incarnation.'[9] At the end of a lighthearted list of lovers, including "Sampson / and Delilah" and "Noah / and Mrs.," is "The Magdalene, / the gardener," followed by Norris's conclusion in the playfully down-home mid-western tone that she has made a hallmark of her verse: "God help us, / we are God's chosen now." The First Epistle of John says famously "we are God's children now," but Norris makes us more by the simple changing of a word. After that startling appearance of the Risen Jesus to Magdalene, Norris is saying, we're simply stuck being God's beloved. That appearance of Jesus as gardener also figures in 'Luke 14: A Commentary,' where he blends into the scenery as if playing hide and seek. Clearly Norris likes this Gospel episode for its hint of how the numinous works (or plays) in our world, flashing out for a surprise transformative instant.

Her poem 'Hide and Seek' makes this very process its subject. The title metaphor appears first as a lightning flash over the field where the monastic community at St. John's is about to bury one of their number, Brother Louis. The poem then moves through a string of metaphorical hide-and-seek experiences, like lightning flashes, to end with thanks "for unsearchable riches / that reach into our lives, love / calling us by name." Yet these last lines of the poem aren't quite its end, because that "love" circles us back to the poem's epigraph, which is a line from Brother Louis himself: "Your true and only Son is love." This is about as indirect an entry as Jesus could make into a poem. Yet without that hide-and-seek appearance of the Son as "love calling us by name," the poem would lose its meaning, which is precisely this incarnational grounding. When asked in an interview about how living at the abbey had influenced her, Norris answered that one effect had been to reveal metaphor to her in a new way, because "when you've got a religion based on the Incarnation, you can't afford to say that metaphor is not important."[10] The Incarnation itself is metaphor, she goes on, not in the sense that it's untrue but "in the sense that it yokes the human and the divine. That's what metaphor does; it's yoking two disparate elements." And in 'Hide and Seek,' many more than two.

The other impact of living at the abbey that Norris mentions is "going to liturgy every day. Really getting into that rhythm has changed my life" and "had a profound effect on my writing." I had sensed this effect in the poems of *Little Girls in Church*, her 1995 collection, even before coming across this interview. I heard them as liturgical poetry, by which I mean not that they're intended for liturgical use but that they feel like Benedictine liturgy. If seven times a day, you chant the psalms and hear a passage read from Scripture, the rhythm of that enormous range of human emotion taken up into prayer inevitably seeps into your whole being. Auden draws on this rhythm in *Horae Canonicae*, though he is using it as an intellectual structure, without the absorption of it into his whole being that marks Norris's work of the 1990s. What she has absorbed isn't just the phrases from Scripture, which are embedded now in her verse, but the entire tone of Benedictine spirituality: its joy that bubbles up from the depths of that daily round, bursting into lighthearted laughter at the most unexpected times. I remember waiting once in the dark chapel of a Trappistine monastery for the nuns to enter for Compline (the Trappists are a reformed Benedictine order, and the Trappistines are their communities of women) and suddenly hearing an outburst of the heartiest laughter from an adjoining room. It was the nuns responding to a talk, perhaps by their abbess, but in that setting I heard it as the exploding delight of the angels singing God's praise. A verse in the middle of her poem 'Land of the Living' shows that Norris has had similar experiences:

> Earlier tonight, a young monk, laughing,
> splashed my face
> with holy water. Then, just as unexpectedly,
> he flew down a banister, and
> for one millisecond
> was an angel—robed,
> without feet—
> all irrepressibly joy
> and good news.

The splash of holy water is the bedtime blessing that all monks and guests receive on exiting a Benedictine monastery chapel after Compline, the last communal prayer of the day.

This poem brings us to another important dimension of Norris's spiritual aesthetic, because the poem begins: "Menstruation is primitive, / no getting around that fact, as / I wipe my blood from the floor / at 3 A.M. in the monastery guest room." Any poem that starts with menstrual blood on the floor is announcing itself as a "women's poem" in the sense developed in the twentieth century's final decades. Menstruation, menopause, childbirth, sex from a woman's viewpoint: these uniquely female experiences were embraced as subjects beginning with the women's liberation movement of the late 1960s. Being of Norris's generation, I remember how liberating it did feel to talk and write openly about these things, after growing up in a society that validated only male experience. At first, our openness was itself the point; Norris's own poems of the 1970s are very much women's poems of this sort. By now, most of us don't feel the need to make such a point of simply *having* a female perspective; rather, this perspective can enter as a dimension of insight that also encompasses more. 'Land of the Living' is a grand example of "women's poetry" at this mature stage of development. Menstrual blood isn't the whole point; it's the starting point for a flow of thought that merges the having (and not having) of children, the laughing monk transformed into an angel, and—in an unexpected way—the Child Jesus.

Musing, first, on that menstrual blood on the monastery floor, Norris sees it as her monthly renewal of not having children. She "celebrate[s]" this "monthly flowering / of the not-to-be"; I "let it go," she says, "without regret." Yet she also goes on to celebrate the flowering of the to-be, in the form of her baby niece in a photo on her mirror, sitting "like the Christ Child / on her mother's lap," looking "amused, and wise" in her "blood-red dress." The surprise of Jesus' entry in this simile isn't of course in the likeness of the poet's sister and niece to a Madonna and Child; thousands of such likenesses have been drawn in literature and art. The surprise is in the image dressing the Christ Child in the color of blood specifically identified as menstrual. With this image, the poem's various celebrations of "letting go" flow together: the poet's letting go of having children, letting herself gladly be "a useless woman"; Jesus' letting go *into* a woman, evoked in an icon of "the black madonna . . . / expectant" with the "good news" that joyfully bursts from the laughing monk; and this monk, "young," whose letting go of having children and even of sex the poet brings into her monthly celebration of the not-to-be as into a liturgical rite, complete with the psalm chant about seeing God's goodness "in the land of the living" of the poem's title. In this richly alive context, the "amused, and wise" smile of the poet's niece as Christ Child seems to be her/his secret knowledge of the metaphorical oneness of these celebratory renunciations.

Kathleen Norris's writing of the 1990s is special for these links it has discovered between women's experience and monastic spirituality.[11] Common to both, she has found, is a groundedness in the basics of nurturing life, a rootedness that works well with her poetic persona's voice of down-home common sense. Many of her poems take place in the kitchen, where she celebrates women's connectedness across generations, often obliquely through apparently trivial objects or quirky habits. The quotidian, her poems say, is full of surprise wonders, if you only know how to see them. In 'Kitchen Trinity' the poet, her mother, and her grandmother become the three divine persons in Rublev's famous icon of the Trinity, which conflates them with the angels who, in the Genesis story, announce Sarah's unexpected pregnancy and so make her (this is the poem's final word) "laugh."

In a 1996 article on Seamus Heaney's poetry, Suzanne Keen comments that Heaney shows us being "caught off-guard by the marvelous."[12] I love her phrase for its catching a typically turn-of-the-millennium spirituality. After a century of taking the rationalist, secular world for granted—that is, of assuming that what we see is what we get—any sight of more, of a marvelous beyond the material realm, is bound to catch us off guard. We're going about our daily business—fixing breakfast or sitting in a committee meeting or shopping at the mall—when: boom! Reality bursts open, the impossible suddenly appears right in front of us, and with Norris's Sarah, we let out an astonished laugh. "You'll be struck dumb / by the ordinary," writes U.S. poet David Craig, who has taken such moments as his subject, "and everything, / will start to matter" ('The Apprentice Prophecies').[13]

The surprise discovery of the sacred in the ordinary is the special gift of a century of unbelief. Precisely because religious faith is no longer assumed, it isn't dull or obligatory, as it had become for the Victorians and their counterparts in other Western countries. It teases, it lures, it intrigues. Such is the story that contemporary novelists are starting to tell, according to critic John McClure, who has been charting the narratives of rediscovery by Don DeLillo, Toni Morrison, Michael Ondaatje, and others.[14] And since the middle of the century we've had the stories of Flannery O'Connor, a master of revealing the mystery lurking in the midst of our ordinary preoccupations. O'Connor didn't take the mystery lightly: toying with the divine was like playing with fire, she thought. Yet her comedy of the grotesque makes both funny and terrifying the experience of the sacred breaking into our private, self-absorbed worlds. Her Holy Ghost is always playing tricks on her characters, pulling their complacent rugs out from under them and leaving them startled in midair, holding their breath and hoping against hope that Someone will swoop a soft cushion under them to ease their inevitable fall.

The poetic world I think is closest to O'Connor's is that of Annie Dillard (1945–). Both writers evoke a genuine terror at the sacred power that catches us off guard, yet within their terror is a comic vision, because what catches us off-guard is ultimately God's love. This comic vision of Dillard's isn't limited to her poetry—an expression of it that has won many readers' hearts is her essay 'An Expedition to the Pole'—but I'll stick to her poetic expressions of it here. Dillard's world is one where we're always blinking in wonder, doing double takes, and being tossed head over heels as the sacred pops up to surprise us. When personalized, the entry of the sacred into Dillard's world does take the form of Jesus (not, as for O'Connor, the Holy Spirit), though he comes in an array of disguises, games, and jokes.

One whole poem that's a joke on how we can never get hold of Jesus is 'The Sign of the Father,' in Dillard's collection of "found poems," *Mornings Like This* (1995). The poem takes scraps from an authentic scholarly text, *New Testament Apocrypha,* and brilliantly rearranges them to show, as Dillard says in a prefatory note, "the absurdly fragmentary nature of spiritual knowledge."[15] I won't quote from the poem because it needs to be read as a whole for its effect: Jesus and his sayings appear in tantalizing snatches, then disppear into an ellipsis or a half-gone word, in a teasing game of hide-and-seek.

Dillard loves the challenge of seeing a poem as a game; I like to imagine her delight at the challenge she took on in a poem that plays a very different sort of trick with Jesus: 'The Man Who Wishes to Feed on Mahogany.'[16] The poem's epigraph is a quotation from a 1969 interview with Borges: "Chesterton tells us that if someone wished to feed exclusively on mahogany, poetry would not be able to express this. Instead, if a man happens to love and not be loved in return, or if he mourns the absence or loss of someone, then poetry is able to express these feelings precisely because they are commonplace." Taking up this quote as a gauntlet thrown down—as if she'd laughingly replied, Oh, so poetry can't express that man's wish to feed on mahogany?—Dillard has composed a stately blank verse poem in which she presents the man's wish as a deep, tender love for the absent adored one. Then, in a metaphorical tour de force, the man and his beloved mahogany turn before our eyes both into a figure for Jesus, whose love for "my fellow creature" weighs so heavily that it "holds him here, / . . . nails him to the world," and into us, we creatures who return his love so longingly that we "desire to drink and sup at mahogany's mass."

Such transformations are right up Dillard's alley. Anything is possible in the world as she sees it: a man craving mahogany is simply no big deal. And what makes anything possible, she implies in two Christmas poems, is the Incarnation. It is *because* God does the wonderfully crazy thing of "emptying" himself into human form, both poems suggest, that all wildly improbable comings-to-life can happen. In 'Christmas,' "tin canisters eat / their cookies; . . . My wrist-watch grows / obscurely, sun- / flower big. . . . Dolls in the hospital / with brains of coral / jerk, breathe and are born." In the Christmas section of 'Feast Days: Thanksgiving—Christmas,' not only do animals talk at midnight ("of course," the poem grinningly shrugs), but "the soil and fresh-water lakes / also rejoice, / as do products / such as sweaters / (nor are plastics excluded / from grace)."

One of the epigraphs in 'Feast Days: Thanksgiving—Christmas' is as follows:

> *Woman, why weepest thou?*
> *Whom seekest thou?*
> —John

With these words of the Risen Jesus to Mary Magdalene, Dillard adds the wonder of the Resurrection to the reasons why anything imaginable can now happen. Dillard is alluding to this Gospel episode where Jesus is "taken / for the gardener," as Kathleen Norris put it in 'Luke 14: A Commentary,' for the same purpose as Norris: their Jesus will pull any trick to wow us. You think you're talking to the gardener, but—oops—it's God. And because it's God, Dillard wants us to realize, you just never know what you might be seeing. Since "God takes the substance, contours / of a man . . . / dying, rising, walking, / and still walking / wherever there is motion" ('Feast Days'), then wherever there is motion anything can move into a different form. Dillard's world is populated by transformations as wild as Ovid's: people turn into animals that turn into plants that turn into gods and back again. The marvelous is always catching us off guard, as Dillard sees it, because that's the only way it will catch us at all.

Dillard's whole enterprise as a writer is to make us marvel. But she's sure that the sacred is too stupendous for us to stare at directly; we can handle only glimpses, and even these usually come in disguise. A favorite poetic trope of hers begins "Once." Once, she'll write, I was doing some ordinary thing (going to the door, digging in the garden) when up popped the utterly extraordinary (the last of the Inca kings in her bathroom, in her hallway an ape wearing her nightgown). Such astonishing moments form the very plot of Dillard's long poem 'Tickets for a Prayer Wheel,' which I'd rate with Auden's *Horae Canonicae* as one of the major spiritual works of twentieth-century English poetry, not least because both are immensely accessible and engaging. In Dillard's poem, a family is trying to figure out how to pray—that is, how to call on the sacred—while the sacred is already swarming through their house, meeting them in wacky disguise at every turn. The poem is simultaneously low comedy and high: low in the slapstick of planting beans on the bookshelf or bumping on the stairs into Saint Irenaeus wearing a necklace of macaws; high in Dante's sense of the *Commedia* as a vision of everything in the cosmos held harmoniously together by a divine love so dazzling that the poet can only break into joyous laughter, in the *Paradiso,* at its flaming brilliance. God swirls through the house of Dillard's poem, taking the form of wind in the beds, or of a picture of the universe that grabs the viewer into its heart, or of Christ:

> We keep our paper money shut
> in a box, for fear of fire.
> Once, we opened the box
> and Christ the lamb stepped out
> and left his track of flame across the floor.
>
> Why are we shown these things?

NINE

Jesus Present

As I was starting to think about this final chapter, a critically acclaimed anthology of contemporary Christian poetry was published: *Upholding Mystery,* compiled by David Impastato. I wrote to Impastato to ask: Is Jesus a prominent figure for these fifteen important English-language poets whom you include? His response was fascinating. If you mean the *person* of Jesus, he wrote back, the answer is no. If you mean an *incarnational presence* in our midst, the answer is yes indeed.

The distinction wouldn't have made sense in Christianity before Romanticism. Incarnation, literally "en-flesh-ment," refers in religions to an embodiment of the divine, a form or figure of transcendence present in the material world. Whereas in Hinduism—to take the contrasting example of a religion finding the divine manifested in a multitude of figures—incarnational presence takes almost countless forms, Incarnation for classical Christianity has meant the unique embodiment of the divine in the person of Jesus. Hence Christianity's capitalized Incarnation. Although Christianity has long seen the whole created world as sacralized by Jesus' taking on human flesh (Ephrem's fourth-century poetry can't stop marveling at the process), no early Christian poet would have conceived of this sacralization without Jesus explicitly at the core. Yet contemporary Christian poets are commonly conceiving of just such a distinction; this was Impastato's point.

In several letters back and forth, we discussed this intriguing situation. Christian poets surely know the Gospels. But in their poetry, by and large, they haven't been drawing on Gospel scenes or the central Gospel character. While their poetry witnesses strongly to what's often called "the sacramentality of the ordinary," that is, to incarnational presence in the sense of God's immanence in everyday life, they are reconceiving this presence through other figures, other images, than that of the Christian incarnational figure.

Richard Wilbur (1921–) is an outstanding example. His poetic vision is grounded in the stuff of the tangible world, in which he sees "the intuitions of the spirit," as he put it in a radio talk in the 1960s.[1] During that talk, he read what has become probably his most popular poem, 'Love Calls Us to the Things of This World,' with its marvelous vision of clean laundry, waving on the clothesline, as angels. Wilbur's route "toward the *mysterium tremendum* leads through the quotidian realities of the world," comments Nathan Scott in his 1992 study *Visions of Presence in Modern American Poetry.* Scott calls Wilbur's religious sensibility "incarnationalist" because its "fundamental norm of consciousness," while "located in a powerful Presence beyond the mind," is "pervasively immanent within the ordinary and the commonplace." Yet Scott observes—as Impastato noted about other contemporary Christian poets—that Wilbur rarely "has recourse to a distinctively Christian idiom."[2]

To me, the most striking instance of Wilbur's deliberate avoidance of exclusively Christian terms for Presence is his poem 'A World without Objects Is a Sensible Emptiness.' The title comes from the seventeenth-century mystic and poet Thomas Traherne, named in the poem as proponent of a world-renouncing mystic way that Wilbur rejects. Wilbur's whole poem is a call to turn from the mirage of "sensible emptiness" to real objects, in which spirit truly dwells. The call is carefully dramatized as a desert journey that draws on the Christmas story but doesn't rely on recognition of the Christmas images to make itself heard. Set in a desert over which the camels of the poet's soul travel toward an elusive goal of "sensible emptiness," the poem warns them away from such chimeras, insisting that "auras, lustres, / And all shinings need to be shaped and borne." To bring in the birth of Jesus through a pun on "borne" is masterfully indirect. And the indirection continues through the imperative with which the poem, and the soul's journey, reach their end: to "wisely watch" for "the spirit's right / Oasis, light incarnate."[3] Jesus is transformationally Present in the poem, but mediated by metaphors, like that "light," which dissolve his uniqueness.

The poem, and Wilbur's poetry as a whole, shows just how in tune he is with the way his own moment in literary and cultural history draws on transcendence. "Religious art in our time," film critic Joseph Cunneen has said in reference to Polish director Krzysztof Kielowski's work, "must inevitably be a very indirect kind of testimony."[4] This is precisely the sort of testimony we've heard from poets like W. H. Auden and Kathleen Norris as well. Indirection is their chosen angle on the transcendental Presence they find in our midst. I can easily imagine the women in one of Norris's kitchen poems taking in the laundry from Wilbur's 'Love Calls Us to the Things of This World,' as their way of touching angels. It's harder to imagine Norris's women setting the table for a Jesus who walks into the poem as into the Gospel scene at Martha and Mary's house. Twentieth-century poets came to know that placing the person of Jesus in the spotlight on center stage would be to risk sending most of their audience nervously toward the exits. Indeed, it would be to risk losing the audience of journal and book editors on whom poets are dependent for gaining a public audience in the first place. Even if the poets' Jesus was traveling light, free of grand doctrinal statements, editors and readers would see him carrying the baggage of a suspect dogma.

For a very practical reason then—to gain and hold an audience—recent Christian poets tend to keep the main character of their faith offstage and let transcendence appear in other guises. Yet this isn't merely opportunism on their part. Indirection is the predominant mode of late twentieth-century poetry, whatever its subject: after modernism, writers and readers alike have been suspicious of meaning that seems too sure of itself. Especially after Eliot's *The Waste Land,* large meanings lay in shattered fragments. So as poetry began cautiously to recover meaning through the century, it was in fragments of the unobtrusive and ordinary stuff of life that meaning was most comfortably found anew. Wilbur and Norris and Auden, David Craig and Annie Dillard: we've noted their attention to the "sacramentality of the ordinary." They find touches of the transcendent in the shards of life we stumble on, like discovering faint traces of a fossil when you turn over a rock. It's as if they pick up a discarded scrap from *The Waste Land* and sit with it a while: let it rest in their palm, finger it, muse on it, and come to see transcendence somehow embedded, embodied, in it.

Understood in this way, their poetry seems a version of the spirituality called "the practice of presence" or "centering prayer," which became increasingly popular as the twentieth century neared its close. In writings by experienced spiritual guides like Thomas Merton, whose books people were buying up as if there were no tomorrow, would-be practioners were counseled to sit still each day for fifteen or twenty minutes, attending to the "holiness of the present moment." It's an age-old spiritual practice, developed most highly by Buddhism but also by the early Christian monastics of the desert. Those desert fathers, as they're referred to, insisted that Jesus Christ was the Presence to be settled into at one's spiritual core; but you won't find the recent guidebooks hammering home this point. The contemporary point is Presence, pure and simple and unpersonified. At the end of a century that began with Christianity discredited, religious institutions and doctrine remained suspect; so sitting quietly alone with transcendence, unencumbered by doctrine, was the preferred mode. Moreover, and more positively, the global consciousness that developed over the course of the century—not only in the interfaith movement, which sought value in all the world's religions, but also in the new environmental awareness—disposed people to sense a worldwide oneness, so that to "practice presence" was to be open to a single transcendent spirit enlivening people all over the globe at the same moment. By the twentieth century's end, then, people in the West were definitely more open to transcendent Presence than they'd been at the century's start; yet they tended to be the more open the less that Presence was bound to a particular religion's incarnation. Even for many practicing Christians, the late twentieth century's strong spirituality of incarnational presence was linked only weakly to the name and person of Jesus.

Yet for all this, there are twentieth-century poets for whom Jesus does embody the transcendent Presence incarnate in our midst. I want to spend the rest of the chapter with some of them, noting where their configurations of Jesus Present are shaped by the context of the century's varieties of unbelief, of searching, of openings to global religious experience. Of course, Jesus has been present throughout the century's poetry; this is precisely what we've been tracing in the book. We've seen him present as modernism's shrunken, impotent figure, his diminishment the very sign of loss of a divine glory nostalgically recalled. We've seen him present as postmodernism's radical skeptic or as its puzzle about the possibility of meaning. An archetypal Jesus has been very much present especially in non-Western cultures, where he appears as archetype of a whole people's suffering or of their hope for rebirth after a crushing political death. Indeed, a politicized Jesus has been present the world over, spokesman for causes ranging from negritude to Marxism, advocate for the downtrodden from Chili to Maori Australia. We've seen him present in Europe after each of its terrible wars, moved to near despair by the century's sins. Even his pointed absences have been defined by his presence as something either sought by the poets or gleefully cast aside.

But in the current chapter, Jesus will be a capitalized Presence. He'll be Wilbur's "light incarnate" but now frankly given its Gospel identity. This is to say that the poets gathered here are likely to be Christians. I haven't made much of the poets' religious orientation in previous chapters, because the figures of Jesus there didn't necessarily depend on the poet's faith. Some of the poets have been Christians (though with varying interpretations of what that means to them), some not. But it seems only logical that if a poet is finding incarnational presence embodied in the person of Jesus, that poet is writing out of, or at least looking toward, Christian faith. There are many such poets to choose from, so I can only hope in what follows to give a sample of their range. I think it will be fun to start off by pairing two poets who in many ways are worlds apart—the Frenchman Charles Péguy (1873–1914) and the Korean Ku Sang (1919–)—to see how, from their different ends of the century and of the globe, they fashion a poetry of Jesus Present. Then I plan to settle into the United States at the millennium's turn, to look at some of the ways that Jesus is Present to our poets. So far I've drawn only minimally on my own compatriots, because of the worldwide range of this study. But I don't want to leave the impression that our own poets haven't been energetically creative in their configurings of Presence in the person of Jesus. Moreover, as literary critics have long pointed out, Presence is a favorite theme in U.S. literature. And, especially for a figure of incarnational embodiment—Presence walking the earth, treading our own pathways—it will be nice to end close to home.

FIRST, THOUGH, TO FRANCE at the start of the century. Charles Péguy, born into a French peasant family, was always proud of these roots, though he managed to make it to college and even considered a university teaching career. Passionate and intense about whatever he did, as a young man he threw himself into starting a socialist bookstore and publishing bimonthly *Cahiers* (*Notebooks*), which he often authored as well. At around age twenty he was proclaiming himself an atheist, but fifteen years later he confided to a stunned friend, "I have found faith again. I am a Catholic."[5] No one knows what led to Péguy's conversion, but its effects soon became evident to all. He would be seen on Paris buses praying the rosary in fervent tears. And in three successive years, beginning in 1910, he published as *Cahiers* his three mammoth poetic "Mysteries" of faith: *The Mystery of the Charity of Joan of Arc, The Portal of the Mystery of the Second Virtue,* and *The Mystery of the Holy Innocents.* At the time, no one paid much attention to these extraordinary products of religious passion. Only after Péguy's death—which he characteristically threw himself into, deliberately charging into German gunfire in a battle he could easily have avoided, being at forty-one past the required age for active duty—did his *Mysteries* enter the canon as France's major religious poetic oeuvres of the century.

I've never come across anything like them in all the literature I've read. The only comparable aesthetic experience I've had is listening to the music of Péguy's compatriot Olivier Messiaen: the paradoxically intimate grandeur of a mystic vision. Messiaen's open harmonics, so original that they keep sounding fresh when heard for the hundredth time, his crafted repetition of phrases to extend time as if forever, his playful bird-calls that are his signature sound: all have their counterparts in Péguy's poetic works. The *Mysteries* do move like music. A note, a phrase, enters, is developed by extended metaphor and playful punning, expands into a meditation on its scriptural and doctrinal meaning, and returns in passages that reprise with the leisure of having all the time in the world. The similarities between the two artists are no accident. Both were seeking to give voice to eternity, but eternity as glimpsed through a Catholic mysticism in the French dogmatic mode. Ever since the Revolution, the French have been sharply divided about Christian faith. A person is either vehemently anti-Church or vehemently Christian (which usually means Catholic). Being on the defensive in an aggresively secular society, French Catholic art tends to have a dogmatic edge, a heightened certainty of tone. In both Messiaen and Péguy it booms. Yet Péguy's genius was to put his booming in the mouth of God, whom he boldly makes the speaker of much of his poetry, while tempering God's proclamations with the tenderness of a parent and the wry humor of a French peasant.

In many ways, there could hardly be a poetic voice and a Christian vision more different from Péguy's than that of Ku Sang. Nor do the patterns of their lives have much in common. Not even their lifespans overlap: Ku Sang's begins in 1919, five years after the end of Péguy's. Born in Seoul, Ku Sang moved as a child to what later became North Korea, then had to flee back to the South because of the tensions preceding the Korean War. He had started a career as a journalist, and his writing against the South's corrupt government in the 1950s landed him in jail. Ku Sang has always been a patriot. This he shares with Péguy, along with being marked by war, though this fate they share with most of the world's people in the violent century that closed the second millennium. Ku Sang and Péguy share also the experience of writing poetry as Christians in the midst of a culture that is basically incomprehending of their beliefs. Ku

Sang was born into a Catholic family, which in Asia means into a minority religion. But unlike Péguy's secular milieu, Asian culture is steeped in spirituality. The Buddhism that surrounds Ku Sang he welcomes into his work. All his verse has the agile feel of Buddhist wisdom, coming across in a lightly amused voice that's a far cry—or, better, a far whisper—from Péguy's booming. Buddhism's compassion and its perception of the world's impermanence also inform Ku Sang's poetry. So although a Christian, he is at home in his society as Péguy never could be, and it's easy to see why Ku Sang became a leader in Korean literary life.

To juxtapose the figure of Jesus in Péguy and Ku Sang is to watch his Presence unfold in lines that are worlds apart yet meet in their reach for language that can touch eternity, in their playfulness of tone (each in his own cultural idiom), even occasionally in metaphor. Here, first, is Péguy's Jesus, from the imagined viewpoint of God the Father, boasting like any peasant father of how his own son has outdone him. Péguy begins with deceptive simplicity, casually referring to the Lord's Prayer, which the Gospel Jesus taught his disciples. I say "begins," but there's really no beginning in Péguy: every passage is an excerpt, even those that open each *Mystery,* because the opening phrase will recur through the books in other passages that roll out into others. Only quoting pages and pages would be fair to Péguy's vision and voice, but I hope the following few lines can give a hint:

I am their father, says God. . . .
Our Father who art in Heaven, my son taught them that prayer. . . .
Our Father who art in Heaven, he knew very well what he was doing that day,
    my son who loved them so.
Who lived among them, who was like one of them. . . .
Who brought back to heaven a certain taste for man, a certain taste for the
    earth.
My son who loved them so, who loved them eternally in heaven.
He knew very well what he was doing that day, my son who loved them so.
When he put that barrier between them and me, *Our Father who art in
    Heaven,* those three or four words.
That barrier which my anger and perhaps my justice will never pass. . . .
Those words that move ahead of every prayer like the hands of the suppliant
    in front of his face.
Those three or four words that conquer me, the unconquerable.
Those three or four words which move forward like a beautiful cutwater
    fronting a lowly ship.
Cutting the flood of my anger.

And there you see what my son has deliberately done, God pretends to complain, though actually proud that his justified anger at sinners has been "cut" by the cutwater (Péguy's God is always punning) of his son's love for them. I am conquered, God says, moving into an image that recurs through the *Mysteries,* because my son has "tied the arms of my justice and untied the arms of my mercy." And so I'm obliged to be merciful, like that father in the story my son told them about the Prodigal Son, says God, going on to pick up the image of hands pointed in prayer as the point of a ship, the cutwater:

And the ship is my own son, laden with all the sins of the world
And the point of the ship is the two joined hands of my son. . . .
And that point is those three or four words: *Our Father who art in Heaven,*
    verily my son knew what he was doing.
And every prayer comes up to me hidden behind those three or four words
    . . .
The wake of innumerable prayers . . .
By innumerable men,
(By simple men, his brothers) . . .

"All of the huge fleet of prayer and penances attacks me" like "a combat fleet," God continues, until "I am disarmed."

It's hard to pull out of Péguy's lines once you're enthralled in them; it would be like pushing the stop button on your CD player in the middle of a symphony. The development goes on: the fleet of prayers draws in every prayer ever uttered by a petitioner (Hail Marys, morning and evening prayers, the whole lot); the father of the Prodigal Son returns "with embraces." And all because "my son . . . acquired a taste for them, and for the earth, and all that."

For Ku Sang, too, everything is transformed because God's son acquired a taste for the earth and its people. Yet Ku Sang's Jesus comes to us from a voice far removed from Péguy's. The narrative voice in Ku Sang's poetry is his own persona, and many of his poems are autobiographical. So we get Ku Sang's Jesus as revealed to the poet at particular moments. An early revelation is recounted in the untitled opening poem of his autobiographical cycle *Even the Knots on Quince Trees:*

A bridled,
foaming,
drooling
cow.

Aged four, my first revelation of really existing
found in a face like that printed by blood and sweat
on a cloth held out by a Jerusalem woman
to a man on his way to execution:
the face of a cow.

The yellow, twilit path slid up over a mountainside,
calligraphic in black and white,
I gazed at the face of the cow as it plodded along the muddy track,

and while I sat there perched on the leading cart
with an ancient cupboard roped down in the wagon behind,
my first buds of knowledge unfolded,
and I wept.[6]

To my eye, this poem could have come only from Asia: from a poetic sensibility steeped both in the calligraphic aesthetic of spare lines tracing the telling detail and in Buddhism's spirituality of compassion. The child's first awareness of his own existence comes in his perception of humiliating suffering in another. How Asian that this other is a cow. It's the adult poet, of course, not the child, who can recognize that the face of this bridled cow plodding the mountainside track was the face of Jesus on his *via crucis*—and who can see why his childhood response to the face of bridled pain was to weep. Elsewhere, too, Jesus is Present to Ku Sang as the figure of heartbreaking failure, but usually knowledge of the Resurrection transforms his tears into hope. "You are the ultimate failure," the poet says to Jesus in the poem 'Jesus of Nazareth,' and I'm "united with you from my mother's womb," a union that sometimes can be, he adds with colloquial lightness hard to translate, "a nuisance." But you also, the poem comes to say, putting Jesus' accomplishment in the context of the East's characteristic perception of impermanence, "bore witness by your Resurrection" to "Love's imperishability." By embracing our creaturely suffering, you overturned all our rational computations of sin and merit, the poet says, making the same orthodox Christian point as Péguy's God does. And for both poets, this forgiving Presence right in creation forges an identity with the poet's own being. Ku Sang has a poem explicitly on the subject, 'The true appearance of the Word,' where he perceives this identity in terms of the Buddhist motif of ignorance and revelation that appears in the poem about the cow. "As the cataract of ignorance falls / from off the eyesight of my soul, / I realize that all this huge Creation / round about me is the Word" and that, through "a mysterious grace of the Word," my own words, "my muttering," is "Reality itself."

Jesus is Present as this intimately transforming Word for Péguy as well, though most of the words, the lines, of each poet are so culture-specific as to be hard to imagine in the works of the other. It's not only a matter of their styles: Ku Sang's spare Eastern delicacy contrasted to Péguy's expansive attempt to get his arms around all of Church doctrine. Even most of the images through which Jesus is Present to each would be utterly out of place in the other's *oeuvre*. Jesus as cow is an image inconceivable for Péguy's elevated Christology; Jesus as the prow of a warship is an image impossible for Ku Sang's gentleness. So it's all the more instructive to find them sharing one particular image—a bud/flower cluster—for Jesus and his Presence in our world.

We'd probably expect to see the buds in Ku Sang, as his native Eastern art is fond of this natural image of delicate potential. The book that contains most of his explicitly Christian poems is entitled *Mysterious Buds,* but they are everywhere. Usually, as in the "first buds of knowledge unfolded" in the poem about the cow, the metaphor refers to the poet's own awakening. But he blooms in "Eternity's land" quite specifically because of the Resurrection, which brings every hope to fruition. "Rooted in you," he address Jesus in 'Easter hymn,' even the dead comes to life:

> On an old plum tree stump,
> seemingly dead and rotten,
> like a garland of victory
> flowers gleam, dazzling.

And in 'The true appearance of the Word,' "the newly-opened forsythia flowers / in one corner of the hedge beyond my window / entrance me utterly, / like seeing a model of Resurrection."

Péguy can use opening buds in nearly the same way, for a bit. A passage from *The Portal of the Mystery of the Second Virtue* (that is, hope, Péguy's favorite of the trio of faith, hope, and charity) has been elaborating hope as Jesus' crown not of thorns but of "flower buds like on a beautiful apple tree":

> Leafy shoots, blossoming early,
> Which are the shoots of soft, fresh buds,
> And which have the smell and which have the taste
>   of leaves and of flowers.
> The taste of growth, the taste of earth.
> The taste of tree.
> And beforehand the taste of fruit.[7]

The lines could almost be from Ku Sang, except for the litany of repetition of "taste." Ku Sang would drop only a single taste, like a pebble, whereas Péguy's style, as André Gide put it so well, "is like the pebbles of the desert which follow and resemble each other so closely, one so much like the other, but yet a tiny bit different." And as we follow along with Péguy's metaphor of hope as "the shoot, and the bud of the bloom / Of eternity itself," it rolls into an image of hope as a little child—as all children, who are Jesus, "alas my son," says God, my son whose skin on the Cross was dried like the bark from which the tender bud emerges. Human hope emerges, for both poets, from the death and resurrection of Jesus seen anew in the mysterious buds that open with each spring. Jesus is Present to both poets as "mystery," into which their poetry—to their amazement—enters. Yet it is characteristic of their differences that Péguy's buds are a theological virtue alive in the Church's teachings, while Ku Sang's are his personal awakening to the mystery.

IT'S A NATURAL STEP (the pun works irresistibly well) to follow Jesus from the bud/flower image clusters in Ku Sang and Péguy to the contemporary U.S. poets I look at next, because I want to focus first on how they find Jesus Present in Nature. But presence in nature is a slippery category, so some cautions are in order. Jesus and nature have been linked in many ways. John's Gospel, for instance, has Jesus say to his followers, "I am the vine, you are the branches." But John isn't giving us here a Jesus Present in Nature so much as an item of Nature present as symbol for Jesus—or, more accurately, as symbol for a theology of how Jesus gives life to humankind. Péguy similarly starts with a theology, then brings Nature in as image for it. Ku Sang, however, gives the impression of starting with Nature. Observing Nature closely, he watches it burst into life, and in this dazzling burst he sees the victorious force of the resurrected Jesus.

To focus better these differences among ways of linking Jesus and nature, it's useful to compare the poetic world of the late-nineteenth-century British Jesuit Gerard Manley Hopkins. I haven't touched earlier on Hopkins's work because its strong incarnational vision doesn't fit with the predominant figure of Jesus in Hopkins's Victorian era, that shrunken figure whose diminishment I traced in my discussion of modernism. Nor is Hopkins's Jesus a Romantic figure, though Nature speaks loudly of divinity in his work. Rather, as Paul Mariani observes in a very helpful book-length commentary on Hopkins, the Nature so famously "charged with the grandeur of God" in Hopkins's most popular poem isn't at all manifesting God "in any vague, Wordsworthian sense."[8] On the contrary, that much-quoted "dearest freshness deep down things" is quite specifically, to Hopkins's mind, the natural and human world's ongoing renewal in Christ's Redemption. Christ is vividly Present for Hopkins—and it is always "Christ," the salvific figure, rather than "Jesus"—as the redemptive figure who bought humankind back at the "dearest" (most expensive) price. Commentators have noted, appropriately, how Hopkins's poetry comes out of his Ignatian sense of God laboring in the world at every instant. The famous 1877 sonnets, especially, which burst with exploding visions of Christ gloriously Present in Nature, come from the Ignation meditation that seeks God through concentrating the senses on, and deep into, the world. Hence the bird that excites the poet's wonder in 'The Windover' is quite definitely a real bird whose flight Hopkins had closely observed, and it is just as definitely Christ, whose "brute beauty and valour and act . . . O my chevalier!" fires up all of life. So although Hopkins is writing out of a European Christian tradition, his vision of incarnational presence seems closer to that of Ku Sang than of Péguy. It is the Korean who shares the Jesuit's attentive focus on Nature's details, out of which—and *in* which—flashes the enlivening redemptive being who dazzles their hearts.

Turning to the figure of Jesus Present in Nature for contemporary U.S. poets, we find a striking difference from Péguy and Ku Sang and even from Hopkins: Jesus is Present in this poetry now in human form. As incarnational as Hopkins's popular "Nature poetry" is—and its vivid incarnational sense is precisely what accounts, I'd guess, for its current popularity—the human person of Jesus doesn't figure in it. But, for reasons I'll speculate on later, the very person of Jesus, his human Presence as incarnate God, is intriguing to many contemporary U.S. poets. First I'll look at a sample of how he is configured as Present in Nature, then move into other ways that he is embodied as transcendent Presence incarnate.

If I were going to explore a broadly conceived incarnational presence in Nature, as treated in contemporary U.S. poetry, the writer who would come to mind is Wendell Berry. But for incarnational presence in Nature as the person of Jesus, Andrew Hudgins (1951–) is the poet who stands out. Among Hudgins's four volumes of verse, his 1991 collection *The Never-Ending* is where Jesus' earthy Presence most grips the poet's imagination.[9] That isn't a misprint: I do mean *earthy*. The earthiness of Jesus' earthly Presence is what Hudgins is eager to get a handle on. 'Christ as a Gardener,' one of my favorites in the volume, has Jesus digging right into the dirt, getting deeply into that role that the Gospel casts him in for a passing instant. "I love the way / that Mary thought her resurrected Lord / a gardener," the poem says, referring to the post-Resurrection appearance to Mary Magdalene that many other poets have also loved. But while most poets love imagining the scene from Mary's viewpoint—Rilke and Várnalis and Norris and Dillard are ones we've met so far—Hudgins takes off on Jesus' gardening role itself. Having just passed through death and come up into a new life *as* gardener, Hudgins's Jesus exults with the physical energy of a kid just freed from school for the summer. He's so giddy in this double sensation of being *of* the earth yet its master that "Before he can stop himself, he's on his knees," plunging delightedly with his whole wounded body into the dirt, weeding and transplanting. "He laughs. He kicks his bright spade in the earth / and turns it over." The theological insight that leaps from the poet's image is marvelous. Christianity's understanding is indeed that the Risen Jesus turns the earth over: not simply the bit of soil in his spade, but the whole earth is turned over, from death to life, by his resurrected being. And in the poem, the turned-over earth responds with a joyous uplifting dance on which Jesus rises to his Ascension, "on midair steppingstones of dandelion, / of milkweed, thistle, cattail, and goldenrod."

There is a delightful German poem in the Romantic tradition, Hans Benzmann's 'Jesus Walks on the Water,' in which Nature's dance also uplifts Jesus, in this case carrying his feet across the waves to the disciples' boat. So it's interesting to note how Hudgins's Jesus compares to his Romantic counterpart in relating to Nature. The Romantic Jesus is moved and sustained by a Nature in tune with his feelings: we saw this in the 'Gethsemane' of Annette von Droste-Hülshoff and in Felicia Hemans's 'Mountain Sanctuaries,' and it's true as well for Benzmann's poem, where the force of an enchanting night filled with the song of crickets "moves even the Holy One" blissfully to join Nature's festive dance. But Hudgins's Jesus is himself the motivating force behind Nature's dancing: it is Jesus' joy in his resurrected being that moves him to "turn over" the Nature that, thus enlivened, then raises him up. Whereas the Romantics' interest in Jesus' humanness is psychological (focused on his feelings), for Hudgins and others today, as we'll see, the interest is theological. Like Hopkins, Hudgins configures Jesus in Nature in order to ponder what on earth it means to have had a truly incarnated and resurrected God.

And a God who, as human, truly died. Hudgins's Jesus is joyous in his transformed and transformative earthiness as gardener, because—as Hudgins probes in several other poems—this Jesus really did die a human death. To confront this core article of Christian faith, Hudgins chooses to meditate on certain paintings that depict a crucified Jesus who appears undeniably dead. "This Christ knows he's dying," he writes of Gauguin's "yellow Christ" in 'The Yellow Harvest.' In 'Dead Christ,' looking at the Mantegna picture, the poet concludes "this one's flesh. He isn't coming back." And in 'Lamentation over the Dead Christ,' Botticelli has Jesus' "body bent so awkwardly / across his mother's lap: there's no god in it." But dwelling on a truly dead Jesus isn't morbid or mournful for Hudgins, as it was for the modernists discussed in chapter 3: Ole Wivel saying "Weep for Jesus" because he was merely mortal; Vladimir Lvov's "yellowed body of the Lord / Hanging on the cross." But Hudgins's "yellow Christ" and the mere "flesh" with "no god in it" are objects of a calmly exploratory meditation. Can we picture the human Jesus so dead, the poet seems to wonder, that he loses the ability to return to life as Risen Lord?

Other contemporary U.S. poets show a similar fascination with Jesus' humanness, pondering what incarnation—en-flesh-ment, embodiment—can have meant for Jesus and hence for us. Scott Cairns (1954–) in fact makes this the enveloping theme of his 1998 collection *Recovered Body*,[10] which takes its epigraph from Auden's *For the Time Being:* "Love Him in the World of the Flesh / And at your marriage all its occasions shall dance for joy." For Cairns, incorporating the heart of current Scripture scholarship on the matter, to "love him in the world of the flesh" requires recovering the densely embodied Hebrew meaning of the Word (*dabar*) who became flesh, a meaning falsely intellectualized in the Greek concept of *Logos* that Christianity adopted. The poems of *Recovered Body* ring many intriguing changes on this theme, but the most interesting for our purpose is the long poem 'Loves,' because its discourse on the need for a newly embodied sense of Jesus is put in the mouth of Mary Magdalen after the episode that has stimulated so many of our poets: Jesus' appearance to her in the garden. Theologians and poets over the centuries have taken Magadalen as the Gospel figure most implicated in bodiliness, inscribing in her character their valuation of our human existence in the flesh. We've seen, for instance, Rilke's Magdalen learning from the resurrected Jesus that she must let go of her attachment to their bodily selves so as to rise with him to a higher, disembodied love. And we've seen the Marxist poet Kostas Várnalis trace on Magdalen's body the course of dialectical materialism's salvation history. Cairns will have nothing of either of these, nor of any other, derivations of the Greek body/spirit dualism that has distorted Christianity's (and all of Western culture's) sense of the holy. His Magdalen, recalling her uniquely physical intimacy with Jesus—"I have kissed/his feet. I have looked long/into the trouble of his face—insists that *there* "in that intersection" of body and spirit, she found the site of the sacred. It was Christ's desire to be the very bodiliness of love, Cairns has her argue, slipping subtly into a pun on giving birth, that "induced" him "to take on flesh."

DENISE LEVERTOV (1923–1997) would have liked this pun, because the question of what might have induced Christ to take on our human flesh is very much her preoccupation as well. But for Levertov, with her deep lifelong involvement in social justice concerns, it is Jesus' sorrowful pain in sharing the human condition that is the salient feature of his chosen bodiliness. The "weight" of the Incarnation is her recurrent metaphor, especially in the Passion/Resurrection poems she composed after her conversion to Christianity in the early 1980s: 'Salvator Mundi: Via Crucis,' 'Ikon: The Harrowing of Hell,' 'Ascension,' and 'On Belief in the Physical Resurrection of Jesus.' Curiously enough, since the natural world figures significantly in much of Levertov's verse, a Jesus Present in Nature is not her interest in these poems. She seems not to have wanted to distract herself from concentrating on his Presence in a human body.[11]

Having made her name during the 1960s and 1970s not only as a poet but also as a political activist, Levertov comes to Jesus in her 'Salvator Mundi' as to someone who would have shared her own dread after taking a step too far and wishing herself back. This, she imagines, must have been "Incarnation's heaviest weight," this the greatest "burden of humanness" for Jesus on his *via crucis:* "this sickened desire to renege," to pull back from what "He, Who was God, / ... had entered/ time and flesh to enact." In 'Ikon,' too, it's the "travail" of being human that interests Levertov, as she pictures Jesus in the traditional icons of the Harrowing of Hell, pulling the dead up out of the ground as he himself reenters the earthly world on his way back to heaven. Like Hudgins in 'Christ as Gardener,' Levertov chooses to imagine Jesus' mind at this first post-Resurrection transitional moment between flesh and spirit, mortality and immortality. At this midway point, having plunged into the depths of humanity in the grave, now back on earth knowing that he'll soon be leaving his own humanity behind, Hudgins's Jesus is all joy at turning the earth over in his Resurrection, whereas Levertov's Jesus is soberly absorbed in the immanent "struggle" to leave flesh behind. This transitional state gives Levertov's Jesus a painfully piercing insight into his humanity, into how hard it is to break "back into breath and heartbeat . . . / closed into days and weeks again." He is "aching for home," and in 'Ascension' Levertov imagines him going there. But the physical effort of the transition is again what grips her. "Can Ascension / not have been / arduous, almost, / as the return/ from Sheol?" the poem asks, going on

Mexico: Easter Journey *(1978), by Betty La Duke (United States, 1933–). La Duke's Jesus here is transformatively present with his mother Mary. Together in this Resurrection image, they are reborn as lovers, turning the Cross into a joyous transition point between flesh and spirit. Much as Levertov, in 'Ascension,' sees Jesus mothering and fathering his birth into new life, La Duke pictures a creative joining of male and female energy. The resulting restorative force, like Hudgins' 'Christ as Gardener,' turns earth into spirit. Birds fly into La Duke's embodied Jesus to partake of his spirit, as his animal mask reveals his multi-layered nature; the flowers of Mary's dress and the stars bounce off of one another the same visual pattern, linking heaven and earth. By permission of the artist.*

to picture the process as the "torture and bliss" of a birth in which Jesus, freed from a gendered body, both fathers and mothers himself.[12] Even when, in 'On Belief in the Physical Resurrection of Jesus,' Levertov imagines Jesus in his fully resurrected state, it's his bodiliness that she holds onto. Now, though, in this her final book of poems, she is seizing on the mystery of embodied spirit as model for poetry itself. The miracle of God assuming flesh in the Incarnation, and continuing to become the "bread of life" in the Eucharist, informs her faith in the very possibility and meaning of metaphor. Symbols cannot speak to her, she asserts, making a point much like Richard Wilbur's in 'A World Without Objects Is a Sensible Emptiness,' unless they are grounded "in bone and blood."

This late aesthetic statement of Levertov's is highly christological. But, as many commentators have noted, long before her conversion to Christianity Levertov's poetry had been incarnational in the sense we explored at this chapter's start: transcendent spirit infused her material world, a mystery she responded to with gratitude and awe.[13] Indeed, a formative influence on her poetics was Gerard Manley Hopkins, whose notions of "inscape" and "instress" Levertov adopted as early as the 1960s to theorize about poetry's task to express the spirit embodied in natural objects. In later essays and interviews, Levertov discussed how, gradually, the unknown source of the world's mystery "began to be defined for me as God, and further, as God revealed in the Incarnation."[14] The turning point toward the capitalized Incarnation occurred—appropriately enough, she could see later, though at the time she thought she was writing a secular poem—during the process of writing her *Mass for the Day of St. Thomas Didymus* in 1979–1980. Still considering herself "an agnostic," she chose the Mass form for its structural appeal. But after a few months of writing the Kyrie and Gloria and Credo and Sanctus, all of which evoke the "unknown" but won't name it as God, "when I had arrived at the Agnus Dei, I discovered myself to be in a different relationship to the material."[15] Actually, a reader can see the conversion begin in the Benedictus, where, wrestling with the problem of human evil that had been anguishing her during her decades of political poetry, she is able to find a grain of "hope" in the "dust" from which the world "utters itself." Then, evidently to her own astonishment, this uttering brings her to the word who "chose to become / flesh," before which "we bow, baffled." Bafflement then is, quite frankly (Levertov's verse is always absolutely honest about her state of mind at the moment), the tone of the Agnus Dei, which takes the form of blunt interrogations about this "Lamb of God." Can our God, she incredulously asks, really be not omnipotence but this weak, defenseless "wisp of damp wool?" Levertov's deep conviction of our human responsibility to heal the world's hurts then leads her to an extraordinary personal relation to this shivering, damp God she has just come to know. The questions stop with: "So be it. / Come, rag of pungent / quiverings, / dim star. / Let's try / if something human still / can shield you." She has accepted responsibility to protect this tender Lamb of God, but she can't yet see him as the person of Jesus or as a salvific figure.

It was evidently through reading Julian of Norwich, the medieval mystic whose book *Showings,* describing her visions, has moved so many recent readers, that Levertov came to see how the "flesh and bone" Jesus could be a figure of strength. In a cycle of six poems engaging Julian with the urgency of someone plumbing the depths of her current conversion process with a close friend, Levertov lets herself stare for the first time at "God's pierced palm." Julian acts in the poem cycle as Levertov's mentor, showing her how to see—with the eyes and with the understanding—the wounded flesh of "God's agony." Because Julian didn't hide from her era's particular sufferings, its dreadful plagues and wars, but rather could see Jesus as the very figure of Love taking on our suffering human flesh in order to conquer "the Fiend," Levertov can follow her mentor in finally welcoming Jesus as an embodied God whom she can embrace as her own. After this, Levertov was able to go on, in the Passion/Resurrection poems we've already touched on, to engage directly the person of Jesus as someone whose relinquishment of self into human suffering could be model and meaning for Levertov's own path of life. This is to say that Levertov came to understand the core Christian paradox of God choosing to become weak in order to conquer sin and death. It's the kenotic paradox of Jesus' voluntary self-emptying, celebrated in the Philippians hymn and in verse after verse of Ephrem's poetry.

Indeed, contemporary Christian poets who choose to configure the person of Jesus tend to do so in ways surprisingly close to the earliest Christian poetry. His unique status as truly divine and truly human fascinates them, charges up their imaginations. Like the Johannine writers, like Clement of Alexandria, like Ephrem, their interest is theological; pondering what it means to have had an incarnated God, they look to Jesus for insight into what our humanity hence must be. There are certainly key differences, deriving from the contrasts in cultural context. Contemporary poets don't need to formulate doctrine or argue against heresies, nor do they seek to make converts. Nor does the typology that energized the Christian imagination of so many centuries turn them on: they see Jesus hidden not in Old Testament figures but in the ordinary things of daily life. Nor is their tone that celebration that comes with the excitement of an utterly new insight: the revelation of Jesus of Nazareth as Lord, as the Word made flesh. They seem, at the end of two millennia in which this central figure of Christianity has been reshaped and reconfigured, very comfortable with the orthodox configurations yet energized by what they mean for human life at this moment.

What energizes these poets, I'd speculate, is finding in the Word made flesh a figure in whom to situate the inherently mysterious human condition of living two natures at once, flesh and spirit. Hudgins, Cairns, Levertov, and other Christian poets who bring the person of Jesus into their work seem relieved to be done with the contortions that his person has been put through ever since the Enlightenment cut his human role as moral teacher off from his divinity. Unlike poets of the subsequent centuries—unlike the Romantics, who had to keep Jesus' humanity elevated to heroic status; unlike the Victorians and modernists who despaired at what they saw, in a merely human Jesus, as loss of their hope for eternal life; unlike postmodern cynics, who dismissed Jesus' mere humanity as a sign of his meaninglessness—contemporary Christian poets can be comfortable once again with Jesus' humanity. They don't see it as a threat to his divine being. When they try to get into the feel of what the experience of humanity must have been like for Jesus, it isn't into the feel in Romanticism's psychological sense so much as into the feel, for Jesus, of his ontological status as incarnate God, as embodiment of transcendent Presence. In this they are supported, whether consciously or not, by contemporary feminist theology, which finds in the Incarnation an affirmation of bodiliness wherein the mystery of God physically joins the human adventure.[16] As contemporaries of postmodernism as well, these poets can interrogate the mystery of Incarnation dispassionately, because interrogation of inherited truths is the postmodern mode. So they can probe this embodied figure of transcendence without either defensiveness or anxiety. Of course, they might struggle with their personal relation to Christian faith, yet they can do so without calling the whole two thousand year old enterprise into question, because they know that questioning was core to this mind-stretching and soul-piercing enterprise from the start. Stimulated by the creative tension of carrying on this probing enterprise in a culture that is often fearful of even touching on the questions, they can confidently explore where and how transcendence might be in our world through the figure of Jesus Present. If Péguy's Jesus "brought back to heaven a certain taste for man, a certain taste for the earth," the U.S. poets' Jesus brings back to earth a certain taste for heaven.

THE METAPHOR OF A "taste" for heaven applies with special pungency to the poet with whom I'll conclude this discussion of Jesus as embodied Presence: Vassar Miller (1924–1998). When I first came upon Vassar Miller's poetry a few years ago, I was dumbstruck that I'd never come upon it before. Here, clearly, was poetry on a par with that of her contemporaries Denise Levertov and Richard Wilbur. Yet Miller has received nothing like their recognition.[17] This is a shame, because she offers to readers a lifetime of masterfully crafted explorations of spiritual (in Miller's case, specifically Christian) experience. Yet it's this very achievement that explains the neglect of Miller's work. As I noted earlier, the secular bias among editors and critics is at least partially responsible for a poet like Wilbur's avoidance of Christian images in embodying his sense of incarnational presence. The poems of Hudgins and Levertov where we've seen the person of Jesus vividly Present were composed after these writers had already made their names with verse more congenial to a secular society. Nor does Jesus figure for them to the extent that he does for Vassar Miller. Early on, she made the deliberate choice to risk unfashionability in order to plunge into the explicitly Christian themes and images closest to her heart. We can't neglect her in a study of the poets' Jesus, because her Jesus is embodied with an intimacy beyond anything we've seen in the past century. The desire that Levertov came to in her sixties—"for flesh to make known / to intellect ... in bone and breath / (and not die) God's agony" (in 'The Showings')—had been compelling Vassar Miller throughout her substantial body of poetry.

To speak of "a body of poetry" in Vassar Miller's case is to use the idiom with unique force. Her own literal body, her physical being of flesh and bone, is very much a context of her verse. Born with cerebral palsy, Miller naturally had a perspective on being human not available to most of us. Not that her poetry often takes her physical handicap as explicit subject. But, living in a body whose limitations she had to continually bump up against, she developed a heightened sense of our human existence in the flesh. And a heightened sense of what it concretely means that the Word became flesh. When Jesus enters Miller's body of verse—which is often—it's as a Body like her own, an embodied Presence known deep in her own bones.[18]

Knowing "in her bones" is in fact how Miller chiefly pictures perception, and not only for the overtly religious matters that concern, I'd estimate, about half of her work. Her "bones," an image scattered everywhere through her collected poems, are the recurrent site and source of experiential knowledge. Indeed, a verse that ends a poem about insomnia ('Tired')—"I have written / these lines without book, / thumbing the thesaurus / of my bones"—could apply generally to her creative process as she presents it. In her explicitly religious works, she'll sometimes situate in her bones key scriptural moments, internalizing them in a startlingly physical sense. A lighthearted instance is 'Carol of Brother Ass,' which envisions the Nativity scene enacted in dance rhythms inside her body, beginning: "In the barnyard of my bone / Let the animals kneel down." More soberly, 'A Duller Moses,' using the Burning Bush as a transforming image for Miller's spiritual experience, ends:

> I tremble ...
> That He, both radiance and incendiary,
> In my heart lies as on the cross He lay
> (Which bed is fouler?), making my bone-heap—
> Oh, monstrous miracle!—God's sanctuary.

The sense of worthlessness conveyed by "my bone-heap" is reminiscent of the seventeenth-century lyric poets, with whom Vassar Miller has a definite affinity. Not only is her spirituality akin to theirs—in its recurrent drama of intense personal relation with a Savior of whom the poet feels unworthy—but, with them, she finds strict verse forms the preferred vehicle for engaging her spiritual struggles. All through the five decades of her career, Miller embraced intricate classical forms like the villanelle, the double sestina, and (her favorite) the sonnet, clearly stimulated by the challenge of stretching language within a given frame. Taut play between frame and imaginative flights becomes in her hands the perfect medium for a faith stretching itself toward the infinite that can only be known, paradoxically, in the limits of time and place, meter and (poetic or bodily) form.

Nowhere is Miller's crafting of her spiritual drama in collaboration with poetic form more impressive than in the remarkable technical achievement 'Love's Bitten Tongue,' a sequence of twenty-two sonnets interlocked in the Renaissance corona form, where the last line of each is repeated as the first line of the next, though always with a new twist of syntax and sense. The poem's plot follows the poet's struggles against an ego she feels as a drag. Since the ego as problem is a core theme of contemporary Western spirituality, the poem speaks for the Christian soul—for Everyperson—at the second millennium's turn. Yet the poem doesn't claim for itself this universality; its authenticity comes from its laying out an intensely personal, genuinely lived spiritual journey. Characteristically for Miller, the ego starts out as a *physical* drag; "deep in the muck of myself" is where she feels helplessly stuck. Or almost helplessly. She is able to pray, and in one sonnet (number 16), setting inside her own body the book of Revelation's scene of the Lamb opening the scroll (5:1–6:1), she seeks from Jesus that typically bone-deep knowledge:

> teach me . . .
> But with an alphabet that has been burned
> Into my bones, a book till now shut
> And You unseal it, O Lamb only worthy
> To read its alphabet scattered until
> I offer it up, steel filings to smithy
> Beaten out on the anvil, syllable
> After slow syllable.

Offering one's bones to be "burned" and "beaten out on the anvil" is a violently painful way of incorporating the Word of God into oneself. But she can invite Christ to inscribe his Word on her very bones because he himself, Alpha and Omega, is the Word made flesh who became, earlier in the poem, "Heaven's incredible wound." As the poem goes on to recount the Gospel story (I'm necessarily oversimplifying a complex drama in which every sonnet would repay a whole page of unpacking), the poet finds herself continuing to be remade in Christ—and he in her. In the final sonnet, he takes on her condition of being stuck "deep in the muck of myself" by appearing to Mary Magdalene as the Gardener "messy with muck." Jesus' role as Gardener, so intriguing to other contemporary poets as well, works for Miller to confront her with a God who has willingly sunk into her own messiness. She sees then that she too must accept that "muck of myself" and "those flesh-splitting throbs, pain, dread" that come with it. So while the poem opened with the prayer "Lord, hush this ego as one stops a bell," it closes with the poet willing to "bow, acolyte to my ego." That is, she acknowledges—if hesitantly—that being joined to her Lord means incorporating that troublesome ego in her worship.

And the 'Love's Bitten Tongue' of the title? It enters the poem as an address to Jesus being stung on the Cross by his own silent groans: "You, my God, lonesome man, Love's bitten tongue / Heaven's incredible wound." Is this the incarnate God as Love biting its tongue to keep from fully speaking its suffering? The Word made Flesh holding back its full power? However we unwrap the figure—surely one of the more resonant images for Jesus that poetry has had to offer—there's a painful tenderness. The human tongue is so intimate and vulnerable a body part, yet also (as organ of speech) so potentially powerful. And, after "bones," it's probably the body part most common in Vassar Miller's poetry. This is because the tongue, metonymic symbol for the human voice and hence for poetry itself, is the point where Christ in the Eucharist touches the poet's flesh. As 'Love's Bitten Tongue' continues, the poet's tongue, graced by the Eucharist, becomes the poetry through which she can give voice to Christ's redemptive suffering known in her own. Poetry is by nature redemptive, Miller has said elsewhere, because in overcoming "the silence of God that Christ endured on the Cross," it "raises the pain of life onto the level of beauty."[19] Word made flesh made sacrament is, in poetry, again made transformative word.

Conclusion: "To Find Words Adequate to the Mystery . . ."

In an essay in the Winter 1995–96 issue of *Image: A Journal of the Arts and Religion,* poet and literary biographer Paul Mariani talks about how artists' language can touch the transcendent:

> In a time when the language of theological discourse among the general populace seems threadbare, suspect, irrelevant, and emptied—like language itself—of much of its former significance, in a time when the language-philosophers and behaviorists seem to have marched through the land like Sherman on his way to the sea, smashing the edifices we once sheltered in, there is much in the way of joy and challenge in the reconstruction and building anew of this aspect of language for those of us who care about such matters. And what is our goal in this quest? To find words adequate to the mystery, a mystery which can still haunt like birdsong at evening.

Theological language has looked threadbare before. Recall that on the eve of Romanticism, theology seemed like a worn-out, drab old rug. Actually, Mariani isn't accusing today's theology of being threadbare. Theology is indeed quite brilliantly alive, with Christian theologians on several continents creatively shaping a new language for humankind's relation to the transcendent. But though there is much in the way of joy and challenge in current theology's reconstruction of language to reach for the mystery, Mariani is correct that its discourse can sound to the general populace simply mysterious in a negative sense. So although nearly two centuries ago, creative theologians like Emerson and Schleiermacher found for their era new words adequate to the mystery, today I sense that it's our poets who are taking on the task.

Creative prose can certainly engage the mystery, too. George Steiner has argued in *Real Presences* that all great art, by its very nature, moves us precisely because it touches on the transcendent.[20] But increasingly I've been sensing poetry as the place where the word can be uniquely in touch with wonder.

Poetry is the art of holding the word still, of handling it, turning it over, opening it up to peer deep into it, of wondering about it and with it and through it. When other verbal arts do this, we praise them as "poetic." So it's not surprising that contemporary poets, even those whose orientation isn't primarily what we'd think of as religious, often comment on their art's bond with transcendence. A poem "gives us a premonition of harmonics desired," Seamus Heaney, for instance, has said; "art is not an inferior reflection of some ordained heavenly system but a rehearsal of it in earthly terms."[21] Joseph Brodsky has made a strikingly similar point, discussing the poetry of Anna Akhmatova. "Poetry, each particular poem, is a miracle: a linguistic one to begin with, and then, if a poet is lucky—a miracle of spiritual intensity and cohesion. . . . As arts go, poetry is not a mimetic but a revelatory one."[22] The contrast between mimesis or reflection, on the one hand, and heavenly premonition or revelation on the other, recalls the distinction influentially articulated years ago by the critic M. H. Abrams in *The Mirror and the Lamp*: between the eighteenth century's aesthetic of imitation and Romanticism's aesthetic of self-creation illuminated by the divine spirit. Yet poetry today has a humbler sense of its own role than in the Romantic era. The contemporary poet's self-image is not of divinity's voice or mediator. Nor is it Rilke's post-Romantic sense that the artist has to *make* transcendent meaning anew. Poets now *find*, touch, the mystery with a word. They want only to "name" things, Richard Wilbur has said in his essay 'On Poetry and Happiness.'[23] And in 'A Wedding Toast,' he puts the point in poetry itself. "[T]he world's fullness is not made but found," he writes, as if directly refuting Rilke. "Life hungers to abound / And pour its plenty out for such as you."

I love that image of life pouring out its plenty over us—maybe because it confirms my sense that poetry is best read in a hammock. One summer I told the students in my graduate seminar on spirituality and poetry that the course requirement was not only the text (*Burning Bright*, Patricia Hampl's rich anthology of Jewish, Christian, and Islamic spiritual poetry) but also a hammock tied between two trees. What I meant was that lying in a hammock disposes the body, and the whole being, to absorb the touch with mystery that is poetry's art. A hammock puts the body and mind in a receptive state: relaxed, we let ourselves be lightly moved, enveloped. The contemporary poet Billy Collins witnesses to the effect in his comically self-deprecating poem 'Reading in a

Hammock.'[24] "Looking up into this little sky of words" of the poetry volume in his hand, he observes that "around the edges of the book is the larger sky . . . and some overhanging branches / that appear to be slowly swaying back and forth, / as if I were the one lying motionless." He makes fun of himself as "a martyr to idleness, tied to these trees," but there's something genuinely helpful about that suspended position, facing upward, that a hammock puts us in. Our body weighted as if we'd landed from above, we gaze up at the place from which we seem to have come: the sky, mythic source of life and of meaning in all religions. Suspended above the ground, we feel *in* this world but not held *by* it, since the hammock's sway gives an elastic sensation of springing us upward. It's the body language of incarnation. This must be why I viscerally feel poetry's word in touch with wonder when I'm reading it in a hammock. Hanging in suspense, vulnerable to wonder's materializing, I hold in my hand poetry's words that touch it, that find its fullness.

If, as I'm saying, poetry is the art that draws words into their touch with wonder, then I can understand why Christian poets tend to see poetry in incarnational terms. I've already noted Kathleen Norris's calling the Incarnation itself metaphor, not in the sense that it's untrue but because metaphor "yokes the human and the divine." Vassar Miller puts the link in terms of the Incarnation as configured in John's Gospel: "Christianity is the religion of the Word-made-flesh and poetry is its most natural voice."[25] We could go on to say that, for this very reason, Jesus is a natural figure for dramatizing poetry's contact with transcendence in the word. As the Word made flesh who is core to Christianity's self-understanding, the Word who *is* the mystery that Mariani urges us to find words for, Jesus embodies the word in touch with wonder.

Denise Levertov has even speculated that we in the West are reaching the end of the time of skittishness about Christian vocabulary that began with the Enlightenment and peaked in the twentieth century:

> A poet speaking from within the Christian tradition and using traditional terms (though not necessarily upholding every orthodoxy) may have more resonance for our intellectual life than is supposed. The Incarnation, the Passion, the Resurrection—these words have some emotive power even for the most secular minds. Perhaps a contemporary poetry that incorporates old terms and old stories can help readers to reappropriate significant parts of their own linguistic, emotional, cultural heritage, whether or not they share doctrinal adherences.[26]

That is, just as African poets at odds with the doctrine that Jesus stands for still found him useful for configuring their people's experience, the West (as Levertov suggests) may return to him, too. He is, after all, the main character of the main story we have told for two millennia.

As if illustrating Levertov's point, the Spring 1998 issue of the highly respected literary quarterly *Hudson Review* printed on facing pages poems by two outstanding U.S. poets of different generations—Anthony Hecht (born at the twentieth century's first-quarter mark) and Mark Jarman (born at the century's middle)—dealing between them with the key elements of the story that Levertov mentions. Hecht's 'Long-Distance Vision' takes an Audenesque look at the Crucifixion as the crucial event that is "somehow always" in our present moment, though we'd rather keep our distance from its telling details. Jarman's 'Cycle' focuses on the Incarnation and Resurrection as historic points around which "everything" still turns, events that touched off a "change no one can stop." So both poems are about the immediacy of this two-thousand-year-old drama. I want to pause over, and close with, Jarman's 'Cycle' because—as a sonnet cycle with the theme of turning and returning to the Gospel events—it takes as its subject the whole of what this immediacy involves. Composed in the corona form, with each sonnet's concluding line picked up as the opening line of the next, and the cycle's final line returning to its first, 'Cycle' enacts in its form Jarman's theme of a recapitulation that is always however with a difference. So, although returning to this Renaissance verse form used by John Donne and Vassar Miller to intertwine their tense personal stories with Christ's, Jarman returns to it with a difference: he lets go of its historically taut tone. Elsewhere (for instance in some of his poems called 'Unholy Sonnets') Jarman does tangle personally with God; but here in 'Cycle' he chooses to return instead to a more objective, in a sense medieval, view of the Incarnation in its cosmic impact. Yet his return to a cosmic Christ is also with a difference, for unlike any medieval poet, Jarman casts a wry postmodern eye on the cosmos as a "dysfunctional family / Of stars and darkness," and he shrugs a comfortable joke about Jesus' strange cursing of the fig tree. ("Perhaps to understand, you had to be there.") The most fundamental return of 'Cycle' is of course to the central character of the Gospel narratives themselves, and it is the ultimate return with a difference: the poem recounts the Gospel drama in such a way as to at once accept its historicity and yank it into a future that manages to make present the past, meanwhile interrogating what on earth it could possibly mean for us at this moment. 'Cycle' ends—and so will I, since a book on the poets' Jesus should give the last word to a poet—wondering about this person who was and is and will continue to be "the puzzle" through which "everything" passes:

> He took on flesh and then he took it off . . .
> He dwelt among us, then he disappeared.
> And we are left to be and keep on being
> Like everything around a central meaning.

Notes

Since my primary audience in this book is the general reader, the purpose of these notes is to acknowledge my sources and to steer readers to further material on the subject, not to engage scholarly debate. In citing sources for the poetry I quote, I've tried to give the most accessible source, in keeping with my hope that readers will seek out the poems themselves.

ONE / JESUS AS CHRIST AND MORE

1. The precise meaning and implications of every New Testament term applied to Jesus are controverted by biblical scholars. The debates are lively, intense, and fascinating, but I can't rehearse them here. I can assure readers that all my points are drawn from the mainstream consensus, as are my designations of certain New Testament passages as poems or hymns. Readers who want more detail on the biblical terms for Jesus are invited to look into Oscar Cullmann, *The Christology of the New Testament* (London: SCM, 1959); James D. G. Dunn, *Christology in the Making* (Philadelphia: Westminster, 1980); and Raymond E. Brown, *An Introduction to New Testament Christology* (Mahwah, New Jersey: Paulist Press, 1994). On the New Testament hymns, background can be found in Jack T. Sanders, *The New Testament Christological Hymns* (Cambridge: Cambridge University Press, 1971) and Daniel Liderbach, *Christ in the Early Christian Hymns* (Mahwah, New Jersey: Paulist Press, 1998) and an overview in Raymond E. Brown, *An Introduction to the New Testament* (New York: Doubleday, 1997), 489–93.

2. Clement's poem can be found in *Divine Inspiration: The Life of Jesus in World Poetry,* edited by Robert Atwan, George Dardess, and Peggy Rosenthal (New York: Oxford University Press, 1998); the hymn from the Acts of John in *New Testament Apocrypha,* edited by Wilhelm Schneemelcher (Philadelphia: Westminster, 1965), vol. 2.

3. The translations of Ephrem's poetry are by Kathleen E. McVey, from her superb scholarly edition, *Ephrem the Syrian: Hymns* (Mahwah, New Jersey: Paulist Press, 1989): Hymns on the Nativity #3, 4, and 16; Hymns on Virginity #22 and 34.

4. The definitive scholarly source for Romanos's verse sermons is the annotated and delightfully translated two-volume edition by Marjorie Carpenter, *Kontakia of Romanos, Byzantine Melodist* (Columbia: University of Missouri Press, 1970).

5. From 'A Hymn after Fasting,' translated by M. Clement Eagan, in *Poems of Prudentius* (Washington, D.C.: Catholic University Press, 1962).

6. A lovely translation of the first eighty-six lines of *The Dream of the Rood* appears in J. A. W. Bennett, *Poetry of the Passion: Studies in Twelve Centuries of English Verse* (Oxford: Clarendon Press, 1982), which also contains a useful summary of the poetic history of the Cross as Tree.

7. An analysis of the *Ordo Virtutum* that includes the entire Latin text and some translated verses is in "Hildegard of Bingen as Poetess and Dramatist," in Peter Dronke, *Poetic Individuality in the Middle Ages* (Oxford: Oxford University Press, 1970).

8. Like everyone who is getting to know Hildegard's poetry of late, I am indebted to the outstanding scholarship and translations by Barbara Newman in her critical edition of the *Symphonia* (Ithaca: Cornell University Press, 1988).

9. My quotations are from my two favorite translations of *Paradiso,* John Ciardi's (New York: Penguin, 1970) and James Torrens's in *Presenting Paradise* (Scranton, PA: University of Scranton Press, 1993). Both books also have immensely helpful commentary, Ciardi's in the form of endnotes, Torrens's in the creative form of an ongoing explication that nestles the poetry within it.

10. My source for the Middle English devotional poems is Bennett's fine chapter on the subject, "The Meditative Movement," in *Poetry of the Passion.*

11. John of the Cross's poetry has been much translated, often not felicitously. For accuracy (though it misses John's meters), I use *The Collected Works of Saint John of the Cross,* translated by Kieran Kavanaugh and Otilio Rodriguez (Washington, D.C.: Institute of Carmelite Studies, 1991).

12. Guevara's sonnets are in any anthology of Spanish verse. La Ceppède's poetry is harder to find. An ample selection, well translated and annotated by Keith Bosley, is in *From the Theorems of Master Jean de La Ceppède* (Manchester, U.K.: Carcanet New Press, 1983). Morsztyn's 'Emblem 39' is in *Five Centuries of Polish Poetry,* translated by Jerzy Peterkiewicz and Burns Singer (London: Oxford University Press, 1970).

13. The translation of *The Divine Narcissus* is by Alan S. Trueblood in his very useful *A Sor Juana Anthology* (Cambridge: Harvard University Press, 1988). But Trueblood was able to include only a small fraction of Sor Juana's immense poetic output. Much of her secular poetry is widely translated elsewhere, but her over one hundred fifty villancicos and other popular religious verse remain largely unavailable in English.

14. There has been lively scholarly controversy over whether the major influence on seventeenth-century English lyric poetry was Protestant devotional practice or Catholic meditation exercises. Reading the classic works of each side—Barbara Kiefer Lewalski, *Protestant Poetics and the Seventeenth-Century Religious Lyric* (Princeton: Princeton University Press, 1979) and Louis L. Martz, *The Poetry of Meditation* (New Haven: Yale University Press, 1954; revised 1962)—I find myself thoroughly persuaded by each as I'm absorbed in each writer's solidly grounded argument. I'm convinced that both have a large measure of truth: that both streams of religious practice were feeding the wells on which this poetry draws. Joseph Summers's still widely respected study, *George Herbert: His Religion and Art* (London: Chatto and Windus, 1954), does say explicitly that in Herbert's England, religious reading from Catholic and Puritan sources alike was shared by all parties (p. 54).

15. For calling attention to and offering this reading of Taylor's poem, I'm indebted to John Gatta's *Gracious Laughter: The Meditative Wit of Edward Taylor* (Columbia: University of Missouri Press, 1989). For a thorough discussion of how seventeenth-century English poets make their inner selves "the stage for the entire typological drama," see Lewalski, *Protestant Poetics,* especially chapter 4.

16. Because official persecution forced Chinese Christian writings underground, they are just now being rediscovered. The existence of Zhang Xingyao's manuscripts was unknown until U.S. historian D. E. Mungello found them in Shanghai in 1986; a few of Zhang's poems are translated in Mungello's *The Forgotten Christians of Hangzhou* (Honolulu: University of Hawaii Press, 1994). Wu Li had long been celebrated as a painter, but his poetry was practically ignored until another U.S. historian, Jonathan Chaves, collected and studied it. Chaves includes the first English translations of a large selection of Wu Li's poems in his *Singing of the Source: Nature and God in the Poetry of the Chinese Painter Wu Li* (Honolulu: University of Hawaii Press, 1993), on which I've drawn for my understanding of Wu Li and for the quotations from his poetry.

17. The quotations from the philosophes are in *Voltaire on Religion,* edited by Kenneth W. Applegate (New York: Ungar, 1974), 25, 130; *The Enlightenment: A Comprehensive Anthology,* edited by Peter Gay (New York: Simon and Schuster, 1973), 42; and Gay's indispensable *The Enlightenment: An Interpretation* (New York: Random House, 1966), 208.

18. For a useful discussion of the interplay between rationalism and insanity in eighteenth-century England, see David Daiches, *God and the Poets* (Oxford: Clarendon Press, 1984), an insightful book with, however, the limitation of treating almost exclusively English-language poets.

TWO / JESUS AS ROMANTIC HERO

1. Quoted by Gordon S. Haight, *George Eliot: A Biography* (New York: Oxford University Press, 1968), p. 42.

2. My discussion of nineteenth-century theological developments draws on Claude Welch, *Protestant Thought in the Nineteenth Century,* vol. 1 (New Haven: Yale University Press, 1972), which I recommend for a fuller account.

3. The German title is quite different: *Von Reimarus zu Wrede: eine Geschichte der Leben-Jesu-Forschung.*

4. *The Quest of the Historical Jesus,* translated by W. Montgomery (London: Adam and Charles Black, 1911), p. 79.

5. *The Life of Jesus,* translated by George Eliot from the fourth German edition (New York: Macmillan, 1892), pp. 779–80.

6. Quoted by G. H. Lewes, *The Life and Works of Goethe* (London: J. M. Dent, 1908), p. 535.

7. Lewes, *The Life and Works of Goethe,* pp. 99–100, 136.

8. My understanding of Goethe's relation to the Romantic lyric draws on the study by David E. Wellbery, *The Specular Moment: Goethe's Early Lyric and the Beginnings of Romanticism* (Stanford: Stanford University Press, 1996), from which I also gratefully take the translations of Goethe's poetry.

9. Though of course there are countless scholarly studies of Blake—as of Whitman, whom I consider later in the chapter—no major work has been done on their treatment of Jesus. So the analyses of these two poets presented here are my own.

10. Not a lot on Droste-Hülshoff's life is available in English. I've made use of Margaret Mare, *Annette von Droste-Hülshoff* (Lincoln: University of Nebraska Press, 1965), which is helpful even though some of its assumptions about women are out of date.

11. Translated from the German by George Dardess in *Divine Inspiration: The Life of Jesus in World Poetry,* edited by Robert Atwan, George Dardess, and Peggy Rosenthal (New York: Oxford University Press).

12. I'm grateful to Susan Wolfson, professor of English, Princeton University, for calling Hemans to my attention. Wolfson is editing a new edition of Hemans's poetry, to be published by Princeton University Press.

13. *The Life of Jesus,* anonymous 1863 translation, reissued by The Modern Library (New York: 1927), pp. 87, 114, 89, 236.

THREE / SLIDING INTO MODERNISM

1. Lyell's effect on Tennyson is discussed by David Daiches in *God and the Poets* (Oxford: Clarendon Press, 1984), in a useful chapter on poetry and science in Victorian England (chapter 6).

2. Unless otherwise noted, all translations of Baudelaire's poetry are by William H. Crosby, in *The Flowers of Evil and Paris Spleen* (Brockport, New York: BOA Editions, 1991).

3. Noted in Lois Boe Hyslop, *Charles Baudelaire Revisited* (New York: Twayne, 1992), a very helpful, concise appraisal of Baudelaire's work.

4. Mauriac's essay, "Charles Baudelaire the Catholic," is reprinted in *Baudelaire: A Collection of Critical Essays*, edited by Henri Peyre (Englewood Cliffs, N.J.: Prentice-Hall, 1962), a marvelous collection including assessments by such major figures as Paul Valéry, Étienne Gilson, John Middleton Murry, Marcel Proust, and Erich Auerbach.

5. The translation is John Middleton Murry's in his essay on Baudelaire in Peyre, *Baudelaire*.

6. The quotations, from various of Baudelaire's essays and letters, are in Hyslop, *Charles Baudelaire Revisited*.

7. Martin E. Marty, *Modern American Religion*, vol. 1 (Chicago: University of Chicago Press, 1986), pp. 13, 29.

8. Like everyone, I'm indebted to Octavio Paz's voluminous and always insightful writing on the history of Latin American poetry. Darío is Paz's subject particularly in his essay "El caracol y la sirena," translated by Lysander Kemp and Margaret Sayers Peden in Octavio Paz, *The Siren and the Seashell* (Austin: University of Texas Press, 1976). The pronouncement about Darío as founder of contemporary Spanish poetry is on p. 19.

9. Quoted in Paz, *The Siren and the Seashell*, p. 33.

10. *Selected Poems of Rubén Darío*, translated by Lysander Kemp (Austin: University of Texas Press, 1965), p. 135.

11. Marty delightfully evokes the spirit of the 1893 Parliament in *Modern American Religion*, pp. 17–24.

12. *Selected Poems of Rubén Darío*, p. 133.

13. Paz, *The Siren and the Seashell*, p. 43.

14. Paul Fussell elaborates this cultural development in *The Norton Book of Modern War* (New York, Norton, 1991), pp. 23–4.

15. Translated by Martin S. Allwood in *Twentieth Century Scandinavian Poetry*, edited by Allwood (Sweden: Marston Hill Mullsjo, 1950), p. 100.

16. Translated by Sarah W. Bliumis in *Silver and Steel: Twentieth Century Russian Poetry*, edited by Albert C. Todd and Max Hayward (New York: Doubleday, 1993), p. 784.

17. By Theodore Ziolkowski (Princeton University Press, 1972); the study covers twentieth-century novels from Europe and the United States.

FOUR / CRISIS OF THE SECULARIZED WEST

1. Translation by David Curzon and Will Alexander Washburn, in *The Gospels in Our Image*, edited by Curzon (New York: Harcourt Brace, 1995).

2. All quotations of Mason's verse are from his *Collected Poems* (Christchurch, New Zealand: Pegasus Press, 1962).

3. Translated by Paul Borum, in *Contemporary Danish Poetry: An Anthology*, edited by Line Jensen et al. (Boston: Twayne, 1977).

4. Translated by George Quasha, in Nicanor Parra, *Antipoems: New and Selected*, edited by David Unger (New York: New Directions, 1985).

5. Translated by Martin S. Allwood in *Twentieth Century Scandinavian Poetry*, edited by Allwood (Sweden: Marston Hill Mullsjo, 1950).

6. 'Dead Christ' is in Hudgins's *The Never-Ending* (Boston: Houghton-Mifflin, 1991). My thanks to the poet for referring me to the fascinating critical study that lies be-

hind this poem: Leo Steinberg, *The Sexuality of Christ in Renaissance Art and in Modern Oblivion* (New York: Pantheon, 1983).

7. From *Collected Poems* (Sydney, Australia: Angus and Robertson, 1971).

8. 'Last Suppers' is in Jarman's *Questions for Ecclesiastes* (Brownsville, Ore.: Story Line Press, 1997).

9. From Tadeusz Rózewicz, *Unease,* translated by Victor Contoski (St. Paul, Minnesota: New Rivers Press, 1980).

10. From the bilingual edition of *In Praise of Darkness,* by Jorge Luis Borges, translated by Norman Thomas di Giovanni (New York: Dutton, 1974). My quotations from this poem are, however, my own translation.

11. This is not at all the point of John Dominic Crossan's *Raid on the Articulate: Comic Eschatology in Jesus and Borges* (New York: Harper and Row, 1976), despite its subtitle. Crossan is less interested in uses Borges makes of Jesus ('Juan 1:14' is mentioned only in passing) than in parallels between the two as parablers. A characteristically 1970s postmodernist product itself, the book aims mainly to shock by treating Jesus as a postmodernist storyteller playfully subverting his audience's hopes for a fixed meaning. (Since Crossan went on to become a leader of the controversial Jesus Seminar, which attempts a new search for the Historical Jesus by stripping away all Gospel episodes of doubtful historicity, it is fascinating to see his intellectual roots in this book celebrating the slipperiness of meaning.)

12. Translated by Norman Thomas di Giovanni, in *Jorge Luis Borges: Selected Poems 1923–1967,* edited by Giovanni (New York: Delacorte, 1972).

13. Interviews with Borges on the subject are cited in Oswaldo Romero, "Dios en la obra de Jorge Luis Borges: Su teologia y su teodicea," *Revista Iberoamericana* 43 (1977): 465–501.

14. Romero quotes this from Rahner's speech, "Thomas Aquinas on the Incomprehensibility of God," at Duquesne University, Pittsburgh, November 9, 1974.

FIVE / CRUCIFIED AFRICA

1. All quotations from Senghor's poetry are from Léopold Sédar Senghor, *The Collected Poetry* (Charlottesville: University Press of Virginia, 1991).

2. Quoted in Ellen Conroy Kennedy, *The Negritude Poets* (New York: Viking, 1975), introduction, p. xx.

3. Quoted in Kennedy, *The Negritude Poets,* p. 17.

4. In Kennedy, *The Negritude Poets.*

5. In *The Chattering Wagtails of Mikuyu Prison* (Oxford: Heinemann, 1993).

6. For Senghor's response to *Epitomé,* as well as for much of the background for this chapter, I'm indebted to the balanced and informative study by Robert Fraser, *West African Poetry: A Critical History* (Cambridge: Cambridge University Press, 1986).

7. In Tchicaya U'Tam'si, *Selected Poems,* translated by Gerald Moore (London: Heinemann, 1970).

8. In Chinua Achebe, *Beware, Soul Brother* (London: Heinemann, 1972).

9. In George Awooner-Williams, *Rediscovery* (Ibadan: Mbari, 1964).

10. Interview with Awooner in Jane Wilkinson, *Talking with African Writers* (London: Heinemann, 1992), p. 27.

11. Christopher Okigbo, *Labyrinths* (London: Heinemann, 1971).

12. Interview with Okri in Wilkinson, *Talking with African Writers,* p. 88.

13. Interview with Achebe in Wilkinson, *Talking with African Writers,* pp. 48–9, 55.

14. In Kennedy, *The Negritude Poets.*

15. In Tchicaya U'Tam'si, *Selected Poems.*

16. In *Poems from Black Africa,* edited by Langston Hughes (Bloomington: Indiana University Press, 1963).

17. Cited in Janice Spleth, *Léopold Sédar Senghor* (Boston: Twayne, 1985), pp. 161–2.

18. Abiola Irele, *The African Experience in Literature and Ideology* (London: Heinemann, 1981), pp. 1–3.

19. Cleghorn's poem is found in *Divine Inspiration: The Life of Jesus in World Poetry,* edited by Robert Atwan, George Dardess, and Peggy Rosenthal (New York: Oxford University Press, 1998).

20. In James Keir Baxter, *Collected Poems* (Wellington, New Zealand: Oxford University Press, 1979); also in Atwan, Dardess, and Rosenthal, *Divine Inspiration.*

21 The English translation is by Sandra Reyes (Columbia: University of Missouri Press, 1984).

SIX / ARCHETYPAL CHRIST

1. *Journal of Arabic Literature* 2 (1971): 76–91.

2. "Ulysses, Order, and Myth," *Dial,* November 1923, pp. 480–3. Though Eliot's explicit subject in this essay is Joyce's *Ulysses,* he's clearly also talking about his own method.

3. Quoted in Issa J. Boullata, "The Poetic Technique of Badr Shākir al-Sayyāb," *Journal of Arabic Literature* 2 (1971): 113.

4. S. Moreh, *Modern Arabic Poetry: 1800–1970* (Leiden: E. J. Brill, 1976), p. 247, has counted some thirty occurrences of the figure of Christ in al-Sayyāb's collection of poems *Unshudat al-Matar.* (Beirut: Dār Majallet Shīr, 1960).

5. 'Madinat al-Sindibad," in *Unshudat al-Matar* pp. 150–9. This translation is in *An Anthology of Modern Arabic Poetry,* selected and translated by Mounah A. Khouri and Hamid Algar (Berkeley:University of California Press, 1974), pp. 93–103.

6. On the political context of 'City of Sinbad,' my thanks to Issa J. Boullata, professor of Arabic at McGill University, in private correspondence and in a doctoral dissertation published in Arabic as *Badr Shākir al-Sayyāb* (Baghdad: Dār al-Shuūn al-Thaqāfīyah al-Ammah, 1987).

7. 'Al-Masih ba'd al-Salb,' in *Unshudat al-Matar,* pp. 145–9. Translated by M. M. Badawi in *Journal of Arabic Literature* 6 (1975): 136–8.

8. "The Scare-Crow Christ," in *Brown River, White Ocean: An Anthology of Twentieth-Century Philippine Literature in English,* edited by Luis H. Francia (New Brunswick: Rutgers University Press, 1993).

9. Translated from the Danish by Martin S. Allwood in *Twentieth Century Scandinavian Poetry,* edited by Allwood (Sweden: Marston Hill Mullisjo, 1950).

10. Translated from the Hungarian by Dalma Hunyadi Brunauer, in *Divine Inspiration: The Life of Jesus in World Poetry,* edited by Robert Atwan, George Dardess, and Peggy Rosenthal (New York: Oxford University Press, 1998).

11. Translated from the Greek by Kimon Friar, in *Modern Greek Poetry,* edited by Friar (New York: Simon and Schuster, 1973).

12. In *H'm* (London: Macmillan, 1972).

SEVEN / JESUS ABSENT

1. Walter Kaufmann's essay "Nietzsche and Rilke," though written in 1959, is still useful on their relation.

2. Translated by David Curzon and Will Alexander Washburn in *The Gospels in our Image,* edited by Curzon (New York: Harcourt Brace, 1995).

3. Letter to Witold von Hulewicz, November 13, 1925, in *Letters of Rainer Maria Rilke,* translated by Jane Bannard Greene and M. D. Herter Norton, vol. 2 (New York: Norton, 1947).

4. In *Collected Poems 1930–1973* (New York: Norton, 1974).

5. In Soyinka's collection *A Shuttle in the Crypt* (New York: Hill and Wang, 1972).

6. In *The Voices of Indian Poets: An Anthology of Indian Poetry,* edited by Pranab Bandyopadhyay (Calcutta: United Writers, 1975); also in *Divine Inspiration: The Life of Jesus in World Poetry,* edited by Robert Atwan, George Dardess, and Peggy Rosenthal (New York: Oxford University Press, 1998).

7. Translated by Kimon Friar, in *Modern Greek Poetry* edited by Friar (New York: Simon and Schuster, 1973).

8. Ewa Czarnecka and Aleksander Fiut, *Conversations with Czeslaw Milosz* (New York: Harcourt Brace, 1987), p. 123.

9. Translated by Czeslaw Milosz and Lillian Vallee, in Czeslaw Milosz, *The Collected Poems: 1931–1987* (Hopewell, N.J.: Ecco Press, 1988). Except where noted, the other poems by Milosz that I quote are also in this collection.

10. Ewa Czarnecka and Aleksander Fiut, *Conversations with Czeslaw Milosz* (New York: Harcourt Brace, 1987), pp. 232–3.

11. These ideas are found everywhere in Weil, but since she wrote mostly in notebooks not meant for publication, citing particular sources is difficult. My quotations are taken from her notes as published in *The Simone Weil Reader,* edited by George A. Panichas (Mt. Kisco, New York: Moyer Bell, 1977), as well as from one of her few completed essays, now published widely as "Forms of the Implicit Love of God: Love of the Order of the World."

12. 'Before an Old Painting of the Crucifixion' is in Momaday's collection *Angle of Geese* (Boston: Godine, 1974).

13. In *Pequod* 40 (1996) p. 82.

14. In *Twentieth Century Russian Poetry,* edited by Yevgeny Yevtushenko (New York: Doubleday, 1993), and in Atwan, Dardess, and Rosenthal, *Divine Inspiration.*

15. In *An Anthology of Modern Arabic Poetry,* edited and translated by Mounah A. Khouri and Hamid Algar (Berkeley: University of California Press, 1974), and in Atwan, Dardess, and Rosenthal, *Divine Inspiration.*

16. Quoted in D. Z. Phillips, *R. S. Thomas: Poet of the Hidden God* (London: Macmillan, 1986), p. 56.

17. Readers familiar with J. P. Ward's fine analytical survey, *The Poetry of R. S. Thomas* (Mid Glamorgan: Poetry Wales Press, 1987) will notice that I owe to him these interpretative terms, as well as some later in my discussion. There is a large body of critical analysis of Thomas's poetry, especially in Britain; to my mind Ward's book is the best overall introduction.

18. The poems I quote from are in *Poems of R. S. Thomas* (Fayetteville: University of Arkansas Press), 1985.

19. *Foundations of Christian Faith* (New York: Crossroad, 1997), p. 64.

20. From Dillard's essay collection *Teaching a Stone to Talk* (New York: Harper, 1983).

EIGHT / BETWEEN ABSENCE AND PRESENCE

1. In James K. Baxter, *Collected Poems* (Wellington, New Zealand: Oxford University Press, 1979).

2. Translated by Albert C. Todd, in *Twentieth Century Russian Poetry,* edited by Yevgeny Yevtushenko (New York: Doubleday, 1993).

3. All the poems by Auden that I quote are in his *Collected Poems* (New York: Vintage/Random House, 1991).

4. Anthony Hecht, *The Hidden Law* (Cambridge: Harvard University Press, 1993), p. 291.

5. Translated by Dalma Hunyadi Brunauer, in *Divine Inspiration: The Life of Jesus in World Poetry*, edited by Robert Atwan, George Dardess, and Peggy Rosenthal (New York: Oxford University Press, 1998).

6. The episode is recounted in Richard Davenport-Hines's excellent biography, *Auden* (New York: Pantheon Books, 1995), pp. 200–201.

7. Quoted in Davenport-Hines, *Auden*, p. 226.

8. *Cross Currents*, Winter 1994–95.

9. This and the remaining poems by Norris that I quote are in her *Little Girls in Church* (Pittsburgh: University of Pittsburgh Press, 1995).

10. "Monks, Meaning and Metaphor," interview with Peter Gilmour, *Critic*, Spring 1995.

11. For Norris's expansion of the subject in prose, see *The Quotidian Mysteries: Laundry, Liturgy, and "Women's Work"* (Mahwah, N.J.: Paulist Press, 1998).

12. *Commonweal*, May 17, 1996.

13. From *Like Taxes: Marching through Gaul* (Washington, D.C.: Scripta Humanistica, 1990).

14. "Post-Secular Culture: The Return of Religion in Contemporary Theory and Literature," *Cross Currents*, Fall 1997.

15. *Mornings Like This* (New York: HarperCollins, 1995).

16. This and the remaining poems by Dillard that I quote are in *Tickets for a Prayer Wheel* (Columbia: University of Missouri Press, 1974).

NINE / JESUS PRESENT

1. The talk was published by Howard Nemerov in his still valuable collection *Poets on Poetry* (New York: Basic Books, 1966) and under the title 'On My Own Work' in Wilbur's collected essays, *Responses* (New York: Harcourt Brace, 1976).

2. Nathan A. Scott, Jr., *Visions of Presence in Modern American Poetry* (Baltimore: Johns Hopkins University Press, 1993), pp. 187, 195.

3. *New and Collected Poems* (New York: Harcourt Brace Jovanovich, 1988; originally in *Ceremony and Other Poems* [1950]).

4. *Commonweal*, August 15, 1997.

5. Quoted by Julian Green, translator's introduction to *God Speaks*, a selection of Péguy's poetry (New York: Pantheon, 1945). Except where otherwise noted, the passages of Péguy that I quote are in this translation.

6. All quotations of Ku Sang's verse are in his *Wastelands of Fire: Selected Poems*, translated from the Korean by Anthony Teague (Boston: Forest Books, 1989).

7. In *The Portal of the Mystery of Hope*, translated by David Louis Schindler, Jr. (Grand Rapids: Eerdmans, 1996).

8. *A Commentary on the Complete Poems of Gerard Manley Hopkins* (Ithaca: Cornell University Press, 1970), p. 94.

9. *The Never-Ending* (Boston: Houghton Mifflin, 1991). All my excerpts of Hudgins' poetry are in this volume.

10. New York: George Braziller, Inc., 1998.

11. 'Ikon: The Harrowing of Hell' is in *A Door in the Hive* (1989), 'Salvator Mundi: Via Crucis' and 'Ascension' in *Evening Train* (1992), and 'On Belief in the Physical

Resurrection of Jesus' in *Sands of the Well* (1996); all published in New York by New Directions.

12. Though the image of Jesus being "born" into a new exalted life at his Resurrection is as old as Christianity, Levertov was probably influenced by contemporary feminist Christology in configuring Jesus as both father and mother of his own birth.

13. Because Levertov's stature as a poet has long been acknowledged, there is an abundance of critical analysis of her poetry. On this point I recommend especially Albert Gelpi, editor's introduction to *Denise Levertov: Selected Criticism* (Ann Arbor: University of Michigan Press, 1993), and Paul Lacey's essay "'To Meditate a Saving Strategy': Denise Levertov's Religious Poetry," in *Renascence,* Fall/Winter 1997–98. This special issue of *Renascence,* devoted to "Spirit in the Poetry of Denise Levertov," is indispensable to anyone interested in the subject.

14. "A Poet's View," originally in *Religion and Intellectual Life* (Summer 1984): 48; reprinted in *New and Selected Essays* (New York: New Directions, 1992), p. 241.

15. "Work That Enfaiths," originally in *Cross Currents* (Summer 1990), pp.152–3; reprinted in *New and Selected Essays* (New York: New Directions, 1992), p. 250.

16. My formulation draws on Elizabeth Johnson, *She Who Is: The Mystery of God in Feminist Theological Discourse* (New York: Crossroad, 1992), p. 168: "The inner dynamic of the doctrine of incarnation sounds a ringing affirmation of the cherished feminist value of bodiliness, even for God . . . Bodiliness opens up the mystery of God to the conditions of history, including suffering and delight. She becomes flesh, choosing the very stuff of the cosmos as her own personal reality forever. She thereby becomes irrevocably, physically connected to the human adventure, for better or worse."

17. She hasn't been totally neglected. Her first poetry collection, *Adam's Footprint* (*New Orleans Poetry Journal,* 1956), received high praise in the literary quarterlies; she was nominated for a Pulitzer Prize in 1961; Levertov herself wrote the preface to Miller's third (1963) collection of poems; Howard Nemerov included her in his *Poets on Poetry* (New York: Basic Books, 1966). More recently, the *Dictionary of Literary Biography* gave Miller a major entry and—most important—Southern Methodist University Press published her complete poems, *If I Had Wheels or Love* (1991), which received deeply appreciative reviews in *Kenyon Review* and *Georgia Review.* But the fact remains that, outside of Miller's native Texas, there has been practically no critical discussion of her work.

18. All my excerpts of Vassar Miller's poetry are in *If I Had Wheels or Love* (Dallas: Southern Methodist University Press, 1991).

19. Nemerov, *Poets on Poetry,* pp. 129–30.

20. *Real Presences* (Chicago: University of Chicago Press, 1989).

21. Title essay of *Government of the Tongue* (New York: Farrar Straus and Giroux, 1989), p. 94.

22. In his introduction to *Remembering Anna Akhmatova,* by Anatoly Nayman (New York: Henry Holt, 1991), p.vii.

23. In *Responses,* his collected essays (New York: Harcourt Brace, 1976).

24. In *The Art of Drowning* (Pittsburgh: University of Pittsburgh Press, 1995).

25. Nemerov, *Poets on Poetry,* p. 115.

26. "Work That Enfaiths," p. 257.

Permissions Acknowledgments

"Song for Holy Saturday," by James K. Baxter, reproduced by permission of Mrs. Jacquie C. Baxter from *Collected Poems* by James K. Baxter (Oxford University Press, New Zealand, 1979).

"Jesus" by James McAuley from his *Collected Poems* copyright © 1971. Used by permission of HarperCollins Publishers.

"That Yellowed Body" by Vladimir Lvov, translated by Sarah W. Bliumis, from *20th Century Russian Poetry* by Yevgeny Yevtushenko. Copyright © 1993 by Doubleday, a division of Bantam Doubleday Dell Publishing Group, Inc. Used by permission of Doubleday, a division of Bantam Doubleday Dell Publishing Group, Inc.

"Even the Knots on Quince Trees" by Ku Sang, from *Wastelands of Fire,* by Ku Sang, translated by Anthony Teague (Forest Books, 1990). Used by permission of Forest Books.

Poetry by Denise Levertov is reprinted by permission of New Directions Publishing Corp.: "Mass for the Day of St. Thomas Didymus" from *Candles in Babylon* copyright © 1982 by Denise Levertov; "Ikon: The Harrowing of Hell" from *A Door in the Hive* copyright © 1989, by Denise Levertov; "Salvator Mundi: Via Crucis" and "Ascension" from *Evening Train* copyright © 1992 by Denise Levertov.

Poetry by Kathleen Norris is used by permission of the author: "Luke 14: A Commentary," originally published in *Cross Currents,* Winter 1994–95; also excerpts from *Little Girls in Church* (University of Pittsburgh Press, 1995).

Poetry by R. S. Thomas is used by permission of the author: "Kneeling" from *Not That He Brought Flowers* (London: Hart-Davis, 1968); "The Coming" and "Via Negativa" from *H'M* (London: Macmillan, 1972).

Translations from Rainer Maria Rilke's "On the Marriage at Cana" and "The Olive Garden" by David Curzon & Will Alexander Washburn, from *The Gospels in Our Image* (Harcourt Brace, 1995). Used by permission of the translators.

Notes on the Artists

Fred Fulsom is featured in Gregory Wolfe, "Fred Folsom: A Profile," *Image: A Journal of the Arts & Religion,* Summer 1992.

Betty La Duke's studio is in Ashland, Oregon; she is the author of *Compañeras: Women, Art and Social Change in Latin America* (San Francisco: City Lights, 1985) and *Africa through the Eyes of Women Artists* (Trenton, N.J.: Africa World Press, 1991).

Cho Kwang-Ho teaches at the Catholic Institute of Art, Seoul, Korea.

Luvon Sheppard teaches graphic art at Rochester Institute of Technology, Rochester, N.Y.

Robert Wagner is featured in Rupert Martin, "Roger's Wagner's Visionary Landscapes," *Image: A Journal of the Arts & Religion,* Summer 1995.

Index

Cairns, Scott, 162–3, 166
Cardenal, Ernesto, 98
centering prayer, 153
Cheney-Coker, Syl, 87
China, Jesuit missions in, 19
Cleghorn, Sarah, 98
Clement of Alexandria, 5
Clough, Arthur Hugh, 50–1, 64, 70
Coleridge, Samuel Taylor, 25, 27, 30–1, 32
Collins, Billy, 171–2
Communism, 65, 86, 98, 104, 120, 121–2, 126
cosmic visions
    Blake, 32–40
    Dillard, 150
    medieval cosmology, 10–13
    Senghor, 85
    Whitman, 39
    See also Jesus, poetic figures of, cosmic Christ
Councils of Nicea, Chalcedon, and Ephesus, 6
Craig, David, 148, 153
Cross. See Crucifixion
Crucifixion
    in African poetry, 87–9
    in Arabic poetry, 104–6
    in Auden, 137, 141–2
    in Baxter, 136–7
    in Demetillo, 106–7
    in Hecht, 173
    in Hudgins, 162
    in medieval devotion, 13–14
    in modernism, 64–5
    in Peterson, 107
    in postmodernism, 70, 72–3, 74–5
    in R. S. Thomas, 110–11
    in seventeenth century Chinese poetry, 20
    in Vinokurov, 137
    in Whitman, 40
Cunneen, Joseph, on indirection in religious art, 152

Dante, 12–13, 150
Darío, Rubén, 58–61, 80
Demetillo, Ricaredo, 106–7

Depestre, René, 93
Dillard, Annie, 134–5, 148–50, 153, 161
distractedness, spiritual problem of, 136–43
Dream of the Rood, 10
Droste-Hülshoff, Annette, 41–6, 69

ecumenism, 67, 153
Eichendorff, Joseph von, 46
Eliot, George (Mary Ann Evans), 22, 23–4, 26
Eliot, T. S.
    Christian poetry of, 138, 139–41
    influence of The Waste Land, 61–2, 91, 101–3, 110, 153
Emerson, Ralph Waldo, 27, 35–7, 48
Enlightenment, 20–2, 23–5, 31, 166, 172
Ephrem, 6–8, 12, 18, 144, 151
evangelicalism, nineteenth century, 21–2, 24, 25
existentialism, 63, 86, 118, 125, 131

feminist movement, 146, 167
Fortunatus, 10
Franciscan devotion, medieval, 13–14
French Revolution, 32, 33

Goethe, Johann Wolfgang von, 27, 28–30, 32, 47
Guevara, Miguel de, 15, 18
Gumilyov, Nikolai, 126

Hecht, Anthony, 172–3; on W. H. Auden, 137
Hegel, Georg Wilhelm Friedrich, 25, 27, 32, 36
Hemans, Felicia, 46–8
Herbert, George, 17, 18
Hildegard of Bingen, 10–12, 18
Hopkins, Gerard Manley, 160–1
Hudgins, Andrew, 74–5, 161–2, 166

Ignation spirituality, 17, 161
Impastato, David
    on incarnational presence, 151
    on postmodernism, 83
Incarnation
    in Borges, 79–81

in contemporary U.S. poetry, 161–70,
172–3
definitions of, 151
in Edward Taylor, 17
in Emerson, 36
in Ephrem, 6–8
in Hildegard of Bingen, 12
in John of the Cross, 14–15
in Ku Sang, 158
as model for poetry, 145, 172
in Romanos, 8
as sacramental presence, 151–3
in seventeenth century Chinese poetry,
19–20
Irele, Abiola, and *The African Experience
in Literature and Ideology,* 97
Irenaeus, 6, 10

Jabrā, Jabrā Ibrāhīm, 101
Jarman, Mark, 75, 77–8, 172–3
Jesus, poetic figures of
as archetype of death and resurrection,
102–5
as archetype of sacrificial suffering,
84–90, 95
as betrayer, 87, 89
as Christ, 3–4, 8, 21
as comrade, 40, 86, 98
as cosmic Christ, 5–6, 7, 8, 10–13, 32,
40, 85, 98, 129–30, 173
as dehumanized, 73–4
as disillusioned, 69–72
displaced by Romantic poet, 29–30
displaced by Satan, 55, 120–1
displaced into humanity's powers,
116–20
as forgotten, 112, 123–7
as imagination, 34
as incarnational presence, 151–3, 162–
70
as jokester, 143–50
as king, 6, 8, 10, 22
as lover, 14–16, 18
as meaninglessness, 73–5
as Messiah. *See* Jesus, poetic figures of,
as Christ
as moral model, 21, 28, 30, 31
as mortal merely, 49, 50–1, 62–5

as mother, 7
as music, 6
as nostalgia, 61, 64
as pathetic, 54, 65
as political activist, 98–100
as politically subversive, 34–5, 97–100,
103–5
as political victim, 31, 87, 165
as puzzle, 75–81
as reconciliation, 92–5
in relation to moral wasteland of twentieth century, 106–11
in relation to nature, 43–8, 69, 159–62
in relation to Tammuz myth, 102
in relation to tribal gods, 90–2
as relativized, 38, 60, 63–4
as shepherd, 5, 6, 7, 9, 16, 34
as teacher, 5, 21
as victim of modern distractedness,
136–43
as waited for, 127–34
as Word, 4, 16, 75, 77, 79–81, 139, 158,
169–70
John of the Cross, 14–15, 18
Juana Inés de la Cruz, 16

Keen, Suzanne, on Seamus Heaney, 147
Kirkeby, Per, 72–3
Ku Sang, 154–60

La Ceppède, Jean de, 15
Levertov, Denise, 163–6, 172
Luther, Martin, 16–17
Lvov, Vladimir, 64–5

Mapanje, Jack, 87
Mariani, Paul
on G. M. Hopkins, 160
on language and transcendence, 170
Marty, Martin E., on Protestant mod-
ernism, 57
Marxism, 120, 137
Mason, R.A.K., 69–71, 74
McAuley, James, 75–7
McClure, John, on narratives of religious
rediscovery, 148
Middle Ages, 10–14, 173
Miller, Vassar, 167–70, 172